Sometime in 1579, anti-theatricalist Stephen Gosson made the curious remark that theatre "effeminated" the mind. Four years later, in a pamphlet twice the size, Phillip Stubbes claimed that male actors who wore women's clothing could literally "adulterate" male gender. Fifty years later, in a thousand-page tract which may have hastened the closing of the theatres, William Prynne described a man whom women's clothing had literally caused to "degenerate" into a woman.

How can we account for such fears of effeminization? What did Renaissance playwrights do with such a legacy? Laura Levine examines the ways in which Shakespeare, Jonson and Marlowe addressed a generation's anxieties about gender and the stage and identifies the way the same "magical thinking" informed documents we much more readily associate with extreme forms of cultural paranoia: documents (like King James' *Daemonologie*) dedicated to the extermination of witches.

"[This book provides] one of the most searching and subtle perspectives on the contributions and limitations of New Historicism . . . Laura Levine is a critic of the first rank."

Patricia Parker

"Intersecting with recent work on the construction of gender in the period, the significance of English transvestite acting companies, and the dramatic repertory itself, this book will force a great many people in the field to re-think what they thought they knew about such issues . . . The questions which frame Levine's analysis are both central to the works examined and yet far from obvious – at least until thus articulated . . . Masterfully written . . . a pleasurable read."

Steven Mullaney

"Levine's book will revise our sense of masculinity in the period. No other critic has anatomized the crisis of masculinity implicit in the anti-theatrical position with such precision, details, and insight, or has developed from that central notion so many relevant insights and provocative readings . . . an original brave voice."

Valerie Traub

CAMBRIDGE STUDIES IN RENAISSANCE
LITERATURE AND CULTURE 5

Men in women's clothing
Anti-theatricality and effeminization, 1579–1642

Cambridge Studies in Renaissance Literature and Culture

General editor
STEPHEN ORGEL
Jackson Eli Reynolds Professor of Humanities, Stanford University

Editorial board
Anne Barton, *University of Cambridge*
Jonathan Dollimore, *University of Sussex*
Marjorie Garber, *Harvard University*
Jonathan Goldberg, *The Johns Hopkins University*
Nancy Vickers, *University of Southern California*

The last twenty years have seen a broad and vital reinterpretation of the nature of literary texts, a move away from formalism to a sense of literature as an aspect of social, economic, political and cultural history. While the earliest New Historicist work was criticised for a narrow and anecdotal view of history, it also served as an important stimulus for post-structuralist, feminist, Marxist and psychoanalytic work, which in turn has increasingly informed and redirected it. Recent writing on the nature of representation, the historical construction of gender and of the concept of identity itself, on theatre as a political and economic phenomenon and on the ideologies of art generally, reveals the breadth of the field. *Cambridge Studies in Renaissance Literature and Culture* is designed to offer historically oriented studies of Renaissance literature and theatre which make use of the insights afforded by theoretical perspectives. The view of history envisioned is above all a view of our own history, a reading of the Renaissance for and from our own time.

Titles published

Drama and the market in the age of Shakespeare
DOUGLAS BRUSTER, University of Chicago

The Renaissance dialogue: literary dialogue in its social and political contexts, Castiglione to Galileo
VIRGINIA COX, University College London

Spenser's secret career
RICHARD RAMBUSS, Tulane University

Shakespeare and the geography of difference
JOHN GILLIES, La Trobe University

Men in women's clothing: anti-theatricality and effeminization, 1579–1642
LAURA LEVINE, Wellesley College

Men in women's clothing
Anti-theatricality and effeminization, 1579–1642

Laura Levine

Assistant Professor of English, Wellesley College

CAMBRIDGE
UNIVERSITY PRESS

Published by the Press Syndicate of the University of Cambridge
The Pitt Building, Trumpington Street, Cambridge CB2 1RP
40 West 20th Street, New York, NY 10011–4211, USA
10 Stamford Road, Oakleigh, Melbourne 3166, Australia

First published 1994

Printed in Great Britain at the University Press, Cambridge

A catalogue record for this book is available from the British Library

Library of Congress cataloguing in publication data

Levine, Laura, 1955–
Men in women's clothing: anti-theatricality, 1579–1642 / Laura Levine.
   p.   cm. – (Cambridge studies in Renaissance literature and culture: 5)
Includes index.
ISBN 0 521 45507 3 (hardback). ISBN 0 521 46627 X (paperback)
1. English drama – Early modern and Elizabethan, 1500–1600 –
History and criticism.
2. Sex role in literature.
3. Female impersonators – England – History – 16th century.
4. Female impersonators – England – History – 17th century.
5. English drama – 17th century – History and criticism.
6. Literature and society – England – History.
7. Masculinity (Psychology) in literature.
8. Theater and society – England – History.
9. Clothing and dress in literature.
10. Women in literature.   I. Title.   II. Series.
PR658.S42L48   1994
822'.309353–dc20   93-27476   CIP

ISBN 0 521 45507 3 hardback
ISBN 0 521 46627 X paperback

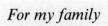
For my family

Contents

Acknowledgements

Chapter 1 of this book appeared in *Criticism* vol. 28. no. 2 (Spring, 1986) under the title "Men in Women's Clothing: Anti-theatricality and Effeminization from 1579 to 1642," and I am grateful to Wayne State University Press for permission to reprint it and to Arthur Marotti for taking an interest in my work at an early stage of its development. I have also had the opportunity to present portions of this book at the Renaissance Society of America Conference, thanks to Stephen Orgel; the Fifth World Shakespeare Congress in Tokyo, thanks to Steven Mullaney and Peter Stallybrass; the Reconfiguring the Renaissance Conference, thanks to Jonathan Crewe; and the MLA.

I am grateful to both the National Endowment of the Humanities and Wellesley College for making it possible to have time to complete the book, as well as to the Beatrice S. Berry Fund for making travel to the Tokyo Shakespeare Congress possible.

I would like to thank Stephen Orgel whose example, insight and faith in the project have enlivened it since its inception and Jonathan Crewe whose agile questions helped it at so many different stages to take shape. I am grateful to Jane Tylus for her extraordinary criticism and to Susan Meyer, Pat Bellanca and Frank Donoghue whose capacity to listen to the manuscript at moments when the lines of its logic seemed invisible to me often brought those lines back into existence. Rory Metcalf, Jeff Stone, Suzanne Bixby and the late Adele Bowers read and reread the book. Valerie Traub and Katherine Maus read it after it was completed, and for their large and penetrating constructions of it I am grateful. Among the colleagues, friends and family who commented on all or parts of the manuscript as it evolved or after it was completed, I would particularly like to thank Lynda Boose, Daniel Fischlin, Jonathan Goldberg, Lorraine Hirsch, Esther Levine, Harry Levine, Joe Levine, Julia Lupton, Pat Parker and Ken Reinhard, as well as the students with whom these ideas took form. My largest debt of gratitude must go to Peter Saenger who has read this manuscript more times than any human being should have to read anything. In a very real way it could not have been written without him.

Introduction

> That time? O times!
> I laugh'd him out of patience; and that night
> I laugh'd him into patience; and next morn,
> Ere the ninth hour, I drunk him to his bed;
> Then put my tires and mantles on him, whilst
> I wore his sword Philippan.
>
> (*Antony and Cleopatra*, II.v.18–23)

This book quite literally began with the passage quoted above, the moment in *Antony and Cleopatra* in which Cleopatra reminisces about dressing Antony in her tires and mantles. The moment alludes outward to a particular stage practice, the practice of boy actors wearing women's clothing, but more than that, it alludes to the point at which one might think Renaissance drama would imagine itself most vulnerable: for six decades, three before and three after *Antony and Cleopatra*, the charge that theatre effeminized the boy actors who played women's parts by dressing them in women's costume was the hallmark of Renaissance anti-theatricality. Cleopatra happily rhapsodizing about dressing the passive, drunken Antony in her women's clothing presents, in distilled form, everything that would have horrified those who attacked the stage. Why would a dramatist invoke such a moment? Not merely "invoke" but embody and heighten precisely the attack launched against his own craft? Of course there are other traditions than Renaissance stagecraft encapsulated in the moment; the effeminized Hercules, whose sexual play with Omphale consisted in the exchange of his hairy mantle for her "dainty" girdle; the same Hercules destroyed by another piece of clothing given to him by a woman, the poisoned shirt dipped in centaur's blood; *The Arcadia's* Pyrocles dressed as a woman, complaining that love of a woman has turned him into one. But that Shakespeare invokes these literary traditions of effeminization to characterize Renaissance stage practice itself only makes the passage more problematic. Why should a playwright invoke the very accusations used against him?

In fact, *Antony and Cleopatra* contains other such moments, moments

1

which only intensify the problem. In IV.xiii Cleopatra, locking herself in her monument and sending word she is dead, scripts a scene of theatre which sends her audience, Antony, to *his* suicide. And there is evidence that this is precisely the effect she has anticipated. "She had a prophesying fear," says Diomedes, "of what hath come to pass" (IV.xiv.120–1).[1] Such a moment seems to cast theatre itself as something so potent and so dangerous it has the capacity to make its spectator go home and kill himself. It casts theatre, in other words, in terms much more bleak than the terms of the attacks. What does it mean for a dramatist to advance such an argument?

As I turned to other plays, in an attempt to determine to what extent such impulses were idiosyncratic to *Antony and Cleopatra*, I was struck by what seemed an even more disturbing instance of theatre validating the attacks of its attackers in *Troilus and Cressida*, although now these attacks had to do with the sexual charges that anti-theatricalists during the period tended to make about theatre, the accusation that it could "whette desire to inordinate lust" and make the "affections" of the spectator "over-flow."[2] In V.ii, in the scene on the walls, Ulysses seems to orchestrate just such a scene of theatre, which engenders in its primary spectator, Troilus, precisely those impulses that attacks against the stage accused theatre of engendering. Hidden in the darkness, Troilus watches Cressida, who is in the process of betraying him, depict for him what is practically a mastur-batory fantasy, a rendition of Troilus himself in bed substituting the glove Cressida has given him for herself. What does it mean for a playwright to stage such a moment? Not to "defend" his practice from the attacks lodged against it, but to embody and rehearse precisely those attacks? What would it mean for a playwright to "defend" his work in the first place? In fact, the question is misconceived, for it assumes that pamph-leteers attack while playwrights "defend." Both halves of the assumption are faulty, it turns out, for attacks against the stage regularly seem to conceive of themselves *as* plays, as both their structures (divided into acts and scenes) and titles indicate – *Playes Confuted in five Actions*, Gosson calls his second and longest attack. In this confused context, what does it mean for a playwright to rehearse the arguments of his attackers? Clearly one possibility is that the playwright is as "contaminated" by the anxieties of the attacks which we think of him as "defending" against as the attackers are themselves. At any rate, this turned out to be the case in *Troilus and Cressida*, which in certain peculiar ways *behaves* like the anti-theatricality it also anatomizes.

Was such "contamination" peculiar to Shakespeare or somehow built into the nature of Renaissance drama itself? In a sense Jonson seemed a likely place to turn to answer such a question, since his anti-theatricality has long been noted, although in terms that have never seemed to me to be terribly satisfying. This is first because descriptions of his anti-theatricality have always been based on *Volpone* and on the poems, and have consequently missed the ways that plays like *Epicoene* and *Bartholomew Fair* actually replicate the specific sexual anxieties that animate pamphlet attacks against the stage.[3] But it is also because of the way accounts of Jonson's anti-theatricality try to salvage Jonson's investment in theatre. In their attempts to try to deal with the problem of Jonson's anti-theatricality (the "problem" being that he wrote plays), critics have always salvaged a coherent Jonson by arguing that Jonson's anti-theatricality was only superficial, directed merely towards the institution of theatre as it was practiced, and not towards that rarified ontological entity, the "essential" play, Jonson's own written text before the industry of the stage compromised it.[4] What such explanations have missed are the actual critiques of anti-theatricality which emerge in Jonson's late plays and which constitute a kind of *anti*-anti-theatricality (a vantage point from which the "logic" of the tracts is rendered absurd and untenable, but from which the fears that motivate that logic are still quite volatile in the playwright himself). This *anti*-anti-theatricality, as it appears both in Jonson and in Shakespeare, provides the beginnings of an answer to why a playwright would rehearse and even heighten or embody the arguments of his attackers.[5] For in rehearsal lies the possibility of a kind of "working out." Playwrights like Shakespeare and Jonson are both contaminated by the anxieties of the attacks they defend against and obsessively bent on coming to terms with them.

If our first expectation coming to this material is that pamphleteers attack and playwrights "defend," and if Shakespeare presents a profound challenge to such an expectation by rehearsing the arguments of his attackers, the second surprise lay for me in the way that Jonson, traditionally assumed to share affinities with anti-theatricality, actually offered a critique of anti-theatricality on just those points on which he might have been assumed to be the most sympathetic, i.e. on the anti-theatrical fantasy that a one-to-one correspondence exists between each "sign" and the "thing" it stands for. To understand this, though, we need to understand more exactly the contradictions built into anti-theatricality itself and the precise role the fantasy of a one-to-one correspondence between sign and thing played in these contradictions.

In fact, at the heart of Renaissance anti-theatricality lay a glaring contradiction. For at the root of pamphlet attacks lay the fear that costume could actually alter the gender of the male body beneath the costume. Theatre "effeminates" the mind, says Stephen Gosson somewhat cryptically in 1579, and four years later Phillip Stubbes makes explicit what Gosson has hinted at: that boy actors who wear women's clothing can literally "adulterate" male gender.[6] In the years of mounting pamphlet war this evolves into a full-fledged fear of dissolution, expressed in virtually biological terms, that costume can structurally transform men into women.

But even as they betray this fear, those who attacked the stage proclaim something very different indeed: "garments are set down for signes distinctive betwene sexe and sexe," says Stephen Gosson.[7] Anti-theatricalists claimed (over and over again, in many places using many citations) that costume was the "sign" of gender, even as they betrayed the deeper and more irrational fear that costume could actually alter the gender beneath. Thus at the heart of Renaissance anti-theatricality lay a contradiction which implied an extraordinary mechanism: the tendency to turn to a theory of knowledge to quell the fear that one's gender could dissolve. For to say, as Gosson does, that garments are set down as "signes distinctive" between sex and sex is to assert that knowledge is possible. And the more worried anti-theatricalists became about the possibility of effeminization, the more dogmatically they turned to an epistemology of signs, a faith in a pure referentiality.

Why should anti-theatricalists turn to this epistemology – to any epistemology at all – to quell such a fear? This has been the question that has haunted the writing of this book. And the question it generated in turn: "What did Renaissance playwrights 'do' with such a legacy?" has provided the structural principle for writing the book and dictated its form: what Shakespeare "did" was imagine the world the anti-theatricalists feared, one in which men really could be turned into women. What Jonson "did" was imagine the world anti-theatricalists wanted, one built on a faith that "signs" really could lead to things, a world built on a faith in pure referentiality.

But to say that what Jonson "did" was "imagine" such a world is to tell only part of the story. For what he did when he imagined this world was to suggest that it was ultimately untenable. Thus at the center of both *Epicoene* and *Bartholomew Fair* are figures who simultaneously embody the worlds the anti-theatricalists long for and are doomed in this very enterprise: Morose, so bent on constructing a language of pure signs that he misses the fact that he is marrying a boy and nearly brings on the very experiences anti-theatricalists fear: homoeroticism, near-castration, and the recognition that he is "no man." Or the puppet Dionysius in *Bartholomew Fair* who has "nothing" under his clothing and who simultaneously represents the supreme anti-theatrical fantasy of sanitization – with no sexual equipment, he is immune from the seductions anti-theatricalists fear – and the destruction of what they cherish: for with "nothing" under his clothing he has no "thing" for the costume, the "sign," to refer to, and thus represents the destruction of referentiality itself.

Why should anti-theatricalists turn to a fantasy of pure reference to quell the fear that gender can dissolve? Why should they turn to an epistemology at all? In some way, it seemed, the epistemology must offer an opposite, an antidote to the fear, but to see this it was necessary to isolate this principle in a series of related texts.

But what texts would these be? In a sense, the fear that costume can alter the gender beneath it is only a specific version of a much more profoundly "magical" idea that representations in general can alter the things they are only supposed to represent. But to dismiss this as "magical thinking" is to miss the way that in the Renaissance such thinking lay, almost literally, at the heart of texts about magic and witchcraft, texts bent on the extermination of witches. Thus King James' *Daemonologie*, the most influential English text on witchcraft, if only because of its author's political stature, shares a fundamental contradiction with anti-theatrical tracts of the period. Although it *claims* that magic itself is merely a series of representations (figures, illusions, pictures merely formal in nature) it *acts* as if these representations had a constitutive power – a power to alter and unman the male body itself.

Daemonologie doesn't, as anti-theatrical tracts do, turn to a coherent and systematic epistemology of signs to quell its fears. But *Newes from Scotland*, the text that in a sense "explains" *Daemonologie*, in its picture of how the king put his beliefs into practice, does just that. Here, the "sign" which is believed to guarantee certainty is not costume, but the "mark" that the devil leaves on a given witch. It frequently takes torture to "discover" this sign, but what is crucial here is the anxiety that makes such a discovery *necessary*. At the heart of *Newes from Scotland* is the same fear that dominates anti-theatrical tracts, but escalated to a more desperate level, the fear of sympathetic magic, that the shirt that is only supposed to stand for the king can actually kill the king, the fear that representations can actually alter the things they are merely supposed to represent.

What can such a text tell us about anti-theatricality? How can it help us to answer the original question, "Why should anti-theatricalists turn to this particular epistemology of signs, to an epistemology at all, as con-solation for the idea that men can be turned into women?" *Newes from Scotland* suggests a general principle of use in answering this question, for more starkly here than anywhere else the epistemology men seek to construct is the opposite of what they fear. If they fear that represen-tations can alter, they are willing to torture to restore the idea that representations merely signify.

If we apply this principle to understanding the specific relation between the fear of effeminization that dominates anti-theatrical tracts and the epistemology of signs anti-theatricalists turn to as consolation, it suggests that here, too, the relation must be one of opposites. Why turn to a system of knowledge at all to quell the anxiety that it is possible to turn into a woman? Why not turn one's rage against women or assert with renewed vigor that one is a man? In fact, anti-theatricalists do both things, but if we turn the question around and ask what the consolation tells us about the fear, the specific consolation offered by an epistemology of signs suggests that the fear of effeminization must be in part about the experience of doubt itself. At stake in the fear of effeminization must be a basic doubt: "What am I?" – as if one of the primitive, fundamental categories of knowledge for these tract writers were, "What am I, man or woman?" The consolation offered by a faith in referentiality must be that it generalizes: if we live in a world where "signs" always lead inevitably to things, then those things must be fixed, always what they are and unsusceptible to change. And if we live in a world in which this is so, then one of the things that must be fixed and unsusceptible to change is gender itself. Thus the naive epistemology at the heart of anti-theatricality seems to promise anti-theatricalists both that the genders will remain fixed and that the doubt that is triggered by the idea of them changing can be erased. Although, as we shall see, even this is an inadequate formulation, since the promise required is really that one gender remain fixed, the one that is so badly feared to be capable of change, masculinity itself.

All of these texts and all of the chapters about these texts are about doubt. Chapter 1, "Men in women's clothing," is about the doubt that men are really men (or able to stay men), about the model of the self that generates this fear, and about the epistemology that serves as a way of containing or managing it. The Jonson chapters are about the way that epistemology generally fails to deliver the certainty or security that those who turn to it look for. The witchcraft chapters are about the violence that erupts when that epistemology can not be successfully established. The Shakespeare chapters are much more centrally about the subjective experience of doubt, what it feels like and why those who choose to create it in others do so: "*Troilus and Cressida* and the politics of rage" is about the cultivation of doubt, not in the way Montaigne employs such a notion, as a purge for violent emotion, but in just the opposite way, about the cultivation of doubt as a means of producing violent rage, because in the experience of that rage men can be trusted to "act" and perform like warriors, and thus like men. But the need for such a performance implies a much more fundamental kind of doubt that is of even greater interest to me, a doubt that is, in a sense, the true subject of this book. For it implies that men are only men in the performance of their masculinity (or, put more frighteningly, that they are not men except in the performance, the constant re-enactment of their masculinity) – or, and these are the implications I am particularly interested in, that they have no way of knowing they are men except in the re-enactment, the relentless re-enactment, of their own masculinity. The texts examined in this book give quite a lot of information about what this state of affairs would feel like and about the particular type of powerlessness they would induce.

As such, they have the potential for offering a kind of corrective or qualifier to what for me has been the most suggestive and important strain of Renaissance criticism in the last couple of decades. Ever since 1975, when Stephen Orgel quoted Elizabeth I as saying "We princes, I tell you, are set on stages in the sight and view of all the world," the tendency to think of power as expressing itself in theatrical ways during the Renaissance has been implicit in New Historicism.[8] But this tendency has steadily grown. From Orgel's citation of Elizabeth to Stephen Greenblatt's repetition of the same passage as evidence that "Elizabethan power ... *depends* upon its privileged visibility" (italics mine), is "constituted" in theatrical celebrations, to Jonathan Goldberg's insistence (invoking Foucault) that "for the period we are concerned with, power is manifested in the spectacle," at least one strand of New Historicism has increasingly come to view power as existing *only* in the theatricalization of itself.[9] Foucault, such an authority for New Historicism, puts the claim in what are perhaps its strongest terms when he tells us we should think of power as "exercised" (enacted, acted out) "rather than possessed."[10] Over a decade and a half of criticism, as the insights of New Historicism have solidified, it has been marked by a tendency to think of power as existing only in the enactment, the performance of itself.

But there are at least two things about this view that are (to me) highly problematic. The first is the failure to acknowledge the epistemology that such an ontology of power logically implies. For if there were really no power except in the theatricalization of power, there would be no knowledge of power except in the theatricalization of power, and in the absence of such a theatricalization, what one would be left with would be a profound sense of powerlessness. Hypothetically, then, if New Historicism were "right," there would be an acute sense of *powerlessness*, not being talked about, but being passed over by the critics in their discussions of Renaissance texts, a sense of powerlessness that is implicit in the texts I consider.

Secondly, as New Historicism has broadened its scope, and in the process extended the number of things it has come to conceive of as existing only in the performance of themselves, it has been marked by a striking omission. As New Historicism has come more and more to construct the Renaissance itself in theatrical terms, it has viewed not only power as existing in the enactment of itself, but selves and reality as well. Consider Greenblatt on *1 Henry IV* (in "Invisible Bullets," but articulating the concerns of *Renaissance Self-Fashioning*) when he says that "it is by no means clear that such a thing as a natural disposition exists in the play as anything more than a theatrical fiction."[11] Or Jonathan Goldberg in an even more comprehensive moment when he says of the Renaissance, "The public sphere, the realm of the gaze, constitutes reality as a theatrical space."[12] But if New Historicism has extended the number of things it construes as existing only in the performance of itself, it has been marked by a striking failure to consider that gender too may exist only in the theatricalization of itself, only insofar as it is performed.[13] Why has New Historicism failed to apply its own insights to the issue of gender, to see the degree to which in Renaissance texts masculinity itself apparently must be staged in order to exist?

Such a proposal has emerged from other quarters, from gay and feminist circles outside of Renaissance studies. Judith Butler makes precisely the point that New Historicism omits, that the "gendered body" has no "ontological status" at all except for the series of actions and performances that create the idea of gender.[14] For Butler this is a liberating possibility, precisely because it is in the failure to repeat these acts (as well as in parody) that the possibility for gender transformation exists. But Butler will not account for the texts this book examines (or for the worlds they depict). Precisely because she is committed to the idea that the "gendered body" has "no ontological status" apart from the acts that create it, she must by definition be equivalently talking about male and female bodies lacking an ontological status apart from the performances that create them. And it is the peculiarity of the texts this book considers to think *only* of masculinity as needing to be performed in order to exist; it is as if femaleness were the default position, the thing one were always in danger of slipping into. The texts I consider call attention to what New Historicism has passed over and left to silence: a kind of *a priori* sense of powerlessness that springs from precisely the fear that there is no real masculinity, no masculine self.[15]

If we ask, "Why is it that it is only masculinity in these texts that needs to be enacted?" the question is susceptible to two kinds of answers. In a general way, for these texts, femininity seems to be the default position, the otherness one is always in danger of slipping into, so nobody ever thinks of it as *needing* to be maintained or performed.[16] But to answer the question with more specificity, we need to ask, "What is the alternative to an enacted masculinity for each of these texts?" That is, for *Antony and*

Cleopatra, castration, the loss of the sword; for *Troilus and Cressida*, the sense that Helen's "white enchanting fingers" can do more than all the island kings to disarm Hector; for *Epicoene*, the loss of all difference; for *Daemonologie*, where the sense of powerlessness is clearest, the sense of the body as a set of holes; for Prynne, the sense of something "other" where the self is supposed to be. These moments are pressure points where the sense of powerlessness that informs these texts is most nearly articulated, the sense of powerlessness that necessitates the enactment of masculinity. Thus, in a sense, the answer to the question "Why is it masculinity only that has to be enacted in order to exist?" lies for each of these texts in the alternative envisioned to masculinity (castration, porousness, effeminization, otherness), a series of terrifying possibilities one is always in danger of slipping into.

These texts themselves point to what it is that New Historicism has eclipsed or passed over and in that sense offer a critique of New Historicism, even as they ratify one of its deepest insights: that of a culture which conceives of itself (almost compulsively) in theatrical terms. But in isolating the fear that there is no masculinity except in the performance of masculinity, they also isolate a key determinant in a series of phenomena we might ordinarily fail to connect: in hostility toward the stage, the persecution of witches, the attempt to construct an epistemology and language of "signs" devoid of connotation and affect, war itself. All of these phenomena in the texts treated in this book spring from the terror that there is no masculine self. It is this fear and the particular kind of powerlessness it generates, and the strategies of accommodation it necessitates and creates, that this book examines.

1   Men in women's clothing

Sometime in 1579, in a pamphlet which was to establish the terms of attack and defense for another sixty years, Stephen Gosson made the curious remark that theater "effeminated" the mind.[1] Four years later, in a pamphlet twice the size, Phillip Stubbes clarified this claim even as he heightened it by insisting that male actors who wore women's clothing could literally "adulterate" male gender.[2] Fifty years later in a one-thousand-page tract which may have hastened the closing of the theatres, William Prynne described a man whom women's clothing had literally caused to "degenerate" into a woman.[3] In the years of mounting pamphlet war about the stage, the vague sense that theatre could somehow soften the responses of the audience had been replaced by the fear – expressed in virtually biological terms – that theatre could structurally transform men into women. How can we account for this fear of effeminization? It at once seems irrational and tends to endow theatre with magical properties: the idea that a man can be turned into a woman is a version of the more basic "magical" idea that one person can be turned into another. But what model of a self would one have to have to maintain that idea?

Curiously enough, critics have ignored the information that such an anxiety provides about anti-theatrical (and perhaps wider Renaissance) conceptions of the self. Explanations of antipathy to the stage have traditionally begun with the idea that anti-theatricalists saw the self as fixed and stable, "uniforme" and "distinct."[4] Jonas Barish, for instance, takes the claim made by William Prynne that God "hath given a uniforme, distinct and proper being to every creature" at face value, as being an accurate depiction of the anti-theatrical view of the self.[5] But a position which tries to explain anti-theatricality from the standpoint of a fixed and stable self gives rise to a glaring contradiction. If those who attack the stage see the self as stable, why do they imagine that theatre has such a tremendous power to alter it? If they see the male self as "fixed," why do they so frequently imagine it being turned into a woman? What is required, it would seem, is a model of the self which accounts for (rather than ignores) the fears of effeminization which anti-theatricalists display.

Such a model would not only have the advantage of explaining these fears, but might additionally explain the rift in Renaissance criticism between those critics of anti-theatricality who maintain that a belief in the concept of "absolute identity" motivated attacks on the stage, and those other critics, writing about a wider range of Renaissance texts, who claim to challenge the very notion of a fixed or stable self.[6] For if the notion of an absolute self is functionally inadequate – if it fails to explain the tracts it undertakes to explain – the opposite notion, "no inherent self," presents a different problem. In recent Renaissance criticism, the most important challenge to the notion of an absolute self comes from Stephen Greenblatt's *Renaissance Self-Fashioning*, which rejects the idea of the self as a discrete (or fixed) ontological entity in favor of the observation that "in the sixteenth century, there appears to be an increased self-consciousness about the fashioning of human identity as a manipulable, artful process."[7] But the problem with the attempt to argue "no inherent self" is that Greenblatt often replicates the very notion he himself considers a fallacy. At regular junctures in *Renaissance Self-Fashioning*, the notion of a self as a manipulable construct seems underwritten by an older sense of the self as a deep "psychic structure." This is particularly so in Greenblatt's last essay on *Othello*, which depends on a set of analogies or "homologies" between Iago and Othello. The first homology, the capacity for "narrative self-fashioning" which the two characters share, is predicated on the idea of "no inherent self," for it springs from the premise that "being" has never been any more than an imaginary language construct.[8] But the second homology, the deep-seated and unconscious revulsion at sexuality, is one which Greenblatt describes as a deep "psychic structure." Lacanian models of the self as a language construct are underwritten by Freudian models of the self as a permanent structure. The notion of a self abides even in the very attempt to get rid of it.[9]

If the notion of a fixed self fails to explain the tracts it is intended to explain, and the notion of "no inherent self" continually betrays its own premises, what model of the self will explain the fears of effeminization which dominate anti-theatrical tracts? We would seem to be looking for something contradictory: something neither absolute, nor devoid of essence, something neither fixed nor capable of playfully shaping itself. If both notions of the self are flawed, although they appear to be opposites, perhaps Greenblatt and Barish share some unstated central assumption.[10] That assumption, I would argue, is a tacit belief in the primacy of the will.

And this is exactly what seems to have been disarmed in anti-theatrical tracts: this is a self which can always be altered not by its own playful shaping intelligence, but by malevolent forces outside its control.

In fact, the model of the self implicitly held by anti-theatricalists is profoundly contradictory, for, according to its logic, the self is both inherently monstrous and inherently nothing at all. To manage this contradiction, the men who held this model of the self seemed to project it outward. And from this point of view, the actor became the ideal repository for such a projection: the male actor, dressed in women's clothing, seemed to lack an inherent gender, and this seemed to make him monstrous. In this way, the fantasy of effeminization which came to dominate anti-theatrical tracts became a repository for a profound contradiction in the way a certain segment of the English Renaissance saw the self.

The idea that a man can be turned into a woman is a version of the more basic "magical" idea that a given person can be turned into another person. This idea is not explicitly magical – it does not self-consciously allude to charms or potions – but it is implicitly so, for it involves a belief in a fairly mysterious process which violates the notion of discrete and individual identity. Anti-theatrical tracts are, in fact, dominated by both explicit and implicit claims about magic. Let us begin with the explicit claims to see if they help account for what seems to be an otherwise irrational belief.

In 1579, Gosson calls poetry Circe's cup, implying that theatre's power is its ability to make men into beasts.[11] In 1580, Anthony Munday asks, "Do wee not use [plays] to counterfeit witchcraft, charmed drinks and amorous potions thereby to drawe the affections of men and stir them up unto lust?"[12] But elsewhere Munday suggests that theatre's power lies not in its ability to make men into aggressive beasts, but in its ability to make them pliant, curiously passive, to take away their volition. They can be made by plays "to like even those whom of themselves [they] abhor."[13] The first two passages, on the one hand, and the third, on the other, suggest two antithetical effects of magic: plays are magic because they make men into aggressive beasts and plays are magic because they make men into puppets, passive will-less robots – in other words, all volition, or no volition. All of the other explicit claims about magic – Rankins' depiction of actors as demonically possessed monsters and Stubbes' claim that no man who hadn't been bewitched by Circe or Medea would put on women's clothing – fall into one or the other of these two antithetical categories.[14]

We might be tempted to dismiss as hyperbole these explicit claims about magic if they weren't mirrored by a second set revolving around the notion of one person's being turned into another. The anecdote with which Gosson ends *Playes Confuted in five Actions* (1582) is a good example, for it suggests that the actor can make the spectator into a mirror image, a version of himself. The anecdote is simply a retelling of Xenophon's story of the play *Bacchus and Ariadne*, but it emphasizes the way the audience can be made compulsively to imitate what happens in the play:

When Bacchus beheld her, expressing in his daunce the passions of love, he placed himself somewhat neere to her, and embraced her, she with an amorous kind of feare and strangeness as though shee woulde thruste him away with her litle finger, and pull him againe with both her handes, somewhat timorously, and doubtfully entertained him.

At this the beholders beganne to shoute. When Bacchus rose up, tenderly lifting Ariadne from her seate, no small store of curtesie passing betwene them, the beholders rose up, every man stoode on tippe toe, and seemed to hover over the playe. When they sware, the company sware, when they departed to bedde; the company presently was set on fire, they that were married posted home to their wives; they that were single, vowed very solemly, to be wedded.[15]

The passage suggests a belief in magic, in the coercive, almost hypnotic, power it imagines the play to have over the audience. The spectator will automatically replicate what he has seen on the stage. The passage insists on this in its formulaic repetition of tiny gestures (rising up, shouting, standing on tip-toe, swearing oaths) as a prologue to larger actions such as going home to bed or getting married. What this presupposes is the magical idea that watching leads inevitably to "doing." There is plenty of support for the belief that watching leads inevitably to "doing" in other anti-theatrical tracts. Anthony Munday cites examples of ancient cities that closed their theatres on this particular premise.[16] But the passage suggests the more radical idea that watching leads inevitably to "being" – to assuming the identity of the actor. The play is dangerous precisely because the spectator becomes a replica of the actor. This is the deeper belief in magic.

If this seems an extreme way to state the case, we might recall that, for Gosson, the process of watching a play involves a physical transformation. The "impressions" in the actor's mind are mysteriously transferred to the gazer.[17] In this way the spectator quite literally takes on the identity of the actor. It looks as if we were dealing with not one but two magical processes. In the first one, watching leads inevitably to doing – to compulsive imitation. In the second, watching leads to taking on the identity of the person watched. The assumption is that "doing" is constitutive. By imitating certain actions, one becomes the thing one is imitating. William Prynne grimly warns his readers that action can shape the doer: "he who puts on a womans rayment ... though it be but once, is doubtlesse *a putter on of womens apparell.*"[18]

If we looked at this anecdote in isolation, we would have the impression that the actor possessed a tremendous power to shape the identities of his spectators, to remake or "unfashion" them into versions of himself. But other anecdotes suggest that the actor's own identity is unstable, that he himself can be shaped or unfashioned by his part. Gosson himself says that the real danger for the actor is that he must become the part in order to play it well. The actor who plays the tyrant, for instance, must actually "whet his mind unto tyranny that he may give life to the picture he presenteth."[19] It is not that the actor himself has the power to shape identity, but that the part is actually constitutive and shapes the man who plays it. The most famous example of this belief comes not in an attack on the stage, but in a defense, Heywood's *Apology for Actors* (1612). Here Julius Caesar, in *Hercules Furens*, actually kills the servant that he was only supposed to pretend to kill. Heywood says: "Although he was, as our tragedians use, but seemingly to kill him by some false imagined wound, yet was Caesar so extremely carried away with the violence of his practised fury, and by the perfect shape of the madnesse of Hercules, to which he had fashioned all his active spirits, that he slew him dead at his foot, and after swoong him, *terque quaterque* (as the poet says) about his head."[20] Here the actor does not shape the part, but the part, the "perfect shape of the madnesse of Hercules," shapes the actor. In the sense that the actor becomes the part that he is playing, this passage too violates the notion of discrete individual identity. Heywood's boast is that through theatre Caesar becomes an actual avatar of Hercules, just as Hercules himself became an avatar of Jupiter.[21] Other critics have cited this passage to argue that defenders of the stage shared the assumption of their opponents that theatre could lead its practitioners to mistake fiction for reality.[22] These critics have argued, in effect, that Heywood's defense is not a defense at all, but a recapitulation of the assumptions of the attacks. I will return to the issue of whether Heywood's defense is a defense, but first I would like to emphasize a different aspect of the anecdote. Like the Bacchus and Ariadne anecdote, it suggests that one person can literally become another, though here it is the actor who takes on the identity of the character, rather than the spectator who takes on the identity of the actor. If we are to understand such anecdotes, we shall have to account for the irrational idea that one person could be changed into another, the spectator into a replica of the actor, and the actor himself into the part. These tracts appear to revolve around the anxiety that there is no such thing as a stable identity, despite the protestations to the contrary which other critics have often identified. No one seems to have any inherent identity and everyone can be converted into someone else.

What concept of the self would it be necessary to have to maintain that one person could actually be turned into another, the spectator into an enflamed Bacchus or the actor into the "shape of the madnesse of Hercules"? Such a self would be pliable, completely manipulable, like a robot that could be programmed from the outside or a fluid that took its shape according to the kind of container in which it was put. In fact, this is exactly what anti-theatricalists do say about the self. Gosson depicts the affections as fluids, held in an inadequate container.[23] Poets are people who make the fluids overflow. But where is the will which would govern affection? Gosson's view of human behavior implies a kind of "domino theory" of the self. Human behavior is a chain of degenerative action in which each act leads automatically to the next – ("from pyping to playing, from play to pleasure, from pleasure to slouth, from slouth to sleepe, from sleepe to sinne, from sinne to death, from death to the Divel").[24] Each action mechanically triggers the next without will or volition. In fact it is as if the will has been permanently disarmed, rendered inoperative. In this sense the self is already a robot. It is easy to reinsert this self back into the Bacchus and Ariadne episode, to imagine the way it could be made to carry out compulsive imitative actions.

An even more powerful sense of the self as neither "fixed" nor self-propelling is evoked by both Munday's and Gosson's depictions of the spectator as literally "carried away." Who on the Sabbath, asks Munday, isn't "carried whether his affection leades him?"[25] But it is not just the affections which the tract writer imagines being "carried away," but parts of the physical body itself: "Are not our eies [at plays] carried awaie with the pride of vanitie?"[26] Gosson uses practically the same words in *Playes Confuted* when he warns us that if we fail to govern delight "we are presently carried beyond ourselves."[27] The language of these tracts reflects the sense of the self as something – almost portable – that can be geographically moved from place to place by others outside, rather than by its own volition.

If we locate a self whose chief characteristics are its abilities to be carried, programmed, poured out of its container into something else, we begin to see how it would be possible to maintain the kinds of claims Gosson maintains in *Playes Confuted*, the claim that the spectator could be made compulsively to replicate the actor. If you believe the self is so tenuous that it can be altered at the slightest touch, then the slightest touch becomes magic, witchcraft, capable of radical, constitutive, mysterious change. But the charge that the spectator could be turned into an enflamed Bacchus or the actor into an enraged Hercules would make sense from a different point of view as well. If we imagined a self already constructed along the lines of an enflamed Bacchus or an enraged Hercules, then anti-theatricalists would be blaming the theatre for making the spectator into the monster they already believed he was. Interestingly, we find confirmation for this model of the self in the very same writers who characterize the self as a manipulable robot. According to this second depiction, the self is pure appetite, perpetually insatiable, "alwaies eating and never satisfied," says Munday, so "anhungered" that it mistakes the wormwood of plays for meat.[28] Plays are bad because they cater to a self that is perpetually voracious anyway, like he that "hearing one half of a sentence . . . is very desirous to have the rest."[29] This is a self characterized not by the absence of volition, as the first self was, but by uncontainable desire, not propelled from outside, but self-propelling. This is a self which must be contained. Gosson imagines it locked up in a (Pandora's) box: "lift upp the lidde, out flyes the Devil; Shut it up fast, it cannot hurt us."[30] This self is not a puppet or a robot, but a devil, a monster.

We seem to have returned to the original antithesis with which we began. We started with two seemingly antithetical claims about theatre's magical properties: theatre was magical because it made men pliant, and theatre was magical because it made men into beasts. We have at least accounted for why the magic should take such disparate, even antithetical forms. Anti-theatrical tracts hold two views of the self. They subscribe simultaneously to a view of the self as pliable, manipulable, easily unshaped, and at the same time to a view of the self as monstrous. The antithetical claims about magic then reflect the two kinds of anxiety about the self – the anxiety that, underneath, the self is really a monster, and the anxiety that, underneath, the self is really nothing at all. It becomes possible to account for the logic of both Gosson's and Heywood's anecdotes, then. The actor or spectator can be turned into another person because he really isn't anything himself. At the same time, he can be turned into a Hercules or a Bacchus because he is already an insatiable monster.

At the heart of the logic that endows theatre with magical powers is an idea which violates the notion of discrete and individual identity, the belief that one person can literally be turned into another. This belief itself turns out to be based on two interrelated ideas, both of which involve magical processes: the idea that watching leads inevitably to "doing" and the corollary that watching leads inevitably to "being" (because action, particularly imitative action, is constitutive). This account by itself would identify the steps in an irrational and magical belief, but would not explain how it was possible to maintain such a view in the first place. But this becomes a little clearer in light of the view of the self revealed in anti-theatrical tracts, a view in which the self can easily be made into anything because it has no inherent nature, and at the same time can be made into anything monstrous because it has an inherently monstrous nature. In other words, it is possible for anti-theatricalists to maintain a view of theatre as malignant magic bent on unshaping and animalizing the self, because they hold the contradictory view of the self as shapeless and animal-like to begin with.

What would it be like to have such a sense of self? Of course the question needs to be qualified before it can become very useful. Perhaps a better question would be, "Would there be any predictable way of ordering the world which would be likely to accompany such a sense of self?" We might speculate, for instance, that the logical contradiction between two equally entrenched and antithetical views of the self might lead to a way of organizing the world designed specifically to eliminate (or at least minimize) the contradiction. In order to "protect" the idea of the self as fragile and indeterminate, for instance, one would effectively have to banish the notion of the self as monster. Perhaps one would accomplish this by projecting the idea of monstrosity onto other things, things outside the self like witches and actors. We would not be surprised, then, to hear Stubbes calling actors monsters or to hear that William Rankins called his tract against the stage *A Mirrour of Monsters*. Alternately, if one were committed to the notion of the self as monster, one might banish all ideas having to do with precarious identity onto other things, things like incubi and succubi with no inherent genders. In order to eliminate the contradiction, one would have to banish at least one of the ideas, simply to keep the other intact. If the more threatening idea were the idea that there was no inherent self, if even a monstrous self were better than no inherent self, one might fasten on a philosophic or religious position which insisted that things had essential natures – for then one of the things which would have an essential nature would be the self. It has long been a critical cliché to say that as attacks against the stage grow more vehement, they switch from arguments about the abuse of theatre to arguments which insist that theatre has an essential evil nature – from convention arguments to essence arguments.[31] What has not been explored is the preoccupation with essentialism itself in later tracts. In *Playes Confuted*, for instance, Gosson is determined to preserve the idea that things have essential moral natures. But in order to protect this notion against the many contradictions which he himself can see it generating, Gosson is often forced to break down into separate ontological entities the single things with which he began. To avoid the morally relativistic claim, for instance, that plays are sometimes good and sometimes evil, or the convention argument that the use of the play determines whether or not it is evil, Gosson is forced to break the term "play" itself into two ontological entities – plays-not-to-be-performed-but-read, and plays-to-be-performed.[32] In this way he can defend the religious plays of Buchanan and Naziancen as plays-not-to-be-performed while maintaining the essentialist position that all performed plays have essentially evil natures. My point is not that these are not different ontological entities – many Renaissance playwrights would have agreed with Gosson's distinction – but that they only become different ontological entities in Gosson's text when there is no other way to reconcile essentialism with the exceptions Gosson needs to make. The fragmentation, the breaking up of the original term, is a recurrent phenomenon and indicates the stress that essentialism itself is under. The fragmentation is a sign of the energy Gosson is willing to expend to protect the idea that things have essential natures. If this is so, perhaps the appeal of the idea is that, if things in general have essential natures, then one of the things that will have an essential nature will be the self. If we were to find, then, that anti-theatrical tracts grew increasingly frantic and threadbare in their attempts to preserve essentialist logic, we might hypothesize a growing anxiety about whether there was such a thing as an essential self. The claims made by Gosson that the mind is "simple without mixture or composition" and by Prynne that we all have "uniforme, distinct and proper beings" would become defenses against the more threatening idea that one self could be turned into another.[33] Essentialist logic, in fact, does get more frantic and threadbare. Of all the tracts which proliferate before the closing of the theatres, Prynne's *Histrio-mastix* is the one most dominated by the essentialist logic that "That which is sinful in itselfe is nowhere, no time lawfull upon no occasion" and yet the one which most frequently works itself into relativistic binds, such as the claim that theatre is an "abuse" of that which is already essentially evil.[34] *Histrio-mastix* is the tract which asserts most emphatically that God has given a "uniforme, distinct and proper being to every creature," and yet the tract which, as we shall see, displays the most anxiety about the gender and boundaries of that "proper being."

One strategy, then, for dealing with contradictory and volatile ideas about the self would be to eliminate one half of the contradiction – either the idea that the self was monstrous or the idea that the self lacked an inherent nature. But another strategy would be to banish both ideas, to manage the contradiction by projecting it outward. Then the idea of a being that was both monstrous and yet had no inherent nature could be preserved, though kept at a suitable distance.

If we found that anti-theatricalists regularly fixed their attentions on things which were both monstrous and lacked intrinsic natures, we would seem to be justified in saying that they had found a repository for their own conflicts about the self. This is, indeed, exactly what they do. Significantly, anti-theatrical tracts from *School of Abuse* onward grow increasingly obsessed with the idea of the effeminized man – the thing that has no inherent nature because it has no inherent gender and is monstrous precisely because of this fact. Phillip Stubbes' *Anatomie of Abuses* calls men who wear women's clothes "monsters, of both kindes, half women, half men."[35] He defines the monstrous itself in terms of that which has no essential nature – because it has no essential gender. At least in this tract we can see the antithesis between the two opposites "monstrous" and "no inherent nature" collapse in the idea of the androgyne. For writers of these tracts, the hermaphroditic actor, the boy with the properties of both sexes, becomes the embodiment of all that is frightening about the self.

My argument, however, would be that anti-theatrical tracts are moving all the time in this direction. One could chart the development of anti-theatricality in terms of the increasing anxiety raised by the idea that there is no such thing as an essential gender. What I have argued so far is that anti-theatricalists found a way to contain the conflict of the contradictory self – the self that was both inherently monstrous and inherently nothing at all – in the image of the androgyne. What I shall argue now is that this "solution" generated its own problem: the anxiety that there was no inherent gender. This anxiety then required a new defense, so anti-theatricalists turned even more desperately than before to essentialist rhetoric. Where they had previously reached for dogmatic essentialist positions to quell the panic that there was no such thing as an essential self, they now reached for the same positions to quell the anxiety that there was no such thing as an essential gender.

The first tract to demonstrate any real concern over the issue of gender is Gosson's *School of Abuse* (1579), which accuses theatre of being both "effeminate" and effeminizing – an association which is itself suggestive, since it implies that things that are like women are likely to turn into women. Gosson poses a kind of puzzle. In his dedication "To the Gentlewomen, Citizens of London," he suggests that looking at women in the audience makes men lose their human identity – they become animals, turn into braying "wild coultes."[36] But looking at plays makes men lose not their human identity but their male identity: theatre "effeminates" the mind.[37] Playwrights design "effeminate gesture to ravish the sence, and wanton speache to whette desire to inordinate lust."[38] In other words, what titillates or "ravishes" is also what emasculates. This is a curious idea. Why should men lose their human identity looking at women, but lose their male identity looking at plays? Is it that men turn into beasts when their sexuality is engaged by looking at women and turn into women when their sexuality is engaged by looking at men? This would make sense, however, only if the passage took for granted a homosexual response on the part of the spectator, and only if such a response were imagined to have a constitutive power. Then the tract would display the magical belief we have encountered before, that "doing" (doing what a woman does when she looks at a man) leads to "being" (being a woman).

As we progress chronologically from tract to tract we shall see that the belief that "doing" leads to "being" – the belief that action is constitutive – becomes more and more pervasive, and that, as it does, it poses an increasing threat to the notion of an essential gender, to the notion of a permanent structure that remains the same regardless of the actions it commits. But the first thing to say about *School of Abuse* is that the assumption of a homosexual response on the part of the spectator would be only speculation, for, unlike later tracts, *School of Abuse* says nothing explicit about homosexuality.

The next two things to notice about *School of Abuse* are also "omissions," at least by the standards of later tracts. First, for all its fear of effeminization, *School of Abuse* says nothing about the Deuteronomic code, the prohibition against men's and women's exchanging costume. No doubt this stems from the fact that Gosson's authorities are still largely classical, not biblical, but the omission is still striking in a tract concerned with effeminization. For there is no suggestion here, as in later tracts, that the costume is itself in any way constitutive, and this suggests that there is still some sense of a fixed gender beneath the costume. The second "omission" is the omission of essentialist logic. *School of Abuse* is a convention attack concerned with the use or "abuse" of theatre, not with the idea that theatre is essentially evil. Of course, this conjunction, the absence of the Deuteronomic code and the absence of essentialist arguments, would only become significant if later tracts tended to pair essentialist claims and citations of the Deuteronomic code. We might then hypothesize that, as tract writers approached the idea that costume was constitutive (that there was no essence beneath the costume), they clung increasingly to the very notion of an essence to defend against their perceptions.

Gosson's next tract, *Playes Confuted* (1582), does cite the Deuteronomic code and does focus on essentialism, though again it says nothing explicit about homosexuality. Gosson says: "The law of God very straightly forbids men to put on women's garments, garments are set downe for signes distinctive betwene sexe and sexe, to take unto us those garments that are manifest signes of another sexe, is to falsify, forge and adulterate, contrarie to the expresse rule of the words of God. Which forbiddeth it by threatening a curse unto the same."[39] Gosson's interest in clothing here is an interest in signs: by signs we are supposed to "declare ourselves."[40] But what is it that the man who puts on women's clothing "falsifies, forges and adulterates?" Is it the "signe" or the gender which the sign stands for? The explicit position here on signs is that they merely signify. They do not constitute. The man who wears women's clothing perverts God's sign, but not the gender it refers to.

This explicit position is belied, however, by the elaboration of the Deuteronomic code through the rest of the tract, for Gosson grows increasingly preoccupied not with scriptural claims, but with the wider issue of female impersonation. If putting on women's garments is bad, adopting "not the apparell onely, but the gate, the gestures, the voyce, the passions of a woman" is much more abominable.[41] Why are these things worse than the violation of the explicit biblical prohibition? We have already seen, in the Bacchus and Ariadne anecdote, that this tract finds the danger in playing a part in the idea that one may actually become the part one plays. If, in order to effect the part of a convincing tyrant, one must become tyrannical, must "whet his mind to tyranny," the fear of learning to "trippe it like a Lady in the finest fashion" must be in the analogous idea that the actor will eventually become a woman.[42]

Although Gosson never explicitly claims that signs are constitutive, never explicitly makes a claim which would challenge the notion of a definite gender beneath the sign, he betrays this anxiety in his fears about female impersonation. It is in this context that his assertions of absolute identity, his claims that the mind is "simple and without mixture," must be understood: as the text circles around the idea that there is no such thing as an essential gender, it increasingly defends against this anxiety with essentialist rhetoric.

Playes Confuted raises two ideas which would seem to have a radical impact on each other. The first is that theatre can turn one person into another and the second is that there is something dangerous not only about dressing, but also about talking and gesturing like a woman. If we brought these two ideas together, we would be led to the conclusion that wearing women's clothing and talking and walking like a woman were dangerous precisely because they could turn men into women. But bringing these ideas together is exactly what Gosson does not do. He raises two radically threatening ideas about the stage and leaves them, as it were, in separate compartments. He is in this sense a transitional figure. He claims that wearing women's clothing is wrong because it is a lie, but he implies that wearing women's clothing is dangerous because it can become the truth. The claim is based on the belief that only signs can be perverted, not the essential genders they stand for. But, the fear is based on the idea that the signs themselves are constitutive, an idea which implies that there is nothing fixed underneath.

This fear is explicitly articulated in Stubbes' *Anatomie of Abuses* (1583), written only a year later. Stubbes claims that the sign can alter the essence, that wearing the other sex's clothing can literally "adulterate" gender: "What man so ever weareth womans apparel is accursed, and what woman weareth mans apparel is accursed also. ... Our Apparell was given to us as a signe distinctive to discern betwixt sex and sex, and therefore one to wear the Apparel of another sex, is to participate with the same, and to adulterate the veritie of his owne kinde."[43] The claim here is that costume is constitutive. Men and women who wear each other's costume, says Stubbes, "may not improperly be called Hermaphroditi, that is, Monsters of both kindes, half women, half men."[44]

It is at this point that what Stubbes calls sodomy enters the discourse – as if it were the cause of that collapse of gender which anti-theatricalists anyway fear. Stubbes says that after plays "every one bringes another homeward of their way verye friendly, and in their secret conclaves (covertly) they play the Sodomits, or worse. And these be the fruits of Playes and Interluds, for the most part."[45] Even here the dramatic metaphor is inextricable from the sexual act: they will "play" the sodomite. Much has been made of this passage and of the elasticity of the word sodomy during the period, but the passage involves virtually the same assumption as Gosson's Bacchus and Ariadne anecdote – that the spectator will go home and imitate the actor, will replicate the actions he has seen on the stage.[46] And unless we want to dismiss as mere convention that boys play women's parts, what the spectator has seen on stage is boys in an embrace.

This theme reaches an explicit crisis in Prynne's *Histrio-mastix* (1633). Citing long lists of precedents for the notion that sodomites titillate themselves by dressing their boys in women's clothing, Prynne claims that theatre is always a pretext for male homosexuality. His list includes the "Male Priests of Venus" who with their companions the "passive beastly sodomites" of Florida "went clad in womans apparell, the better to elliciate, countenance, act and colour their unnaturall execrable uncleannesse."[47] It includes the sodomites of Florida themselves who, for dressing themselves in women's clothing, have gone down in posterity's record as "very monsters of nature."[48] Finally, it includes the magical Incubi "who clothed their Galli, Succubi, Ganymedes and Cynadi in woman's attire, whose virilities they did oft-time dissect, to make them more effeminate, transforming them as neere might be into women, both in apparell, gesture, speech, behaviour... And more especially in long, unshorne, womanish, frizled lust-provoking haire and love-lockes..."[49] The passage associates male homosexuality with the loss of masculine gender in a number of ways: first, through the associations attached to the

Incubi and Succubi who have no inherent gender, second, through the associations of castration – or as Prynne puts it, "dissection" – and, third, through the notion that we have already encountered that "doing" what a woman does leads to "being" what a woman is. What is most striking about the passage, however, is its apparent conviction that locked away within the man – tucked away somewhere inside his own body – is a woman herself, waiting apparently for the appropriate attire and the removal of those "virilities" which would allow her to assume her proper shape.

What becomes clear is that the focus on homosexuality, the preoccupation with sodomy, is itself an attempt to provide a rationale. The work of social historian Alan Bray provides us with corroboration for such a claim, for Bray persuasively argues that the mythology of sodomy was so fantastic, that the sin itself was rarely even connected with homosexuality as it was practiced.[50] Sodomy in the tracts of Stubbes and Prynne, then, functions as a metaphor or scapegoat, or an attempt to give an account for the much more disturbing idea at the center of these tracts, that under the costume there is really nothing there or, alternatively, that what is there is something foreign, something terrifying and essentially "other."

Perhaps the most telling claim on this subject comes in Prynne's own particular reworking of the Deuteronomic code: "If then a woman's putting on or wearing of man's apparell . . . incurres an anathema . . . doth not a man's attyring himself in woman's vestments . . . *much more demerit?*" (italics mine).[51] If it is worse for men to wear women's clothing than for women to wear men's, it is male identity per se that is at stake. It is as if the passage's secret conviction were that the only people with real selves were women. Or, as Prynne's depiction of a warrior dissolving into a woman suggests, it is as if clothing were so constitutive that, when the man began to remove it, he found a woman underneath in the body itself. Prynne says of a man in woman's clothing: "Doth not that valiant man, that man of courage who is admirable in his armes, and formidable to his enemies degenerate into a woman with his veiled face? he lets his coate hange downe to his ankles, he twists a girdle about his breast, he puts on women's shoes, and after the manner of women, he puts a cawle upon his head; moreover he carries about a distaffe with wooll, and drawes out a thred with his right hand, wherewith he hath formerly borne a trophie, and he extenuateth his spirit and voyce into a shriller and womanish sound."[52] In a curious way we have come back to the terms with which we began, for this particular image of the effeminized man betrays the original conflict it was meant to conceal, the antithesis between a monstrous self and a "no inherent self." There is nothing essential about this "valiant man's" identity: it slips away from him with his clothes. At the same time there is something permanent and, therefore, essential and clearly monstrous locked away "inside" him, his capacity – envisioned almost as a bodily structure – for womanishness itself.

It is no longer a question of violating scriptural injunctions, but an unmanageable anxiety that there is no such thing as a masculine self. Thus, of all the tracts written during the English Renaissance, Prynne's is the most underwritten with ideas of monstrous androgyny, boys in delicate dresses worshipping Venuses with beards, and men with breasts tyrannized by effeminate tyrants in skirts. The visions of breakdown have become disordered in *Histrio-mastix* on the deepest possible biological level. It is, then, in this context of a frantic defense against the perception of something horrendously "other" at the core of the self that Prynne's assertions of absolute identity, his claims that God "hath given a uniforme, distinct and proper being to every creature," have to be understood.

The original problem was how to account for the fear of effeminization in anti-theatrical tracts, and the original answer was that the preoccupation with the idea of the effeminized man was a way of managing contradictory attitudes about the self – the idea that the self was inherently monstrous and the idea that the self was inherently nothing at all. By projecting conflicts about monstrosity and indeterminacy onto boys on stage, anti-theatrical pamphleteers made the contradictions in themselves more manageable, and in this way the fear of effeminization which came to dominate anti-theatrical tracts disguised a profound conflict about the nature of the self.

This would account for the anxiety about effeminization in the first place, but not for why, as we have just seen, it should grow. Why do these tract writers become steadily *more* obsessed with the idea of the effeminized man? Why do the images of androgynous breakdown – of boys with breasts and man-woman monsters – multiply from 1579 to 1642? How do we account for the sheer momentum? Is it just a question of Stubbes reading Gosson and elaborating, of Prynne reading Stubbes, getting scared and elaborating again? If the images of androgyny proliferate from tract to tract, if the pictures of Venuses with beards and tyrants in skirts multiply with giddying frequency from line to line, if they are invoked by the hundreds instead of the dozen in *Histrio-mastix*, perhaps they are failing to serve their original function.[53] Perhaps more are required because they have ceased to contain the original conflict they were meant to contain.

At what point would this happen? At what point would the container cease to contain? It would happen at the moment, both in the period and in the individual, when a cultural prejudice – a mode of containing

contradictory ideas about the self – burgeoned into a personal symptomatology.[54] Of course this moment cannot be fixed in a single passage or
even in a single tract. But anti-theatrical tracts seem to be moving steadily
in this direction all the time. What is important is the relation between the
cultural prejudice and the personal pathology, the way that the pathology
is never only "personal," but an index to the culture's system of beliefs
and values.

What begins as a cultural critique dissolves by the time we get to
Histrio-mastix into case history. For personal fears of effeminization in
School of Abuse are still contained within a public and national ideal of
military valor. Gosson yearns for the "olde discipline of England," for a
past when "English men could suffer watching and labour, hunger and
thirst... They used slender weapons, went naked, and wer good soldiours."[55] Costumes are merely the symbol of the decline from this ideal.
They do not have the power to constitute reality.[56] In contrast, by the
time that Gosson himself writes *Playes Confuted* just a few years later, his
interest in war as a literal institution seems to have evaporated. The idea
of the military has become merely a metaphor for Gosson's own fluctu-
ating sense of victory and humiliation, his own depiction of himself as a
writer. He is Callicratides, admiral of the Lacedemonians who said that
turning back was worse than defeat. He is Hercules cleaning the Augean
stables of theatrical filth. He is Agamemnon begging Walsingham to help
him sack Troy in his pamphlet war.[57] The military is neither a literal
institution with the power to quell anxieties about effeminization, nor is it
free from the anxieties about impotence which it once served to quell. And
by the time Prynne describes his soldier "degenerating" into a woman, the
interest in war itself has become purely symbolic, subordinate to the
whole host of fears about gender and the body which we have already
seen in Prynne's work.

From the viewpoint of this increasing fear of effeminization, we can
now return to the anecdote about Caesar's being carried away with the
"violence of his practised fury" and being shaped by the "madnesse of
Hercules" in Heywood's *Apology for Actors*. We are now in a position to
understand the sense in which this anecdote really is a "defense."
Although it grants one of the claims of its opponents – that one self can be
transformed into another – it repudiates another claim. It repudiates the
claim that a man, let alone a soldier, can be turned into a woman. The
growing intensity of the fear of effeminization in anti-theatrical tracts can
be gauged by what Heywood thinks is a reassurance and a defense. He
argues that, though the self may be transformed into someone else by
theatre, it will be transformed not into a woman, but into a superman. As
we shall see, in *Troilus and Cressida*, it is just this kind of transformation
that Ulysses attempts to stage.

2   *Troilus and Cressida* and the politics of rage

In Act V, scene ii of *Troilus and Cressida*, Ulysses takes Troilus to watch Cressida betray him. The scene is explicitly presented as a scene of theatre, watched by multiple audiences – Troilus watching Cressida, Ulysses watching Troilus and Thersites watching all three. The effect of the scene is to plunge Troilus into what the Renaissance would have recognized as the crisis of skepticism itself, a moment of acute and paralyzing doubt in which all bases for judgments as Troilus has known them dissolve: "Was Cressid here?" he asks, "This is, and is not, Cressid."[1]

Ultimately, this doubt congeals into rage, and ultimately this rage leads Troilus into battle. As such, the scene raises a series of implicit questions about Shakespeare's conception of theatre's relation to its own audience. Why does Shakespeare picture theatre as an instrument of rage? Why does he envision it as something which plunges its spectator into paralyzing doubt? To answer these larger questions, it will be necessary first to answer a smaller one: What is Ulysses doing in the scene on the walls? Why does he seek to engender in Troilus a doubt so radical as to amount to Pyrrhonism itself?

In the pages which follow, I am going to be examining three possible answers to this question. The first looks at Ulysses' actions in moral terms, as offering a purge or a cure for pride. The second looks at them in exactly the opposite way, not as moral but as political, as a method of winning the war. The third explanation, and the one I will be advocating, looks at the scene on the walls neither as moral nor as primarily political, but as a response to an identifiable set of cultural anxieties during the period, anxieties articulated by, among others, Stephen Gosson, for instance when he claims that theatre "effeminates" the mind.[2] The scene on the walls is Shakespeare's anatomy of a cultural anxiety. By depicting not only it but all the scenes Ulysses stages as defenses against the anxieties of effeminization that lay at the heart of anti-theatricality, Shakespeare offers a critique of anti-theatricality itself. But this critique, I will suggest, is contaminated by the very anxieties it anatomizes. For

26

Troilus and Cressida's argument and practice are at odds. And if the play anatomizes the scenes Ulysses stages, it also behaves in ways which are disturbingly like them.[3]

Medicinable derision

What the scene on the walls brings about in Troilus is the collapse of a criterion or standard. For at the beginning of the long speech that starts at line 133, Troilus' criterion for whether it is Cressida or not is a belief in the reality of ideals or essences, or what he calls "souls" ("If beauty have a soul, this is not she; / If souls guide vows ... This was not she" [V.ii.138–42]). But by the end of the scene, this criterion has become dislodged. For where Troilus has explicitly rejected the "attest of eyes and ears" in insisting that it is not Cressida, he implicitly accepts it when he acknowledges that it is Cressida ("O Cressid! O false Cressid! false, false, false!" [V.ii.177]). What the scene on the walls enacts is the loss of one criterion and its replacement by another. In between, what Troilus is left with is radical doubt, or what he calls "madness of discourse." In between he is criterionless.

It is this moment of being criterionless that interests me as a depiction of what it means to be a spectator, since for both classical and Renaissance skeptics it was the condition of life itself: since both reason and the evidence of the senses were fallible, man's condition was one of uncertainty. If we had a guaranteed criterion to tell us which judgments were true and which were not, knowledge would be possible. But since we do not, we are left in perpetual doubt. The Academic skeptic said, "It is impossible to know anything with certainty," and instead of seeking certainty, tried to construct a kind of probability model. The Pyrrhonic skeptic said, "It is not even possible to know whether it is possible to know anything."[4] For the Pyrrhonist, the cultivation of doubt was a practice in itself, and what the scene on the walls produces in Troilus is something very like this practice. What does it mean to think of theatre in this way? Why does Shakespeare present it as an instrument of radical skepticism? Why does Ulysses wish to produce in Troilus radical doubt?

From one standpoint, the most obvious explanation for a scene of theatre which seeks to engender radical doubt in its spectator is the goal of curing pride. From what standpoint would this explanation be so obvious? From the standpoint of Pyrrhonism itself. Both classical and Renaissance advocates of Pyrrhonism thought of it as a purge. Montaigne compares it to rhubarb which expels evil humors and then carries itself away in the process.[5] The method by which the Pyrrhonist accomplishes this purge is the cultivation of perpetual doubt. He develops the mental habit of apprehending contradiction, of balancing opposed sets of evidence pro and con in his mind at the same time and by doing so suspends his judgment and attains a kind of ataraxy, peace or tranquility.[6] This, Montaigne says, everybody knows is the greatest good. For Montaigne, the process is specifically a cure for pride, "man's original malady," and even more specifically a cure for the particular kind of pride that imagines that it is possible to know something. Other antidotes Montaigne recommends include blindness, darkness, ignorance, confusion and being stripped of all one's power. But better than any of these is to live in perpetual doubt.

It is tempting therefore to read the scene on the walls as Montaigne might read it. Troilus' "This is, and is not, Cressid," his complaints about "bi-fold authority," his complaint that "cause sets up with and against itself" and his habit of citing opposed pieces of evidence pro and con about whether it is actually Cressida or not, all look like the habits of the Pyrrhonist mind. It is tempting, then, to read the scene on the walls as an attempt to purge pride, tempting if only because Ulysses stages at least one other play-within-a-play scene in *Troilus and Cressida* which he explicitly calls a purge for pride and which, like the scene on the walls, seeks to accomplish its ends by throwing the spectator into a state of radical doubt.

That scene is the pageant of Greek warriors, the parade of Greek generals who stroll past Achilles refusing to recognize him ("Know they not Achilles?" Achilles asks), and actually there are two parts to the performance, the parade itself and Ulysses' "interpretation" afterwards, an interpretation which is as much a staged performance as what it purports to explain, complete with stage prop of book and Ulysses in the role of philosopher sage. Both parts of the performance, pageant and "interpretation," seek to create doubt, specifically the doubt that it is possible to have a self, discrete and separate from the community that defines us.

Even before Ulysses "explains" the pageant he's devised, Achilles has begun to flirt with the idea that he has no intrinsic value, no separate self. "What, am I poor of late?" he asks. "'Tis certain [that] ... not a man, for being simply man, / Hath any honor, but honor for those honors / That are without him, as place, riches and favor – / Prizes of accident as oft as merit" (III.iii.75–83). But no sooner has he begun to doubt the idea of honor "for being simply man" than he retreats into the proposition that the case doesn't apply to him ("'tis not so with me, / Fortune and I are friends" [III.iii.87–8]).

Even before Ulysses' "interpretation," then, this scene of theatre has suggested to its spectator a diminished sense of worth and denied to him a separate existence apart from the community that grants him his "honor." Ulysses' "explication" seeks to induce these reactions even more energetically. "A strange fellow here," Ulysses says in his role of scholar

> Writes me that man, how dearly ever parted,
> How much in having, or without or in,
> Cannot make boast to have that which he hath,
> Nor feels not what he owes but by reflection...
>
> (III.iii.95–9)

Ulysses assaults both the possibility of the spectator *having* a separate self and the possibility of his *knowing* who or what he is. When Achilles tries to construe his message solely as an argument about knowledge, when he tries to sanitize it with conceits about the eye's purity making it impossible to see itself, Ulysses restates it as an argument about power, emphasizes the powerlessness implicit in not being able to know who or what you are. The position is familiar, he says, but this particular author proves "that no man is *lord* of any thing... / Till he communicate his parts to others; / Nor doth he of himself know them for aught, / Till he behold them formed in th' applause" (III.iii.115–19, italics mine).

The pageant of Greek warriors is a kind of rehearsal for the scene on the walls, then, not only because it seeks to engender radical doubt, but because it assaults the spectator's belief in the possibility of a separate self. And the very crux of Troilus' experience in the scene on the walls is the fragmentation of his belief in the possibility of a single whole Cressida:

> This is, and is not, Cressid!
> Within my soul there doth conduce a fight
> Of this strange nature, that a thing inseparate
> Divides more wider than the sky and earth,
> And yet the spacious breath of this division
> Admits no orifex for a point as subtle
> As Ariachne's broken woof to enter.
>
> (V.ii.146–52)

What the passage rails against (but ultimately registers) is the idea that two separate and opposite Cressidas can reside in the same body – even the pun on "Ariachne," the malapropism which conflates Arachne and Ariadne, dissolves the idea of a discrete separable identity, and, as we shall see, it is not only Troilus' belief in the possibility of a self that begins to erode in the scene on the walls, but his sense of his own self as well: "I will not be myself," he says, "nor have cognition of what I feel" (V.ii.63–4).[7]

Ulysses is quite specific about the purpose of the pageant of Greek

warriors. He is doing it to cure Achilles' pride. Not only does he tell
Agamemnon that he has "derision medicinable" to put between his
"strangeness" and Achilles' pride, but his whole justification of the
lottery plot is that Achilles' "seeded pride" must be cropped, that this will
"physic" him. It is tempting then to see the pageant of Greek warriors and
the scene on the walls alike as purges, assaults on the self to correct
excesses of self, theatres which create disorder in the service of greater
order. This is, after all, a familiar enough theory of drama, drama as
physic, drama as cure. And it is a theory of drama particularly suited to
make sense of a theatre that engenders radical doubt, a crisis of Pyrrhonism, since Pyrrhonism understands itself specifically as a cure for pride.

But there are a number of problems with this idea, beginning with
Ulysses' own inconsistency. For though he is good at engendering the
experience of Pyrrhonism in others, he himself speaks like no skeptic, as
when, for instance, he claims that the "providence that's in a watchful
state / Knows almost every grain of Pluto's gold" (III.iii.196–7), or when
he claims that the state can keep pace with thought or unveil thoughts in
their cradles. As part of that state, he is far from doubting his own
capacity for knowledge. Nor is his commitment to quelling pride in others
necessarily even consistent. A large piece of the lottery plot is the play-
within-the-play scene dedicated to the puffing-up, the flattering of Ajax.[8]
At the very least, then, to "cure" Achilles' pride, Ulysses seems to need to
"infect" Ajax with the same pride. And even Achilles himself is frequently
the object of Ulysses' flattery, as when, for instance, he tells him that his
"glorious deeds but in these fields of late / Made emulous missions
'mongst the gods themselves" (III.iii.188–9).

But perhaps a more interesting problem with seeing the scene on the
walls as a purge is that the very metaphors Ulysses uses suggest that he
wants Troilus not to purge his emotions but to "contain" them. "Contain
yourself," he says, "Your passion draws ears hither" (V.ii.180–1). He
conceives of Troilus' emotions as a set of fluids, conceives of them always
in physical terms, always in danger of becoming "enlarged" ("Let us
depart.... / Lest your displeasure should enlarge itself / To wrathful
terms" [V.ii.36–8]), always in danger of "overflowing" ("You flow to
great distraction. Come, my lord" [V.ii.41]). He conceives of Troilus in
the same terms that anti-theatricalist Stephen Gosson does the psyche
when he describes it as a cup in danger of overflowing.[9] And far from
wanting Troilus to purge these affections, he says at least that he wants
Troilus to contain them.

But if, as Ulysses' metaphors suggest, the emotions are fluids held in a
container, in fact, Ulysses does everything possible to make this container
overflow, from showing Troilus the scene in the first place, to goading him
with descriptions of Cressida's looseness, to putting pressure on that

"container" by urging patience. "You have not patience, come" (V.ii.42). "You have sworn patience" (V.ii.62). Though Ulysses' rhetoric is the rhetoric of an anti-theatricalist, his actions are the actions of the player or playwright *as an anti-theatricalist would see the player or playwright*, the person who produces in the spectator uncontainable affect, whets desires to inordinate lust. What Ulysses does, in other words, is create as much pressure as possible, both from without and from within, first by stimulating the "fluids," and then by urging containment. He wants Troilus neither to "purge" nor to "contain" his affections. He wants the container to break.[10] The largest problem, then, with arguing that Ulysses seeks to cure pride by engendering Pyrrhonism, is that Pyrrhonism itself is supposed to promote peace or ataraxy, and the scene on the walls produces neither, but jealous rage.

Part of what Ulysses asks Troilus to "contain" during the scene on the walls is in fact exactly the titillation that anti-theatricalists said plays produced in the spectator. "Contained" within the scene on the walls is a masturbatory fantasy with Troilus as its subject. Cressida depicts Troilus to Troilus alone in the darkness, substituting the glove for her:

> O all you gods! O pretty, pretty pledge!
> Thy master now lies thinking in his bed
> Of thee and me, and sighs, and takes my glove
> And gives memorial dainty kisses to it,
> As I kiss thee. Nay, do not snatch it from me.
>
> (V.ii.77–81)

Just as the fantasy is about to reach its crisis ("As I kiss thee") it is cut off, frustrated. The moment is quite literally like Stephen Gosson's description of theatre's capacity to render the spectator like one that "hearing one half of a sentence ... is very desirous to have the rest."[11] The technique is to raise anxiety and then to channel it into rage against a third person, here Diomedes. Troilus articulates that rage at the end of the scene when he vows to fight Diomedes ("That sleeve is mine that he'll bear on his helm. / Were it a casque compos'd by Vulcan's skill, / My sword should bite it" [V.ii.169–71]).

In a sense, then, the scene on the walls can be seen as a kind of contest between Ulysses' attempts to make Troilus "overflow" to distraction and Troilus' own attempts to contain the rage the scene before him is producing. Troilus' first defense against this rage is patience itself: "I will be patient" (V.ii.47); "There is between my will and all offenses / A guard of patience" (V.ii.53–54);[12] "I am all patience" (V.ii.64); "I did swear patience" (V.ii.84). But though he asserts his patience again and again, what the scene enacts is in fact the breakdown of patience. What the scene depicts is the progression in Troilus of an increasingly radical set of defenses until he is left with his own rage.

Even within the first eighty lines of the scene, the nature of this "patience" changes from simple patience, a restraining of emotion or impulse, to the *loss* of emotion or impulse, a gradual dimming of cognition ("I will not be myself, nor have cognition / Of what I feel; I am all patience" [V.ii.63–4]). What follows – that esperance that doth "invert th'attest of eyes and ears" – implies a widening of the defense, the need to deny what is "without" as well as what is "within." But even this defense breaks down into a moment of deeper, more radical doubt. "Was Cressid here?" he asks (V.ii.125). Not even the certainty of denial, but a question, just as Pyrrhonic skeptics during the period said the statement "I know nothing" made an assertion to knowledge and thus framed their Pyrrhonism in the form of a question ("Que sais-je?").[13] In what follows, Troilus offers an even more radical defense (what Kleinians would call "splitting," the breaking-up of the loved person into good and bad object: "This she? No this is Diomed's Cressida," says Troilus [V.ii.137]). This is more radical, because the very need to split up Cressida suggests it is no longer possible to deny what is "without," the "attest of eyes and ears."[14] But this too breaks down. For though Troilus seeks to support his position with the rhetoric of essentialism ("If beauty have a soul ... if souls guide vows") this too breaks down into radical doubt, paralyzing skepticism, incoherence:

> O madness of discourse,
> That cause sets up with and against itself!
> Bi-fold authority, where reason can revolt
> Without perdition, and loss assume all reason
> Without revolt. This is, and is not, Cressid!
>
> (V.ii.142–6)

The lines neither assert nor deny nor try to split Cressid up. They are an instance of the paralysis itself, a last-gasp defense against the rage Troilus will ultimately be left with at the end of the scene and from which he can no longer protect Cressid ("O Cressid! O false Cressid! false, false, false!" [V.ii.177]).

We have a potential answer to one question then: the relation between doubt and rage. In the scene on the walls, Shakespeare seems to conceive of doubt as the last stage in a progression toward rage, both the last weapon in Troilus' attempt to protect Cressida from his sense that she is "false, false, false" and something which is itself "maddening." What we really need to account for, then, is not a theatre which plunges its spectator into a state of radical doubt, since that doubt will anyway only be a stage on the way to rage, but a theatre which provokes its spectator to uncontainable rage. What does it mean for Shakespeare to think of theatre in this way?

Flowing to distraction

Perhaps if the scene on the walls cannot be seen as a moral tool in the service of curing pride, it is simply a political one in the service of winning the war. There would be corroboration for such a claim, if the play were, for instance, to align the release of uncontainable rage with the destruction of the person in whom that rage were released. In fact, Ulysses himself makes just that equation. At the end of the degree speech, he describes a self in disorder, a self in which the higher faculties have collapsed and brought into dominance the lower faculties, which, in turn, collapse, until what is left is the universal wolf:

> Then everything include itself in power,
> Power into will, will into appetite,
> And appetite, an universal wolf
> (So doubly seconded with will and power)
> Must make perforce an universal prey,
> And last eat up himself.
>
> (I.iii.119–24)

The vision is essentially one of the self as a set of dominoes, the self with the will rendered inoperative, the same vision Gosson articulates when he pictures the player degenerating "from pyping to playing, from play to pleasure, from pleasure to slouth, from slouth to sleepe, from sleepe to sinne, from sinne to death, from death to the Divel,"[15] and the same vision Troilus himself articulates when he tells Cressida, "But something may be done that we will not / And sometimes we are devils to ourselves" (IV.iv.94–5).

But this is exactly the process that Ulysses brings about in the scene on the walls when he destroys the "guard of patience" that stands between Troilus and all his offenses (and destroys not only the "guard of patience," but, as we have seen, all the other defenses – dimming of cognition, denial of ocular evidence, splitting, skepticism itself – that Troilus seeks to erect between himself and his rage). It is precisely the release of uncontainable aggression, the "universal wolf" that Ulysses aligns with the destruction of the self, and it is precisely the universal wolf that he releases in Troilus at the end of the scene on the walls. The very language Troilus uses to describe his rage replicates Ulysses' vision of destruction at the end of the degree speech, the water making a sop of all the solid land:

> Not the dreadful spout
> Which shipmen do the hurricano call,
> Constring'd in mass by the almighty sun,
> Shall dizzy with more clamor Neptune's ear,

In his descent, than shall my prompted sword
Falling on Diomed.

(V.ii.171–6)

The language of the speech replicates not only in general ways the "evil mixture" in which the planets wander to disorder, but replicates with some specificity Ulysses' description of the "bounded waters" lifting their bosoms higher than the shore and making a "sop of all this solid globe." We could say, in fact, that what Ulysses brings about in Troilus is "evil mixture" itself, "This is, and is not, Cressid."

We could say, then, that the production of doubt in the spectator is itself only in the service of the production of rage, and that this rage is, in turn, in the service of destroying the spectator's self, and this is, in turn, in the service of winning the war. But the problem with this formulation is that Ulysses doesn't only turn such scenes of theatre against his enemies. Neither the production of rage nor the destruction of the self is peculiar to the scene on the walls, but rather a regular feature of every other scene of theatre Ulysses stages. We have already seen the way the pageant of Greek warriors assaults Achilles' "self," but in seminal form, Ulysses' re-enactments of Achilles' and Patroclus' satires to Nestor and Agamemnon do the same thing by presenting back to the spectators who are also the subjects of the performance images of their own worst selves.[16] In Agamemnon's case, that self is merely pompous – Ulysses represents him as speaking like "a chime a-mending" – but the vision of Nestor as helpless and fumbling in a night alarm, coughing and spitting "and with a palsy fumbling on his gorget" is calculated to titillate the anxiety of the spectator who is also its subject. Ulysses' true skill, however, lies in his ability to translate that anxiety into rage against a third person – Achilles, whom he pictures to Nestor not only as laughing "in pleasure of [his] spleen" but as requesting the performance in the first place. Similarly, just as the scene on the walls provokes Troilus to uncontainable rage, so the conspiracy scene, the puffing-up of Ajax, both seeks to and succeeds in enraging its spectator. Here, the self-proclaimed purpose of the scene is to enrage: "He's not yet through warm," says Ulysses. Nestor adds, "Force him with praises – pour in, pour in" (II.iii.221–4). Though, logically, the effect of the praise should be to soothe rather than enrage, both the goal and the effect of the scene are to make Ajax "warm." ("If I go to him [Achilles], with my armed fist / I'll pash him o'er the face" [II.iii.202–3]).[17]

But there is another, even larger problem with understanding the scene on the walls as a political instrument in the service of winning the war. For if Ulysses destroys Troilus' "self" in the scene on the walls, he also brings into being a formidable opponent, by drawing into battle someone who has been in flight from it throughout the whole play: "Call here my varlet, I'll unarm again. / Why should I war without the walls of Troy, / That find such cruel battle here within?" says Troilus (I.i.1–3). A scene later, we see him sneaking across stage, clearly not having been to battle. And though he spouts the rhetoric of war in the Trojan council scene, by Act III he has still not gone to battle. Pandarus asks who's afield, and Paris says, "Hector, Deiphobus, Helenus, Antenor, and all the gallantry of Troy ... How chance my brother Troilus went not?" (III.i.135–8). It is specifically the scene on the walls that gets Troilus into the war, gets him to do for rage what he would not do for love.

What is interesting about this is that it is almost as if this is just what Ulysses is trying to bring about. For he has just (at the end of IV.v) described Troilus' capacity for jealous rage and, more importantly, *the way that capacity facilitates Troilus' military prowess.* Repeating what Aeneas has told him, he suggests that it is the specific quality of Troilus' wrath – its jealous and justificatory nature – that makes him more dangerous than Hector. He calls Troilus

> Manly as Hector, but more dangerous,
> For Hector in his blaze of wrath subscribes
> To tender objects, but he in heat of action
> Is more vindicative than jealous love.

(IV.v.104–7)

Yet it is just this capacity for "jealous love" that Ulysses actualizes in the scene on the walls, just this capacity for rage he realizes in Troilus.

There is a model for just such a theatre during the period, and we have already had a glimpse of it in Heywood's anecdote about Caesar playing Hercules and growing so carried away with the "practised fury" of Hercules that he kills the servant in fact that he was only supposed to pretend to kill:

Yet was Caesar so extremely carried away with the violence of his practised fury, and by the perfect shape of the madnesse of Hercules, to which he had fashioned all his active spirits, that he slew him dead at his foot, and after swoong him, *terque quaterque* (as the poet says).

This is a theatre that produces uncontainable rage, but the first thing to say about it is that for Heywood such rage does not destroy the self, but enhances it, does not diminish the actor who is filled with it, but empowers him. This is because a large part of theatre's value for Heywood lies in its capacity to "fashion" soldiers, to "enflame" the hearts of the spectators with military ardour. "To see a souldier shap'd like a souldier ... To see a Hector all besmered in blood," says Heywood wistfully. "Oh, these were sights to make an Alexander." At the heart of the text is a vision of history in which warriors *become* warriors by

watching theatre – Caesar by watching the actions of Alexander per-
formed before him, Alexander by watching those of Achilles, Achilles
Theseus, Theseus Hercules and Hercules by watching those of his father
Jupiter.[18]

But why would Ulysses want to fashion a warrior of Troilus? Why
would he want to actualize his military prowess? Why would he want to
draw him into the war? It makes sense to stage a theatre which enrages
your spectator and draws him into war if your spectator is one of your
own men, Nestor, Ajax, or Achilles, but why should Ulysses want to
militarize a Trojan? What we really need is an explanation that will
account for all the scenes of theatre Ulysses stages which enrage their
spectator, an explanation that will account both for what Ulysses does to
his enemies, and for what he does to his own men.[19]

White enchanting fingers

Perhaps Ulysses' comments to Achilles at the end of the pageant of Greek
warriors will provide a clue. He tells Achilles: "And better would it fit
Achilles much / To throw down Hector than Polyxena" (III.iii.207–8).
War is better than love, Ulysses argues, "throwing down a man" better
than "throwing down" a woman.[20] His next lines are even more suggestive. He tells Achilles that it will grieve young Pyrrhus at home when the
Greekish girls taunt him by singing "'Great Hector's sister did Achilles
win, / But our great Ajax bravely beat down him'" (III.iii.212–13).
Ostensibly the issue at stake is the female mockery, but the syntax reveals
a deeper anxiety: Does the line "Great Hector's sister did Achilles win"
make Polyxena or Achilles the subject of the verb? Who is it that does the
winning? Who is it that is active and who is passive?

Patroclus identifies the anxiety buried within the syntax a moment
later:

> To this effect, Achilles, have I mov'd you.
> A woman impudent and mannish grown
> Is not more loath'd than an effeminate man
> In time of action.

> (III.iii.216–19)

The play then articulates the same fears which dominated anti-theatrical
tracts for sixty years, the fear that action is constitutive, that men who
dress or act or behave like women will turn into them. Achilles himself
articulates this fear of effeminization in its strongest terms:

> I have a woman's longing,
> An appetite that I am sick withal,

> To see great Hector in his weeds of peace,
> To talk with him and to behold his visage...
>
> (III.iii.237–40)

By the end of the scene, the very desire for peace itself has become effeminate, a "woman's longing" – the phrase itself suggests pregnancy urges.

In a world which regards peace itself as effeminate, a theatre which stirs men to rage will serve a defensive purpose. For indeed fears of effeminization in *Troilus and Cressida* are not confined to any one character or camp, but are articulated by nearly everyone in the play: by or about Ulysses, Thersites, Troilus, Paris, Patroclus, Achilles and Paris. The play begins with Troilus accusing himself of being "weaker than a woman's tear... / Less valiant than the virgin in the night" (I.i.9–11). During the Trojan council scene Priam tells Paris he speaks like one "besotted" ("You have the honey still, but these the gall" [II.ii.144]). And when we do see Paris, he is, in fact, "besotted," unable to arm for battle because his "Nell" – Helen has become a kind of household slattern – will not let him go (III.i.136–7). Ajax calls Thersites "mistress Thersites," and Thersites in turn calls Patroclus Achilles' "brach," his "male varlot," his masculine whore (V.i.15).

But if anxieties of effeminization are not peculiar to one figure or camp, what they do share is that they are all associated with love, heterosexual or homoerotic.[21] Patroclus suggests that Achilles' homoerotic love for Patroclus himself will be seen as the cause of his effeminacy "in time of action:"

> I stand condemned for this;
> They think my little stomach to the war,
> And your great love to me, restrains you thus
>
> (III.iii.219–21)

although Ulysses implies it is Achilles' love for Polyxena and his attendant oath that keep him out of battle:

> ACHILLES: Of this my privacy
> I have strong reasons.
> ULYSSES: But 'gainst your privacy
> The reasons are more potent and heroical.
> 'Tis known, Achilles, that you are in love
> With one of Priam's daughters.
>
> (III.iii.190–4)

Thersites' reaction an act later as he watches Achilles decide to keep that oath suggests the degree of panic that the world of the play registers at the idea of a man refusing to fight out of love for a woman. He thinks first of

Menelaus, the "goodly transformation of Jupiter there ... the bull, the primitive statue and oblique memorial of cuckolds" (V.i.53–5). The line begins with one kind of metamorphosis and ends with another. It begins with the idea of a voluntary metamorphosis, Jupiter into a bull to rape Europa, a metamorphosis self-willed and aggressive, an assertion of masculine power. It ends with the opposite kind of metamorphosis, the cuckolding of Menelaus, a metamorphosis not actively sought, but passively endured, a reminder of feminine power, masculine powerlessness. But it is as if this very powerlessness, and the transformation which brings it about, were contagious.[22] For the scene ends with Thersites' fantasy of his own metamorphosis:

To an ass, were nothing, he is both ass and ox; to an ox, were nothing; he is both ox and ass. To be a dog, a moile, a cat, a fitchook, a toad, a lezard, an owl, a puttock, or a herring without a roe, I would not care; but to be Menelaus, I would conspire against destiny. Ask me not what I would be if I were not Thersites, for I care not to be the louse of a lazar, so I were not Menelaus. Hey-day! Sprites and fires! (V.i.60–8)

The very idea of Achilles keeping his oath to a woman triggers a series of passive and humiliating transformations, transformations which are not simply degrading, but virtually contagious for the spectator Thersites who stands watching.

But the most eloquent emblem of love's danger, its disorganizing power, is articulated by Paris when he woos Helen "to help unarm our Hector":

> Sweet Helen, I must woo you
> To help unarm our Hector. His stubborn buckles
> With these your white enchanting fingers touch'd,
> Shall more obey than to the edge of steel,
> Or force of Greekish sinews. You shall do more
> Than all the island kings – disarm great Hector.
>
> (III.i.148–53)

The passage offers the perfect emblem for beauty's dangerous disorganizing power, which is conceived of as more dangerous than the dangers of war.

We have a new answer, then, to why Ulysses stages scene after scene of theatre calculated to drive the spectator to uncontainable amounts of rage. Ulysses' theatre offers a defense against the anxieties of effeminization which he and everyone else around him articulate. In a world where Helen's white hands can do more than all the island kings to disarm Hector, in a world where beauty is more dangerous than war, love more disorganizing than battle, effeminization more dangerous than death, a theatre which draws men into battle will insure that they are really men, a theatre which enrages them will protect them from the more disorganizing powers of love. What this implies, though, is a world in which masculinity must be enacted, acted out, actually performed in order to exist.[23] And Shakespeare's particularly nihilistic vision of the Trojan war is his assessment of the *cost* of that performance. He simultaneously exposes the premise built into anti-theatricality, that men must *act* like men to be men, must perform their gender if it is to exist, and at the same time depicts the nature of the world that that premise, escalated to its logical conclusion, would lead to.

The scene on the walls is Shakespeare's anatomy of a cultural anxiety. Where anti-theatrical tracts argue that theatre effeminates men by drawing them away from battle, Shakespeare suggests it is precisely the fear of effeminization that gets them into war in the first place. But the play also offers a critique of the very *possibility* of anti-theatricality, of being "outside" the theatre. For it is the anti-theatricalist in the play, Ulysses – who blames the fact that the Greeks are losing the war on the satires Achilles and Patroclus are putting on in their tent – who stages scene after scene of theatre. In Ulysses himself, Shakespeare suggests that anti-theatricality is, in effect, impossible, for the very anxieties that fuel it seem to need to be "staged" – enacted and compulsively re-enacted in order to be allayed.

We would expect *Troilus and Cressida*, then, to differentiate itself from the various plays Ulysses stages, behave differently toward its own spectator. But there are disturbing parallels between the scene on the walls and *Troilus and Cressida* itself. For it is not only Troilus who is thrown into a state of radical doubt by what he sees before him, not only Troilus who is presented with two contradictory Cressidas, but the spectator of *Troilus and Cressida* as well. For the scene on the walls is itself framed by two mutually exclusive interpretations of Cressida, and by juxtaposing them the play implicitly asks us to choose between them, all the while making it impossible for us to do so.

This is, and is not, Cressid

Perhaps the central problem that confronts any spectator of *Troilus and Cressida* is "What *is* Cressida?" She vows eternal love to Troilus and betrays him within the space of twenty-four hours. Is she lying? Did she mean what she said when she said it and then "change"? Her actions are framed by two diametrically opposite interpretations offered of her within the play itself: Thersites says she is a whore (a "commodious drab" [V.ii.194]). Troilus says it wasn't the "real" Cressida ("This she? no, this is Diomed's Cressida" [V.ii.137]). Troilus' interpretation rejects the evidence of the senses, what he calls "invert[ing] th' attest of eyes and ears" (V.ii.122). Thersites' depends on the evidence of the senses. He accuses Troilus of "swagger[ing] himself out on's own eyes" (V.ii.l36). Troilus' interpretation is incoherent, Thersites' reductive. Troilus seems mad, his rejection of the evidence of the senses seems like willed blindness. On the other hand, the one character in the play with an absolute claim to knowledge also "seems" mad: completely interior, intuited and incommunicable, what Cassandra "knows" also defies the evidence of the senses, and the play never once calls this knowledge into question. Whose criterion for making an interpretation is the play validating? What is Cressida?

There are half a dozen moments when we have to make critical decisions about whether Cressida is telling the truth when she says she loves Troilus, but none of them yield up definite answers one way or the other. Both in their own right and taken cumulatively, these moments are "teases," creating a series of contradictions which, like Ulysses' annihilation of the conceptual category "self," virtually annihilate the concept of character, provoking, as critics have evinced, a considerable amount of frustration in the spectator.[24]

Alone on stage, at the end of I.ii, Cressida makes a speech which offers to explain all her future inconsistencies and choices:

> But more in Troilus thousandfold I see
> Than in the glass of Pandar's praise may be;
> Yet hold I off. Women are angels, wooing;
> Things won are done, joy's soul lies in the doing.
> That she belov'd knows nought that knows not this:
> Men prize the thing ungain'd more than it is.
> That she was never yet that ever knew
> Love got so sweet as when desire did sue.
> Therefore this maxim out of love I teach:
> Achievement is command; ungained, beseech;
> Then though my heart's content firm love doth bear,
> Nothing of that shall from mine eyes appear.
>
> (I.ii.284–95)

There are only two possibilities for interpretation here. Either Cressida is telling the truth, or she is not. If she is telling the truth, she loved Troilus at least at the beginning of the play, and at least at the beginning was neither a liar nor a whore. If she is lying, it is possible to think of her as consistent throughout the play. She is what Thersites says she is: lies and lechery. If we believe she is telling the truth, we get an inconsistent Cressida, but a consistent basis for making interpretations. (When people are alone on stage with no one to lie to, we assume that they are telling the truth.) If we say the speech is not true, we get a consistent Cressida, Thersites' "whetstone," but we get an inconsistent criterion for interpretation. (If even the things characters say alone on stage can be lies, there is no particular criterion for knowing when they are lying to each other.)

The fact that the speech takes place alone on stage (a kind of enormous "aside" to the audience) really does make it seem as if it offers the "key" to Cressida's subsequent actions, as if she were saying: this is what you need to know about me for later when there will be other people around. But the scene that the speech closes has just argued against the very possibility of knowing what a person is, against the very possibility of interpretation itself. At the end of I.i, alone on stage, Troilus asks: "Tell me, Apollo, for thy Daphne's love, / What Cressid is, what Pandar, and what we" (I.i.98–9). He asks, in effect, what a person is, and I.ii – organized around Pandarus' somewhat hysterical refrain, "have you any eyes? do you know what a man is?" (I.ii.252) "Do you know a man if you see him?" (I.ii.63–4) – both reiterates the question and says it is impossible to answer. For Pandarus' claim that Troilus is a better man than Hector is predicated on the belief that it is possible to know *what* a man is (and therefore what a person is). But every time Pandarus himself tries to assert something about the "man," Troilus, Cressida reduces him to either a tautology, "I say Troilus is Troilus" (I.ii.66), or a contradiction, "he's not himself" (I.ii.76), or a scaled-down version of the original claim that Troilus is a better man than Hector (as in the inversion "Hector is not a better man than Troilus" [I.ii.79–80]) or to the attribution of a subjective judgment to someone else, "Helen loves him better than Paris" (I.ii.107–8) – not even better than Hector, but better than Paris! All the attempts Pandarus makes to make claims about what a person is, based on reason, fail. But they are juxtaposed to his failure to make claims about what a person is based on the evidence of the senses. For when Pandarus actually sees Troilus, he misidentifies him:

CRESSIDA: What sneaking fellow comes yonder?
(Enter Troilus [and passes over the stage].)
PANDARUS: Where? Yonder? That's Deiphobus. 'Tis Troilus! There's a man, niece! Hem! Brave Troilus, the prince of chivalry! (I.ii.226–9)

What the scene has just enacted is the impossibility of making an inter-pretation based on either rational grounds or empirical ones, the specific impossibility of knowing what a person is. The very existence of such a scene as a frame for Cressida's disclosure of what *she* is (for the one moment in the play that *seems* to present itself as a yardstick for reading her future contradictions) calls that moment and hence that yardstick into question, and thus dislodges the only criterion that we have for judging her future inconsistencies.

Even if we overlook this, the speech itself seems to generate a series of contradictions in the scenes which follow. The next time we see Cressida and the next time we have to make a decision about whether to believe what she says is during the vows scene. There she says to Troilus, "Prince Troilus, I have lov'd you night and day / For many weary months" (III.ii.114–15). Either she is lying (as Thersites would say, and as the stagey stilted quality of the lines may suggest) or she is telling the truth. But in either case, the lines contradict what she has said in her soliloquy. If she is lying, if she doesn't love him, then the lines certainly contradict what she said in her soliloquy about firm love. But if she is telling Troilus the truth, the lines also generate a contradiction. For she has just said that she will conceal her love. If she loves him, why doesn't it matter any more that men only want what they can't have? And if she is supposed to be acting here, if she is already insincere, already behaving in ways that are consistent with Thersites' interpretation, why is her "act" not even consistent with itself?

What is crucial here is that either way the speech in I.ii generates a series of contradictions, and this speech is the closest thing we get to a criterion, an interpretive purchase on what Cressida is. What the play does is simultaneously develop two contradictory Cressidas, titillate the expectation that we could choose between them (or between Thersites' and Troilus' interpretations, or between their criteria for making interpretations) and then frustrate this expectation. In this way *Troilus and Cressida* recreates in us the very doubt that Ulysses engenders in his spectators, the very experience of a dissolving criterion.

Thus the play provides possible support for the initial speech being the truth, and it also provides challenges to the speech being the truth. All the bawdy jokes about Cressida dragging Troilus back to bed in IV.ii might be suggestions that she is a whore, but they might just as easily represent her fear of being discovered. Her line "You men will never tarry" (IV.ii.16) might be evidence that she has gotten around and that there are other men, or Pandarus' "How now, how go maidenheads?" (IV.ii.23) might be better evidence that she was a virgin. Her grief at finding out that she has been "changed" for Antenor might be as genuine as it seems in IV.ii or it might be aestheticized and theatricalized as it seems in IV.iv when she says "The grief is fine, full perfect, that I taste, / And violenteth in a sense as strong / As that which causeth it" (IV.iv.3–5). The kiss scene (IV.v) might be proof that she is a whore, but it also bears disturbing similarities to a gang rape. At any rate, all the kissing in the scene goes on before Cressida ever gets a chance to speak. And when she does speak it is to resist her kissers, particularly Ulysses, who is the one to call her a whore.

The play then provides us with two simultaneous but opposite

Cressidas. In another play, we might refer these contradictions to Cressida's psychological complexity, but she isn't presented in any psychological complexity apart from the contradictions themselves. Notwithstanding what Ulysses says about Cressida "wide unclasp[ing] the tables of [her] thoughts / To every ticklish reader" (IV.v.60–1) the play insists on her ultimate unreadability, her unknowability, her openness. In this sense, like the scene on the walls, the play is a tease. Like Troilus, we are left with two Cressidas, and the same kind if not the same degree of frustration. But in the service of what does the play seek to produce this frustration? In Ulysses' scenes the production of doubt was itself only an instrument in a politics of rage, a politics which sought to elicit a counterperformance from the spectator, sought to produce rage in order to produce masculinity, which was construed as existing only in the *act* of displaying itself. To what degree is Shakespeare implicated in this politic? To what degree are the anxieties of a period's tract writers his anxieties too? To the degree that *Troilus and Cressida* exposes the fear behind Ulysses' scenes of theatre, it offers an analysis and critique of anti-theatricality itself. But to the extent that it behaves like the theatres it depicts, it is contaminated by the very anxieties it anatomizes, implicated in the practice it exposes.

Even as it anatomizes the militarism of a world in which men must be drawn into battle to remain men, *Troilus and Cressida* seeks to engender similar sentiments in its own audience, to titillate its own male spectators' aggression.[25] It offers, then, both an analysis and an instance of the anxiety which informs Gosson's warning to his reader: "bee not careless; plough with weapons by your sides; study with a book in one hand, a dart in the other; enjoy peace with provision for war."[26]

In an even deeper way, *Antony and Cleopatra* seems implicated in this kind of anti-theatricality. For if *Troilus and Cleopatra* behaves like Ulysses in its compulsive production of doubt, *Antony and Cleopatra* presents as history, as actual, what was, in effect, the central cautionary tale at the heart of the period's anti-theatrical literature itself, the story of the warrior who loses his masculinity because he fails to perform it, to "act" like a man. (If *Troilus and Cressida* offers a glimpse of a world in which masculinity must be performed in order to exist, *Antony and Cleopatra* depicts a world in which this particular performance is in the process of breaking down.) How Shakespeare reconciles this anti-theatricality with his own dramatic form and the degree to which a "defense" of theatre is possible in this context are the subject of the next chapter.

3   "Strange flesh": *Antony and Cleopatra* and
     the story of the dissolving warrior

Midway through his thousand-page *Histrio-mastix*, Prynne tells the story
we are by now familiar with, the story of the warrior who "degenerates"
into a woman: "Doth not that valiant man, that man of courage who is
admirable in his armes, and formidable to his enemies degenerate into a
woman with his veiled face?" Prynne asks. He explains the process by
which this transformation takes place; "he lets his coate hange down to
his ankles, he twists a girdle about his breast, he puts on women's shoes,
and after the manner of women, he puts a cawle upon his head." Not
content to assume the costume of a woman, the warrior also adopts her
customary behavior and "drawes out a thred with his right hand, wherewith he hath formerly borne a trophie." Ultimately what began as custom
becomes organic change: the warrior's voice changes register. "He
extenuateth his spirit and voyce into a shriller and womanish sound."[1]
   There are a number of startling things about this passage – the equation
it makes between what it means to be female and what it means to be
slovenly (as if the man who sloppily allowed his coat to hang down to his
ankles were the man who implicitly dressed like a woman); the way that it
conceives of the man as simply "degenerating" into a woman, as if the
woman were somehow there all along waiting to assume her proper shape.
But what is most striking about the passage is the way it simply assumes
that the adoption of effeminate behavior will lead to biological change in
the warrior's gender itself. The story is a cautionary tale, a warning that
the adoption of behaviors appropriate to the opposite sex will transform
one into that sex, a warning that action itself is constitutive, so much so
that *even* that "valiant man of courage," the most masculine person in the
culture, can be transformed.
   The Roman Philo begins Shakespeare's *Antony and Cleopatra* with a
similar story intended to illustrate a similar warning, when he says that
Antony's "captain's heart" is become the "bellows and the fan / To cool a
gipsy's lust." Philo too begins with a description of behavior. Antony is
abandoning the behavior appropriate to men, the behavior of war, and
turning instead to the behavior of love:

44

>   Those his goodly eyes,
> That o'er the files and musters of the war
> Have glow'd like Plated Mars, now bend, now turn
> The office and devotion of their view
> Upon a tawny front.
>
>   (I.i.2–6)[2]

Literally the description is one of behavior, of a gaze changing, of eyes changing from one "front," the front of war, to another, the tawny "front" of love. But here too behavior is conceived of as leading to physical change: not only do the eyes cease to glow, not only does the "captain's heart" beneath them shrink, becoming insufficient to burst the buckles on his chest, but that heart is become the "bellows and the fan / To cool a gipsy's lust." What does such a claim mean? As if to answer, a string of eunuchs appear, literally fanning Cleopatra. Metaphorically, through the image of the fan, the play begins by comparing Antony to a eunuch. The play opens with Philo telling the same story Prynne does, the story of a man whose masculinity is draining out of him, the story of the dissolving warrior.

But Philo is not the only person in *Antony and Cleopatra* to tell such a story about Antony. From his opening claim to Caesar's charge that Antony is "not more manlike than Cleopatra," to Cleopatra's memory of dressing Antony in her tires and mantles, to Antony's own impassioned cry in Act IV that his body is like a cloud that cannot hold its visible shape, the play registers the dissolution of his masculinity. Not only do individual moments argue that Antony is becoming effeminate, but, taken cumulatively, they tell a story in which effeminate behavior leads to constitutive change. The play simply treats as fact, as history, the cautionary tale at the center of anti-theatricality itself.

But doesn't such a treatment necessarily imply an *endorsement* of anti-theatricality? To treat a set of fears as fact – isn't this implicitly to ratify the danger of theatre? The question is complicated by a second. For even as the play validates the anxieties of the anti-theatrical tracts, it offers a critique of these very anxieties in the figure of Caesar, the explicit anti-theatricalist in the play. For in Caesar, Shakespeare offers a portrait of an anti-theatricalist whose attacks contain within them a longing for the very things he attacks. In Caesar, the play casts anti-theatricality itself as a posture, a front, for all the things that anti-theatricality itself expressly repudiates.

But if the play manifests an anti-theatricality on the one hand and a critique of anti-theatricality on the other, what criterion does it ultimately offer us for mediating between these two impulses? Does it eventually offer some kind of "defense" of the stage? If *Antony and Cleopatra* offers any "defense" of the stage, it doesn't do so by repudiating the charges made by attacks of the period, by claiming that theatre is immune from the evils attributed to it. The play offers no moral or ethical defense of theatre, but rather what is virtually an *ontological* defense. By imagining a world in which things simply fail to exist apart from their own theatricalizations, their own enactments, Shakespeare simply identifies theatricality as the constitutive condition of existence itself.

Such a proposition is not new to Renaissance studies. For some time New Historicism has been presenting variations on this theme, variations in which power in the Renaissance manifests itself in theatrical ways, or selves construct themselves in theatrical ways.[3] In fact, as the insights of New Historicism have crystallized and broadened, criticism has been characterized by a tendency to depict the Renaissance as constructing reality itself in theatrical terms. But what these formulations ignore are the consequences of such a position for the issue of gender: what would it mean to live in a world in which gender – or more specifically masculinity – existed only insofar as it was performed, enacted?[4] What it would mean, the following essay suggests, is living in a profound state of *powerlessness*, just the opposite of the "improvisational power" we have come to associate with the insights of New Historicism. *Antony and Cleopatra* depicts just such a world, a world where masculinity exists only as a highly codified performance, and it presents the moment of crisis in which that performance breaks down.[5]

Unqualitied with shame

Philo's opening claim offers a hypothesis which the rest of the play is busy testing, the hypothesis that Antony is being effeminized by Cleopatra. In the earliest sections of the play we get only the most indirect corroboration for Philo's hypothesis, a kind of glimpse of Cleopatra's effeminizing power in the abstract, but without the full force of that power being directed toward Antony.

In the soothsayer scene, for instance, Egypt is represented as a potentially effeminizing place, as the Egyptian women sit around thinking up ways to cuckold and weaken their men. There is an aura of sterility that hangs over these women, as when Charmian asks the soothsayer how many children she'll have and he tells her "If every of your wishes had a womb / And fertile every wish, a million" (I.ii.38–9). Wishes do not have wombs in Egypt, and the "womblessness" of female desire seems to translate itself into a need to wither and weaken the men. Thus Charmian prays to Isis to make Alexas marry a frigid woman that cannot "go" and to "let worse follow worse till the worst of all follow him laughing to his grave" and he end up "fiftyfold a cuckold" (I.ii.63–7). In its vision of a sterile female sexuality and the malignant intent this sterility generates toward men, the play offers a kind of diffused corroboration for Philo's claim.

We see the same thing in the moments in which Mardian the eunuch, the real proof of Cleopatra's effeminizing power, appears. In these scenes, there is not just a sterility to sexual desire in Egypt, but an actual sense of danger built into the truncated impulse, the wish without womb. Cleopatra tells Mardian that it is lucky for him that being "unseminar'd," his freer thoughts cannot fly forth of Egypt (I.v.11–12). What is the danger in the thought of a eunuch, the thought that is itself "unseminar'd," castrated, cut off? It is as if there is a rage wrapped up in the impulse that cannot act, the thought cut short, that at all costs must be "contained" within Egypt, a sexual rage that somehow becomes synonymous with Egypt itself. The literal eunuch Mardian stands at the center of the play as a reminder of the real danger of emasculation at the hands of Cleopatra. For though she says she takes "no pleasure / In aught an eunuch has" (I.v.9–10), she takes considerable pleasure in anatomizing what a eunuch can and cannot do, in making him admit that though he has "fierce affections" he can only "think" (not do) what "Venus did with Mars" (I.v.17–18).

In these early scenes, then, the play suggests the reality of Cleopatra's effeminizing power, diffused onto a whole landscape or displaced onto a eunuch, without displaying it as a force being channeled explicitly in Antony's direction.[6] But by Act II, the play has begun to show that force aimed in Antony's direction, has begun to display Cleopatra's effeminizing power as the specific thing dissolving Antony's soldiership.

Implicit in this vision is the belief agreed upon by virtually everyone in the play that Antony has been the soldier par excellence, the embodiment of the military ideal itself. Pompey says Antony's soldiership is twice that of Caesar and Lepidus (II.i.34–5). Cleopatra calls him the "greatest soldier" (I.iii.38). And even Caesar yearns nostalgically for the Antony at Modena who fought famine with "patience more / Than savages could suffer" (I.iv.60–1) and bore it "so like a soldier" that his cheek "lanked not." In the imagined world before the opening of the play, Antony is, in effect, Prynne's "valiant man," his "man of courage." But that valiance is dissolving even as the play moves forward, dissolving at the hands of Cleopatra.

At the heart of this process is Cleopatra's capacity to evoke appetite, that force capable of making men behave and act not like men, but like women. She is represented throughout the play as food itself, a morsel for a monarch (I.v.31), Antony's "Egyptian dish" (II.vi.126), the sponsor of "monstrous" feasts (II.ii.182), the woman who while other women cloy the appetites they feed "makes hungry" where most she satisfies (II.ii.235–7). Pompey both invokes her capacity to demilitarize Antony by engaging his appetite and suggests this process is already under way. He invokes her to tie up Antony in a field of feasts, to keep his brain fuming, to literally sharpen Antony's appetite so that the sleep and feeding that result will incapacitate him for battle ("Sharpen with cloyless sauce his appetite, / That sleep and feeding may prorogue his honor, / Even till a Lethe'd dullness" [II.i.25–7]). He says as well that she has already done just that, that Antony in Egypt sits at dinner and "will make / No wars without-doors," has ceased in effect to *act* the part of a soldier (II.i.12–13).

Just as anti-theatricalists during the period feared theatre for its capacity to make the spectator "anhungered," "alwaies eating and never satisfied,"[7] like he that "hearing one half of a sentence . . . is very desirous to have the rest,"[8] Cleopatra makes hungry where most she satisfies. Pompey identifies this capacity to "make hungry" as the specific source of her effeminizing power and in so doing implicitly identifies her with that property that Renaissance anti-theatricalists feared most about the stage.

But though she has been identified with the unmanning power of the Renaissance stage, that power itself has not yet been specifically grounded in any theatricality of her own. She has from the very beginning of the play been associated with a histrionic power that Enobarbus calls her "infinite variety" and Antony describes as every passion "fully striv[ing] / To make itself . . . fair and admir'd" (I.i.50–1). And it is the distinctive feature of this theatricality that Cleopatra conceives of reality itself as a scenario waiting to be improvised and shaped, conceives of reality as a script she is in the process of fashioning and Antony as the material out of which she must fashion it ("I'll seem the fool I am not," she tells Charmian, "Antony / Will be himself," she says as if she were permitting him to play himself [I.i.42–3]). A moment later we see her working him into a scenario which, were it successful, would keep him from battle: "If you find him sad, / Say I am dancing; if in mirth, report / That I am sudden sick," she tells Charmian in order to make him stay in Egypt (I.iii.3–5). What is implicit in this conception of reality as a script is a view of Antony as an actor capable of being made to "act" whatever performance he is scripted into. It is true that Cleopatra vacillates between a view of Antony as Caesar's actor whom he may command to "take in that kingdom, and enfranchise that; / Perform't, or else we damn thee" (I.i.23–4) and a view of him as her own ("play one scene / Of excellent dissembling, and let it look / Like perfect honor" [I.iii.78–80]). But what is never at issue from Cleopatra's point of view is that Antony is only an actor, waiting to be installed in someone else's script.

Notwithstanding this, in these earliest moments, the play doesn't specifically cast Cleopatra's theatricality as the source of her effeminizing power. Only Caesar specifically attributes the fact that Antony is "not more manlike / Than Cleopatra" to the revels in Alexandria. It is not until II.v, when Cleopatra reminisces about dressing Antony in her tires and mantles, that a larger argument about the effeminizing power of her theatricality in particular begins to unfold.

She is talking about the way she drank Antony to his bed, then assumed his sword while she dressed him in her female clothing, and the lines follow a fantasy about fishing, in which she imagines Antony as the penetrated fish and herself as the hook doing the penetrating: ". . . we'll to th' river; there, / My music playing far off, I will betray / Tawny-finn'd fishes; my bended hook shall pierce / Their slimy jaws; and as I draw them up, / I'll think them every one an Antony, / And say 'Ah, ha! y'are caught'" [II.v.10–15]). The fantasy apparently suggests to her an actual memory suffused with similar pleasure, a nostalgia equivalent to Caesar's nostalgia for Antony at Modena – it is interesting the way Antony is always the object of nostalgia, as if to have a relation with Antony were always inevitably to have a relation to one's own past. The fantasy suggests to her a memory which elicits a nostalgia for the same pleasure which Prynne's valiant warrior presumably experiences in dressing up as another gender:

> That time? O times!
> I laugh'd him out of patience; and that night
> I laugh'd him into patience; and next morn,
> Ere the ninth hour, I drunk him to his bed;
> Then put my tires and mantles on him, whilst
> I wore his sword Philippan.
>
> (II.v.18–23)

The passage explicitly identifies Cleopatra's theatricality as the core of her effeminizing power. For what she does in costuming Antony as a woman is no more than what she has already done by tying him up in a field of feasts. Not only does the passage depict her in a hyperbole of Renaissance stage practice, dressing the passive drunken Antony in her female clothing, but it displays that stage practice, the convention that provided the focus for anti-theatrical paranoia, as the logical extension of those appetites which are already effeminizing Antony, as if the women's clothing itself were only the outward sign of an effeminacy within.[9]

Then there is the matter of Cleopatra wearing Antony's sword. So far, in all of what has preceded, Antony has been like Prynne's valiant man in his early stages of degeneration, has adopted effeminate behavior, drunk and revelled and ultimately donned female clothing. But he has not yet suffered constitutive change, as we would expect him to if the play truly replicated the story of the dissolving warrior. Hypothetically, how would the play present such a change? How would it be apprehendable? In Cleopatra's assumption of Antony's sword, the play begins to provide a vocabulary through which we might mark such a change. For at the center of the Roman world is an economy in which swords are explicitly identified with phalluses and phalluses with swords. "Royal wench!" says Agrippa of Cleopatra in II.ii. "She made great Caesar lay his sword to bed; / He ploughed her, and she cropp'd" (II.ii.226–8). In this formulation, the man who lays his "sword," his phallus, in the bed, is the man who puts his literal sword "to bed," i.e. away. The sexually active man is implicitly the inactive warrior.

But if this is so, then it is also the case that the inactive warrior, the man who has put down his sword, is implicitly the eunuch, the impotent man. The play hasn't yet argued that Antony has become this, only that Cleopatra builds her erotic play around such a fantasy. But if we were to see Antony's sword literally weakened or stolen or assumed in subsequent acts of the play, we would have a basis for arguing that in the vocabulary of the play a constitutive change has taken place. In fact, this is exactly what occurs, for in the scenes that follow, Antony will complain that his sword has been "weakened" and "robbed" and we will see it literally being removed from his "wound."

So far, all of what we have heard has been rumor, Caesar complaining that Antony is no more manlike than Cleopatra, Pompey claiming that Antony will make no wars without doors, Cleopatra reminiscing about dressing Antony in her tires and mantles. But we do not need to depend on rumor, for at the center of the play is a virtual dramatization of the story of the dissolving warrior, a dramatization consisting of the trio of disastrous military decisions that Antony makes. At the center of this trio, and indeed at the center of the whole play, is Antony's inexplicable decision to fight at sea. The apparent basis for it is Antony's accommodation to Cleopatra and to her desire to display her navy. But there is a problem even at this level of explanation, for the play goes to great lengths to present Antony as being the first to say "we / Will fight ... by sea" (III.vii.27–8) and Cleopatra as only afterward chiming in "By sea, what else?" (III.vii.28). (The moment is important because it establishes his priority in making the decision.) On another level, the explanation for Antony's insistence on fighting at sea seems to lie in his somewhat useless sense of personal gallantry and the play's recurrent juxtaposition of this to Caesar's pragmatism. (Thus, when Canidius asks Antony why he'll fight at sea, Antony says, in effect, for the challenge: "For that he dares us to't" [III.vii.29].) In the course of the scene, however, so many reasons are supplied and exhausted for not fighting at sea ("Your mariners are muleters, reapers, people / Ingross'd by swift impress" says Enobarbus, "In Caesar's fleet / Are those that often have 'gainst Pompey fought" [III.vii.35–7]) that when Antony can still only say "by sea, by sea" (III.vii.40), his obsession finally seems (like Iago's hatred of Othello) larger than any of the reasons supplied for it, seems like an example of his dissolving captainship, rather than a decision susceptible to psychological explanation. It is as if by making the explanations available to explain the decision inadequate, Shakespeare elevates the action to the status of a negative exemplar, an example of dissolving captainship itself.

But even the decision to fight at sea presupposes an earlier decision, Antony's allowing Cleopatra to come to battle in the first place. Interestingly, Shakespeare presents this decision as the logical extension of the tires and mantles scene. For here we have a swapping not of clothing appropriate to the opposite gender, but of roles appropriate to the opposite gender. Hence Cleopatra's insistence that she will go to the wars not only in person, but will more specifically "appear there for a man" (III.vii.18). If she has sought to assume the costume of a man in the tires and mantles scene, she seeks to assume the behavior and usurp the actual authority of one here. It is as if the scene offered a fulfillment of that moment earlier in the play in which Cleopatra replaces Antony ("Hush, here comes Antony," says Enobarbus, and Cleopatra arrives instead, replacing him just as Charmian says "Not he, the queen" [I.ii.79]). It is as if, in the mind of the play, the image of a woman kept rising up where the man were supposed to be ("'tis said in Rome," Enobarbus tells Cleopatra, "that Photinus an eunuch and your maids / Manage this war." [III.vii.13–15]) It is as if in some primitive way, women and eunuchs kept appearing where men were supposed to be, just as Prynne's image of a warrior degenerating into a woman implied a woman underneath all the time waiting to assume her proper shape.

Thus the decision to allow Cleopatra to come to battle is dangerous not only for all the reasons Enobarbus tells Cleopatra it will be ("Your presence needs must puzzle Antony, / Take from his heart, take from his brain, from's time, / What should not then be spar'd" [III.vii.10–12]), is dangerous not only because of Cleopatra's capacity to stimulate sexual appetite, and appetite's capacity to demilitarize ("If we should serve with horse and mares together, / The horse were merely lost; the mares would bear / A soldier and his horse" [III.vii.7–9]). The decision is dangerous because it implies a more serious kind of transvestitism than the one Cleopatra has reminisced about, a transvestitism not of costumes but of roles, a transvestitism based on adopting the behavior of the opposite sex.

And this adoption of the behavior appropriate to the opposite sex is implicit in Antony's final disastrous military decision as well. For if Cleopatra's insistence on appearing "for a man" constitutes an exaggeration of one side of the tires and mantles scene, her assumption of Antony's sword, Antony's following her when she turns tail, constitutes an even grosser exaggeration of the other aspect of the tires and mantles scene. For he plays the role of a woman when he follows rather than leads. Even Cleopatra says "I little thought / You would have followed" (III.xi.55–6). And Antony acknowledges his role as "follower" when he says, "Egypt, thou knew'st too well / My heart was to thy rudder tied by th' strings" (III.xi.56–7). Those watching Antony conceive of his effemination as if it were contagious: "Our leader's led, / and we are women's men," says Canidius (III.vii.69–70). Thus the decisions that from a literal standpoint are responsible for Antony's defeat as a warrior, his decline as a captain, are the decisions that are presented as extensions of the theatrical transvestitism that Antony and Cleopatra have already practiced.

But all of this is just effeminate behavior, the behavior of a warrior exchanging roles with a woman, playing the part of a woman. We have no evidence yet that anyone watching such a performance imagines that it will lead to transformation, constitutive change. And yet this is exactly what those watching Antony do seem to believe. For Scarus, the battle itself is a performance, an "action" of shame in which manhood violates itself (III.x.21–3). Iras suggests the same dissolution of masculinity when she says Antony is "unqualitied" with "very shame." For Canidius, the transformation is not one of gender but of identity. At the beginning of the play, Philo, apologizing for Antony, has told Demetrius, "Sir, sometimes when he is not Antony / He comes too short of that great property / Which still should go with Antony" (I.i.57–9). For Canidius, it is as if Antony had simply ceased to be Antony. "Had our general / Been what he knew himself" it had gone well, he says (III.x.25–6). For Antony, too, it is as if he has literally left himself. "I have fled myself" (III.xi.7) he says; "Let that be left / Which leaves itself," (III.xi.19–20), as if his self were not a thing that inhered in his person but something independent requiring a separate set of actions or conditions in order to exist. And in a world in which swords are phalluses and phalluses swords, he begins to confess his own impotence when he tells Cleopatra she has made his sword weak with affection ("You did know / How much you were my conqueror, and that / My sword, made weak by affection, would / Obey it on all cause" [III.xi.65–8]).

If there is a transformation, if as in Prynne's story of the dissolving warrior this is a world in which effeminate behavior leads to constitutive change, we are moving closer to an account of that transformation all the time as we move closer to Antony's point of view. For if the first acts of the play present Antony's effeminization through the testimony of rumor and the center of the play offers a dramatization of the story of the dissolving warrior in the set of disastrous military decisions Antony makes, the last scenes of the play that Antony appears in offer a psychological portrait of what it feels like to be an effeminized man. In these scenes, what is dramatized is the attempt (and attendant failure) to flee the knowledge of one's own effeminization. The "drama" lies in the movement between Antony's exertion to conceal the knowledge of what is happening from himself and the strength of that knowledge as it makes itself inescapable. Thus Antony vacillates between an energetic denial and an overwhelmed acknowledgement of his own effeminization.

Initially, Antony's attempts at denial take the form of displacement. It is the land that is ashamed, not Antony. It is the land that "bids [him] tread no more upon't," that is "asham'd to bear" him (III.xi.1–2), just as it is Caesar, the "boy," the "young man" who is having problems with his sword, Caesar who at Philippi wore it only like a dancer rather than (like Antony) fighting in the brave squares of war. In these moments, Antony's attempts to ward off his own sense of shame and effeminacy take the form of a displacement of these qualities onto places and people. But as these attempts at displacement fail and Antony cannot avoid the idea that he has "lost command" and "fled himself" and that his sword has been "made weak," and as Thidias arrives offering new slights to Antony's already precarious masculinity, Antony is forced to turn to more and more radical means to displace his sense of impending effeminization. Thus it is necessary to actually whip Thidias to maintain that it is he, not Antony, who is losing his masculinity ("Whip him, fellows, / Till like a boy you see him cringe his face / And whine aloud for mercy," says Antony [III.xiii.99–101]). He is bent on reducing Thidias to a boy, to a daughter, to anything but a man ("If that thy father live," he tells Thidias, "let him repent / Thou wast not made his daughter" [III.xiii.134–5]). Thus, in this scene in which he begins by acknowledging "Authority melts from me" (III.xiii.90), the threat posed by Thidias actually provokes him to a reassertion of his old identity ("I am / Antony yet" [III.xiii.92–3]) and into the more radical measures of whipping Thidias ("Cried he? and begg'd 'a pardon?" [III.xiii.132]) and stripping Thidias of his masculinity to maintain his own.

Of course Antony has sought to maintain that he is "Antony yet" in other ways as well, has sought to restore his identity as "Antony" by staging it, has sought to regain his "sword," his phallus, through "showing" it. Almost immediately after turning tail, he becomes obsessed with the idea of sword-show with Caesar, a show which is explicitly designed to stage (and thus reconstitute) his "self." Caesar wears the rose of youth on him, Antony complains, and his "coin, ships, legions / May be a coward's, whose ministers would prevail / Under the service of a child as soon / As i' th' command of Caesar" (III.xiii.22–5). The complaint here is that it is impossible to know Caesar's "self" as distinguishable from his effects: "I dare him therefore / To lay his gay comparisons apart," says Antony, "And answer me declin'd, sword against sword, / Ourselves alone" (III.xiii.25–8). The claim implies a belief in an essential self independent from the trappings and attributes of power. But what is extraordinary about the speech is its assumption that it is the staging, the re-enactment of this self, that is going to bring it into existence.[10] By the same token, it is Caesar's construction of Antony as what he is, not what he was, that enrages Antony: "He makes me angry with him; for he seems / Proud and disdainful, harping on what I am, / Not what he knew I was" (III.xiii.141–3). And the fantasy behind the sword-show is that he can bring that past self, the Antony of "Antony yet," back into existence. He never gets the sword-show of course, never gets the opportunity to restage his "self" or "show," and thus make vital and real again his sword.

Thus the play makes synonymous two kinds of degeneration, the degeneration of masculinity (of a manhood which "violates" itself, of a warrior who loses command, of a sword made weak) and the degeneration of a self (Antony saying he's fled himself, Antony thinking of himself as a mangled shadow, Antony failing to reconstruct himself as "Antony yet," Antony wishing he could be not himself, but made of the many men "clapp'd up together in / An Antony" [IV.ii.17–18]). For in the end, Antony is ultimately unable to defend himself against either process. In what is perhaps the most profound acknowledgement of loss in the play, he registers the sense that even his body cannot hold its visible shape:

ANTONY: Sometime we see a cloud that's dragonish,
A vapor sometime like a bear or lion,
A tower'd citadel, a pendant rock,
A forked mountain, or blue promontory
With trees upon't that nod unto the world
And mock our eyes with air. Thou hast seen these signs,
They are black vesper's pageants.
EROS: Ay, my lord.
ANTONY: That which is now a horse, even with a thought

The rack dislimns, and makes it indistinct
As water is in water.
EROS: It does, my lord.
ANTONY: My good knave, Eros, now thy captain is
Even such a body. Here I am Antony,
Yet cannot hold this visible shape, my knave.

(IV.xiv.2–14)

The degeneration of images (bear, lion, citadel, rock, water in water) suggests the inability of Antony's body to hold a fixed shape, suggests in more eloquent terms than any the dissolution he has undergone. A moment later Antony makes explicit the emasculation this process implies. "Thy vild lady!" he tells Mardian, effeminized at the hands of the same lady, "has robb'd me of my sword" (IV.xiv.22–3).

If we look at the play through Antony's account of it, it tells the same story Philo does, the story of a man who begins by acting like a woman and ends as a eunuch, the same story Prynne does, the story of a man who loses his gender by behaving like a woman. And what such a story implies is that there is no masculinity "in itself," but masculinity only insofar as it is enacted (and re-enacted). This is a world in which action itself is constitutive, in which the doer becomes what he does and behavior leads to constitutive change. And such a performance has none of the liberating associations we have come to identify with performative notions of gender, but is itself highly codified, culturally rigid, externally defined.

It could be argued that Antony's account of what happens is just that, an account, a series of metaphors, to describe a series of sensations, perceived losses, not a set of actual facts. But in uncanny ways, the action of the play ends up replicating the very claims Antony makes. "With a wound I must be cur'd" (IV.xiv.78) he says, and in a kind of literalization of Scarus' conceit of "manhood violating itself," a kind of autoeroticism that is also a castration, he falls on his sword. (It is as if being made whole, being restored to manhood, lay for him in being penetrated by that very "sword" he complains has been weakened and robbed.) But why should this be? Why should Antony conceive of this "wound" (with all the associations the word has of castration) as "cure?" Perhaps it is as if (as in theories of totemism) he believed he could repossess that sword and the masculinity it signified by literally putting it back inside his own body.[11] The suicide is one more attempt to repossess the masculinity he has been losing throughout the whole play.

But if Antony seeks to restore his own masculinity by putting it inside him, by making it enter his own body, in the end it is taken out again, removed from his wound and passed on to Caesar. Decretas pulls Antony's sword out of his wound and tells Caesar "This is his sword, / I

robb'd his wound of it; behold it stain'd / With his most noble blood"
(V.i.24–6). It is not just Antony who complains that his sword has been
weakened and stolen, but the culture around him that re-enacts this theft,
that acts out the loss of masculinity that the weakening of the sword
implies. And it is not just that Antony loses his masculinity, but that he
actually loses it to someone else.

What the story of the dissolving warrior implies – both as it appears in
tracts like Prynne's and as it appears in Shakespeare's treatment of it – is
that there is no masculinity in itself but only masculinity insofar as it is
staged and performed. To the extent that Shakespeare exposes this belief
as the premise built into cautionary tales like Prynne's, he offers a critique
of anti-theatricality by suggesting the degree to which performative
notions are built into anti-theatricality itself. But to the degree that he
presents such a story as Antony's story, as history itself, he exhibits a deep
and pervasive anti-theatricality, exhibits the very set of anxieties he has
implicitly criticized. If *Troilus and Cressida* is his vision of a world in
which masculinity must be enacted in order to exist, *Antony and Cleopatra*
is his vision of a world in which masculinity not only must be enacted, but
simply cannot be enacted, his vision of a world in which this particular
performance has broken down.

In the narrative I have presented I have emphasized the way in which
action itself is constitutive and makes the doer into the thing he does.
Such a story is implicitly anti-theatrical, for it suggests the danger of
theatrical action to its practitioner, the actor, who is always in danger of
becoming what he acts out. But, in fact, this line of argument is framed by
another in *Antony and Cleopatra* which is, if possible, even more profoundly anti-theatrical and which suggests an even greater danger posed
by theatre to the spectator. For it is in response to Cleopatra's theatricality that we see Antony dressed like a woman, in response to her tricks at
sea that he behaves like one and turns tail, and in response to her most
potent scene of theatre that he ultimately destroys himself. "To th'
monument," Cleopatra tells Mardian. "Say that the last I spoke was
'Antony'" (IV.xiii.6–8). Her elaborately staged mock suicide triggers
Antony's very real one. There is even a suggestion that she calculated
precisely this effect. "She had a prophesying fear," says Diomedes,
looking at Antony impaled on his own sword, "of what hath come to
pass" (IV.xiv.120–1). Here Shakespeare offers his deepest attack on
theatre, exhibits his most profound anti-theatricality. For here, Cleopatra
scripts a scene of theatre so destructive it drives its audience to kill
himself. What more incriminating a stance to theatre would it be possible
to take?

But if this is so, how does Shakespeare make sense of his own dramatic form, the very theatrical practice that brings such dissolution about? In theory we would expect him to offer a "defense" of theatre, something which redeems it from the attacks of the time, rather than offering a bleaker attack than the attacks do themselves. Instead, what Shakespeare does is offer a critique of the very fears he demonstrates, an *anti*-anti-theatricality. That critique is made through the figure of Caesar, the mouthpiece of anti-theatrical rhetoric in the play. For in Caesar, Shakespeare offers the portrait of an anti-theatricality which contains within it a longing for the very things it attacks, an attack on appetite which contains within it a tacit glorification of appetite, an ideal of masculinity which contains within it a homoerotic longing that ideal itself repudiates, an attack on theatre which contains within it a fierce longing for theatricality – what amounts to a virtually theatrical way of constructing the world. Three times in *Antony and Cleopatra*, Shakespeare presents Caesar as attacking what he secretly longs for. In this way, the play casts anti-theatricality itself as a walking contradiction and calls into question the structure of the attack itself as a mode of thought.

Strange flesh

Caesar's first attack is an attack on appetite itself, a repudiation not only of Antony's sexuality but of sexual appetite per se. His disgust can be felt through every aspect of his attack, his description of Antony's passion as a "tumble" on the bed of Ptolemy, his rage at Antony giving a kingdom for a "mirth," and his explicit charge of "voluptuousness." The very terms of the attack suggest Caesar's need to repudiate sexual appetite, for words like "tumble" suggest both the animalistic and accidental nature of what Antony is doing, words like "mirth" picture Antony's passion as a joke and even the charge of voluptuousness stems from Caesar's need to *dis*-identify himself from sexual appetite, his rage that Antony is contaminating him through his lusts (Antony must not excuse his faults, Caesar says, "when we do bear / So great weight in his lightness" [I.iv.24–5]).

At stake in the fear of general revelry, then, in the charge that Antony "fishes, drinks, and wastes / The lamps of night in revel" (I.iv.4–5), is a much more specific set of fears about the destructive power of appetite. Thus, when Caesar complains that Antony keeps the turn of tippling with a slave, or "reel[s] the streets at noon . . . / with knaves that smell of sweat" (I.iv.20–1), he acts as if the indulgence of appetite were capable of destroying the boundaries between classes. More crucially, when he complains that Antony is "not more manlike / Than Cleopatra; nor the Queen of Ptolomy / More womanly than he" (I.iv.5–7) he acts as if the satisfaction of appetite were capable of destroying the difference between the sexes. It is important to note that this is a view of appetite as having a constitutive power, the power of being able to turn one thing into another. It is important to note as well that this view of things presupposes that at least in some originary sense, the genders themselves were quintessentially separate. In an ideal world (one protected from appetite) they could remain so.

In all of this, it should be said, Caesar is right in the mainstream of Renaissance anti-theatricality as it expressed itself in pamphlets and tracts of the period. For the watchword of these tracts was the claim that the sexes belonged to different ontological categories, so fundamentally different as to be "discernible:" costume they insisted was a "signe distinctive to discerne betwixt sex and sex," a claim which presupposed that the sexes were fundamentally different in the first place.[12] And, as a class, these tracts shared a general abhorrence of appetite precisely because they conceived of it as destroying this difference, of "effeminizing" those in whom it was excited.

Was there anyone immune from this effeminizing power? Soldiers are the "images of God," says Gosson, quoting Homer.[13] He yearns for the "olde discipline of England" when men "used slender weapons, went naked and wer good soldiours," when "they fedde upon rootes and barkes of trees," and "had a kind of sustenance in time of neede of which if they hadde taken but the quantitie of a beane or the weight of a pease, they did neither gape after meate nor long for the cuppe a great while after."[14] The soldier is the best that culture has to offer, precisely because he is the last holdout against effeminacy (or, put differently, because he has the capacity to withstand appetite itself). But the "soldier" in his true self exists only in the past. Compare what we were with what we have become, says Gosson. "Our wrestling at armes is turned to wallowing in ladies lappes."[15] Anti-theatricality, at least in part, is an attempt to bring back this soldier, to militarize men.

Caesar's own rant against appetite depends on precisely this military ideal. Just as Gosson does, he praises the capacity to withstand appetite ("Thy palate then did deign / The roughest berry on the rudest hedge," he tells Antony, "Yea, like the stag, when snow the pasture sheets, / The barks of trees thou brows'd" [I.iv.63–6]). Just as Gosson does, he locates this military ideal only in the past. The Antony at Modena speech which directly follows Caesar's attack is itself an evocation of the old Antony, the Antony at Modena who conquered first the enemy consuls Hirtius and Pansa, and then that much more formidable enemy appetite itself:

> When thou once
> Was beaten from Modena, where thou slew'st
> Hirtius and Pansa, consuls, at thy heel

> Did famine follow, whom thou fought'st against
> (Though daintily brought up) with patience more
> Than savages could suffer.
>
> (I.iv.56–61)

But if this first attack of Caesar's is premised on the repudiation of appetite, Caesar seems to yearn for exactly what he would repudiate.[16] For though he praises the Antony of Modena, for his ostensible conquest of appetite, what the speech seems to contain within it is a glorification of perverse appetite. "Thou didst drink / The stale of horses and the gilded puddle / Which beasts would cough at," says Caesar nostalgically (I.iv.61–3). He yearns for a world of perverse appetites, a world of regressive, infantile sexuality: "On the Alps / It is reported thou didst eat strange flesh, / Which some did die to look on" (I.iv.66–8). This is a world not only of regressive infantile urges, but of cannibalistic enraged appetites, a world of orality gone amok.[17] Yet it is all somehow "contained" within the ideal of the soldier:

> And all this
> (It wounds thine honor that I speak it now)
> Was borne so like a soldier, that thy cheek
> So much as lank'd not.
>
> (I.iv.68–71)

There is another incongruity in Caesar's nostalgia for Modena which is even more troubling. For in Plutarch, Caesar and Antony fought on opposite sides at Modena:

Cicero on the other side being at that time the chiefest man of authoritie and estimation in the cities, he stirred up al men against Antonius: so that in the end he made the Senate pronounce him an enemy to his contry, and appointed young Cesar Sergeaunts to cary axes before him, and such other signes as were incident to the dignitie of a Consul or a Praetor: and moreover sent Hircius and Pansa, then Consuls, to drive Antonius out of Italy. These two Consuls together with Caesar, who also had an armye, went against Antonius that beseeged the citie of Modena...[18]

Yet here, Caesar manages to make it sound as if they shared a lost and important (even intimate) past together. What is this nostalgia about that elides Caesar's earlier enmity towards Antony? What is the connection between this nostalgia and the celebration of perverse appetite the speech betrays? Or between this nostalgia and Caesar's fantasy that Antony and he will show themselves in the field together? If Caesar's repudiation of appetite "contains" within it a glorification of appetite, we might hypothesize that the nostalgia and the ideal of appearing in the field together contain some similarly disruptive impulse, figured perhaps in the image of eating strange flesh or in Caesar's anger at Antony for forgetting he had

partners ("hardly gave audience, or / Vouchsaf'd to think he had partners" [I.iv.7–8]). In a sense, we will have to wait to test that hypothesis
until we look at Caesar's second attack. But before moving to that, it is
worth simply noting the way the attack in I.iv has concealed or "contained" within it a celebration of precisely the thing repudiated, appetite
itself. Something quite similar occurs in II.ii, only now the "thing concealed" emerges in much more specific terms as a longing for Antony.

Caesar's second attack on Antony, which takes place in II.ii as Caesar
and Antony try to negotiate, is not an anti-theatrical attack proper, but
an extension of the first attack and revolves around three separate
charges: the charge that Antony's brother and wife made war on Caesar,
presumably in Antony's name; the reiterated charge that Antony rejected
Caesar's messenger; and the charge that Antony refused to lend arms for
battle. (Antony has broken the "articles of [his] oath," Caesar says, "to
lend me arms and aid when I requir'd them" [II.ii.88].) Ostensibly, then,
the charge is a political attack, based on the charge that Antony has
construed himself as a political and military entity separate from Caesar.
But if Caesar begins by being unable to tolerate Antony as a separate
political entity, he ends by being unable to tolerate Antony as a separate
person, by seeing him as a limb of his own body.

This can be felt both in the way that Caesar poses his charges and in the
way that Antony responds to them. When Antony asks Caesar, "My
being in Egypt, Caesar, / What was't to you?" he is asking, in effect,
"What did it matter that I was separate from you?" (II.ii.35–6). Caesar's
answer is that to be separate is to be hostile, to "practice" on his state:

> No more than my residing here at Rome
> Might be to you in Egypt; yet if you there
> Did practice on my state, your being in Egypt
> Might be my question.
>
> (II.ii.36–9)

(This is a view of the world in which anything which defines itself as
"other" is instantly perceived as inimical to the self.) When Caesar
complains that Antony's brother made war on him ("You were the word
of war" [II.ii.44]), Antony retracts, changes strategies and tries to argue
instead that after all he was not separate ("Did he not rather / Discredit
my authority with yours"), argues in effect that he was merely an extension of Caesar (II.ii.48–9). (This is the response to a world which sees
otherness as hostile. In response to such a world it will be necessary to *be*
an extension, to define oneself as if one were another's limb.) When
Caesar repeats the charges he has made in Act I, that Antony conceived of
himself as separate, wouldn't hear the messengers or vouchsafe "to think
he had partners" (I.iv.8), Antony's answer is that he "did want / of what I

was i' th' morning" (II.ii.76–7), didn't know what he was, separate or not separate. (This is the result of living in such a world: eventually one loses the knowledge of what one is.) Even within the attack itself, then, what we feel is Caesar's pressure for Antony to define himself, even perceive himself as if he were part of Caesar.

But the full force of Caesar's longing emerges most strongly in the wish that immediately follows the attack, the wish he articulates for a symbolic marriage with Antony. For even before Agrippa proposes Antony's marriage to Octavia, Caesar himself has expressed the longing for a "hoop" or symbolic wedding ring to bind him to Antony ("if I knew / What hoop should hold us staunch," he tells Antony, "from edge to edge / A' th' world, I would pursue it" [II.ii.114–16]). But by the time Agrippa proposes it, this ring has become not a voluntary band, but an "un-slipping knot" ("To hold you in perpetual amity, / To make you brothers, and to knit your hearts / With an unslipping knot, take Antony / Octavia to his wife," he says [II.ii.124–7]). And by the time Enobarbus describes it in II.vi, the knot has become a noose. When Menas asks him, "Then is Caesar and he [Antony] forever knit together," (II.vi.115), Enobarbus says that the "band that seems to tie their friendship together will be the very strangler of their amity" (II.vi.120–2). The symbolic marriage that Caesar craves with Antony, then, is itself increasingly figured as some-thing dangerous, something with the capacity to strangle and kill. Perhaps this explains Caesar's depiction of appetite as cannibalism in the Antony at Modena speech. For in a world in which homoerotic longings are themselves conceived of as fatal, it will be necessary to represent desire even to oneself as cannibalism, regression, in order to keep such longings at a distance. In such a world it will be necessary as well to rationalize such longings within a military ideal of display, appearing in the field together, or to contain them within a nostalgia for a shared past which is largely invented.

To say this is, in one sense, to say what has been said before in other contexts: that at given times in given cultures, such longings cannot be represented even to the self directly but must be mediated through a third term.[19] That third term is Octavia, and the proof that she exists primarily to mediate an unacknowledged (and unacknowledgeable) longing lies primarily in the way she loses an independent reality throughout the play. She is an object to be bequeathed: "A sister I bequeath you" (II.ii.149); a piece of business: "Yet ere we put ourselves in arms, dispatch we / The business we have talk'd of," says Antony, and Caesar immediately under-stands him to mean Octavia (II.ii.165–6). She is a piece of cement: "Let not the piece of virtue which is set / Betwixt us, as the cement of our love / To keep it builded, be the ram to batter / The fortress of it," Caesar says

(III.ii.28–31). She is a role, a function, Caesar's sister, Antony's wife. She is finally no inherent thing, but simply whatever Caesar's thoughts constitute her as: "Sister, prove such a wife / As my thoughts make thee, and as my farthest band / Shall pass on thy approof" (III.ii.25–7) – Be what my thoughts make thee.

But what are Caesar's thoughts? He puts it succinctly when he says "Let her live / To join our kingdoms and our hearts" (II.ii.150–1), as if Octavia had no other reason to live. Meditating on other, more direct ways to love, Caesar considers the possibility of an unmediated love between himself and Antony: "For better might we / Have lov'd without this mean, if on both parts / This be not cherish'd" (III.ii.31–3). Finally, only parting from Antony in III.ii can he say, "You take from me a great part of myself" (III.ii.24). What "part" of Caesar's self is Octavia? The feminine part? The part he cannot acknowledge? Not only are the lines sexually suggestive, not only do they suggest Caesar's narcissism (the way not only Antony, but Octavia is conceived of as a "part" of himself), but they point to the sense in which for Caesar Antony is finally not separable, but inextricably bound up with his own identity.

Caesar is moving closer and closer to this knowledge throughout the play, but it can only become knowledge at Antony's death. Thus even when he is first brought the news of Antony's death, he understands only that Antony's identity is not separable from *other* identities: "The death of Antony / Is not a single doom," he says, "in the name lay / A moi'ty of the world" (V.i.17–19). It is Maecenas who first construes Antony's identity as inseparable from Caesar's: "When such a spacious mirror's set before him, / He [Caesar] needs must see himself," he says (V.i.34–5). What takes place in Caesar in V.i is a compulsive groping to define what Antony is in relation to him: "Thou, my *brother*, my *competitor*, / In top of all design, my *mate* in empire, / *Friend* and *companion* in the front of war" (V.i.42–4, italics mine). The rapid progression and discarding of roles suggests the grasp to define relation (brother, companion, mate, competitor) and finally erupts into a series of hybrid body images in which Antony's body finally becomes inextricable from Caesar's, becomes truly a "part" of it, becomes not "strange" flesh, but familiar flesh: "The arm of mine own body, and the heart / Where mine his thoughts did kindle" (V.i.45–6). The inextricability of limbs, the hybrid geography of the lines point to both the inextricability of the identities and the jarred, disordered way in which the sexual longing needs to be realized. The syntax breaks down. The bodies are mixed for the same reason that the desire in the Antony at Modena speech is figured as perverse: disallowed, that is the only way it can be represented, the only way it can be understood.

Thus Caesar becomes an example of the theory of love both he and

Antony articulate during the play, the theory that love is only felt after it is too late to attain the object. "Thus did I desire it," says Antony at Fulvia's death, "she's good, being gone; / The hand could pluck her back that shov'd her on" (I.ii.122–7). Or here is Caesar on the love of the fickle masses: "The ebbed man, ne'er lov'd till ne'er worth love / Comes dear'd by being lack'd" (I.iv.43–4). The desire can only be articulated, even experienced, after it cannot be fulfilled. Thus it is a peculiarity of the play that the moment that is, from one point of view, the culmination of the whole string of things that Cleopatra does to effeminize Antony is also the moment in which Caesar is symbolically able to possess Antony: "This is his sword / I robb'd his wound of it; behold it stain'd / With his most noble blood," says Decretas, announcing Antony's death to Caesar (V.i.24–6). In an economy in which swords are phalluses and phalluses swords, this is the moment in which Caesar is truly given a "part" of Antony's self. Possession can only be imagined in death, after the fact, after it is no longer possible.

In II.ii, then, the play offers us its second instance of an attack which conceals within it a longing for the thing attacked. Only here both the "thing" attacked and the "thing" longed for are Antony himself. But that the thing longed for should be Antony poses a significant threat to the ideal of masculinity which Caesar articulates in the Antony at Modena speech, because that ideal depends on the belief that men and women spring from different ontological categories (and the particular threat posed by homoeroticism lies in the idea that the man who "does" what a woman does when she has sex with a man risks becoming like that woman).[20] Of course, this would only be a threat in a world which believed that "doing" what a woman "does" made one into a woman. We have already seen in the story of the dissolving warrior that this is the operative belief in this world, but, as we shall see in a minute, Caesar in particular subscribes even more broadly to this view of action as constitutive, as making the doer into the thing he does.

What would it take to maintain Caesar's ideal of masculinity? In a sense Caesar has already told us: it would take the complete repudiation of sexuality: "Antony, / Leave thy lascivious wassails" (I.iv.55–6). The play has already suggested that Caesar's repudiation of appetite contains within it a glorification of appetites Caesar himself sees as forbidden. It now identifies these appetites as specifically homoerotic. Thus Caesar's fantasy of showing himself in the field with Antony becomes the defense against his longing to give Antony a "part" of himself. But it is the defense the play casts as destructive, certainly not the homoerotic longings it seeks to contain. For it is Caesar's *flight* from homoeroticism, from all eroticism, that requires the rigid ideal of masculinity in the first place, and this is an extraordinary insight into and critique of that ideal of masculinity itself.[21]

Shakespeare juxtaposes the ideal to the longings it seeks to contain and exposes the discrepancy. But since it is the play's anti-theatricalist in which the discrepancy takes place, the exposure constitutes a critique of anti-theatricality itself. There is a fundamental contradiction inherent in anti-theatricality which Shakespeare exposes, a contradiction between the claims that these pamphleteers make about gender and the cautionary tales about dissolving soldiers that they tell. For if anti-theatricalists like Gosson and Prynne claim that there is a fundamental difference "betwene sexe and sexe," they fear that this difference exists only insofar as it is performed, relentlessly acted out, a fear implicit in Prynne's apparent belief that the wearing of female clothing is enough to make the warrior's voice change register. Shakespeare hints at this contradiction in his treatment of the story of the dissolving warrior, in exposing the degree to which performative notions are built into anti-theatricality itself. But he heightens this contradiction in his depiction of Caesar, an anti-theatricalist whose essentialist claims about masculinity are a means of policing the very longings he himself betrays. If the story of Antony is the story of a man who cannot hold on to his masculinity, the story of Caesar is the story of a man who holds on to his too tightly, so tightly that the holding on itself is revealed as a defense. Shakespeare characterizes the hypermasculinity at the heart of anti-theatricality itself as a defense.

If Caesar's first attack is an attack on appetite which contains within it a secret glorification of appetite, and his second attack is an attack on Antony which contains within it a longing for Antony, his third attack, explicitly an anti-theatrical attack, contains within it an intense longing for theatricality, perhaps the most intense longing for theatricality in the play.

If Caesar parrots the rhetoric of anti-theatrical attacks in I.iv, in III.vi he attacks the actual enthronement ceremonies and coronation performances that Antony and Cleopatra are putting on in Alexandria. ("I' th' marketplace on a tribunal silver'd / Cleopatra and himself ... / Were publicly enthron'd" [III.vi.3–5]). At its simplest level this attack springs from a rage at the aspirations to literal power Antony and Cleopatra exhibit, the bequests of land ("Unto her / He gave the stablishment of Egypt" [III.vi.8–9]), the bequests of title ("His sons he there proclaim'd the kings of kings" [III.vi.13]), and the enthronement ceremonies themselves. Nor is the attack devoid of the sexual disgust that Caesar expresses elsewhere throughout the play. This is apparent even in the language of the speech as Caesar distances himself not only from Caesarion "whom they *call* my father's son" (italics mine) but from sexuality itself:

> At the feet sat
> Caesarion, whom they call my father's son,
> And all the unlawful issue that their lust
> Since then hath made between them.
>
> (III.vi.5–8)

(Antony and Cleopatra's children are not children but "issue," and it is not they but their "lust" which has produced them. Even the phrase "at *the* feet" dehumanizes them, presenting them as animals or objects, like a statue.)

But what Caesar really rages at is Cleopatra's presentation of herself as a goddess: "She / In th' abiliments of the goddess Isis / That day appear'd and oft before gave audience" (III.vi.16–18). On its most profound level, the attack springs from a conviction that it is the representation which Antony and Cleopatra generate that is itself threatening: what goes on in the "public eye." What is at stake here is the power to stage oneself. And the assumption is that this staging is not just the outward manifestation of what one is, but the enabling force. Which is to say that at the core of Caesar's anti-theatricality lies a deeply theatrical way of organizing the world.

This itself becomes apparent as soon as Octavia appears in the second half of the scene. We feel it partly in Caesar's conception of her not as a person, but as a role: "Caesar's sister," "The wife of Antony" (III.vi.43). We feel it more palpably in the desire Caesar articulates for theatrical effects: "The wife of Antony / Should have an army for an usher, and / The neighs of horse to tell of her approach / Long ere she did appear" (III.vi.43–6). One could call it in fact a desire for very theatrical, even supernatural effects: "The trees by th' way / Should have borne men, and expectation fainted, / Longing for what it had not; nay the dust / Should have ascended to the roof of heaven / Rais'd by your populous troops" (III.vi.46–50). The sentiment here is the same one Caesar expresses at Antony's death when he says the breaking of so great a thing should have made a greater crack, should have shaken lions into civil streets and citizens into their dens. It is the sentiment Cleopatra expresses when she tells the messenger that if Antony is dead he should have come like a fury, "not like a formal man" (II.v.41). It is not just a desire for theatrical effects, though it is certainly this as well. It is an expectation that the universe will manifest itself theatrically, that each crucial event will have a theatrical manifestation, will, more than that, only exist through its theatrical manifestation. Caesar explicitly articulates this belief a moment later. He tells Octavia:

> But you are come
> A market-maid to Rome, and have prevented

The ostentation of our love, which, left unshown,
Is often left unlov'd.

(III.vi.50–3)

The belief here that the "love" won't exist at all unless "shown," demonstrated, acted out, lies at the heart of Caesar's way of organizing the world. And if "love," as we have seen, is not a special case, but rather an example of a belief system (in which masculinity fails as well unless "acted out"), then power too won't exist unless acted out, continually maintained, "shown," and Antony and Cleopatra's enactments become not simply the signs but the actualizations of their power.

From this point of view, Caesar's obsession with *staging* a battle in which Antony seems to defeat himself ("Plant those that have revolted in the vant / That Antony may seem to spend his fury / Upon himself" (IV.vi.8–10) is almost inevitable, since it is the enactment of the idea that will give it reality. From this point of view, Caesar's greater and even more sustained obsession with leading Cleopatra in triumph makes sense as well. For it is in the performance of her as "monster," "spot," that she becomes these things. In the triumph, Caesar can enact upon others all the fears he himself must manage. If he fears that Antony dissipates the boundaries of class by tippling with a slave, he can rewrite those boundaries by making Cleopatra part of the varletry. If he fears that Antony can dissipate the boundaries of gender by being "not more manlike than Cleopatra," he can have Cleopatra "boyed" in the posture of a whore. If he fears as perverse and cannibalistic the appetites he carries within him, he can stage and thus constitute appetite itself as Cleopatra's by making her the monster, the spot, the whore. Through staging Cleopatra as "other," Caesar can ignore what is "other" at the heart of the self.

In this third scene, then, in which the play juxtaposes Caesar's attack on theatre to the longing for theatre he immediately displays, it suggests that anti-theatricality itself is in effect just another guise of theatre, although in a sense this was implicit all along in Shakespeare's treatment of the story of the dissolving warrior, since to expose the premise of that story – that masculinity has to be enacted in order to exist – is to suggest the degree to which performative notions of gender are implicit in anti-theatricality itself. In Caesar Shakespeare heightens this discrepancy. Not only does he characterize the rigid ideal of gender which characterizes anti-theatrical tracts as itself defensive, but he characterizes the pose of anti-theatricality as just that, a pose. In so doing, he casts anti-theatricality itself as a walking contradiction. This is Shakespeare's *anti*-anti-theatricality, the suggestion that no one stands "outside" the theatre, least of all those who profess to. In this play there are only rival theatres and, theatrically speaking, it is Cleopatra who gets the final word.

But a critique of anti-theatricality is not the same as a defense of the stage. If the play exhibits an anti-theatricality on the one hand and a critique of anti-theatricality on the other, what criterion does it ultimately provide to allow us to mediate between these two impulses? What is its attitude toward theatre itself? Does *Antony and Cleopatra* ultimately salvage theatre from the attacks of the period, the attacks it itself advances?

Nobleness well-acted

To answer this question we need to look at the play's most profound critique of theatre, the performance Cleopatra scripts and arranges which sends Antony to kill himself: "send him word you are dead," Charmian advises her, "the soul and body rive not more in parting / Than greatness going off" (IV.xiii.4–6). And Cleopatra instructs Mardian not only on what to say to "rive" Antony's soul and body, but how to say it: "go tell him I have slain myself; / Say that the last I spoke was 'Antony' / And word it, prithee, piteously" (IV.xiii.7–9). Here, Shakespeare offers a critique of theatre which goes beyond those offered by the attacks of the period. For here he imagines a theatre so destructive, so implicitly hostile to its own audience that it causes its spectator to kill himself. Such a theatre may pose as catharsis, as a purge for violent emotion – Diomedes tells the dying Antony that Cleopatra did what she did when she saw that his rage "would not be purg'd" (IV.xiv.124) – but its effect is to cultivate grief, to produce an emotion so violent, that it can only be satisfied in death. Diomedes even suggests that this may have been the intention when he says that Cleopatra anticipated her own effect, "had a prophesying fear / Of what hath come to pass" (IV.xiv.120–1).

Taken in isolation, such a moment is profoundly anti-theatrical. But what is striking about Cleopatra's performance is that in a sense it cannot be taken in isolation, for from the very beginning of the play, she has been rehearsing it, imagining it, dreading it, acting it out. "Cleopatra, catching but the least noise of this, dies instantly," Enobarbus tells Antony when he announces his plan to leave Egypt. "I have seen her die twenty times upon far poorer moment. I do think there is mettle in death, which commits some loving act upon her, she hath such celerity in dying" (I.ii.141–4). In one sense, the "celerity in dying" is just a sexual joke: the conceit of death performing a loving act upon Cleopatra no more than a personification of the Renaissance sense of the word "to die." But in a more basic sense, Enobarbus is simply calling attention to what we witness throughout the play, Cleopatra's continual rehearsal of her own death: "Help me away, dear Charmian! I shall fall. / It cannot be thus long, the sides of nature / Will not sustain it" (I.iii.15–17). "Cut my lace,

Charmian, come!" (I.iii.71). "Lead me from hence; / I faint, O Iras, Charmian!" (II.v.109–10). She has, from the very beginning of the play, been haunted by the idea of death, both her own ("I see, / In Fulvia's death, how mine receiv'd shall be" [I.iii.64–5]) and Antony's ("Antonio's dead! If thou say so, villain, / Thou kill'st thy mistress, but well and free, / If thou so yield him, there is gold" [II.v.26–8]). Even the assurance that Antony is "well" is construed as proof of death: "we use / To say the dead are well" [II.v.32–3]. The perpetual rehearsal of the moment of death, then, suggests both a need for and an attempt at mastery, as if, as in repetition compulsions, the belief were that in rehearsing her death again and again she could master it. Looked at within this continuum of rehearsals, then, the mock suicide represents one more attempt at mastery, represents an attempt to act out and to master a fear of death that has haunted Cleopatra throughout the whole play.

But the mock suicide itself is also a rehearsal, a rehearsal for Cleopatra's final performance, the actual suicide she stages in V.ii. For she does not simply die, but rather stages her death. Everything about the death scene, beginning with the way it is ushered in with a request for props and costume ("Give me my robe, put on my crown" [V.ii.280]) calls attention to it as a performance.[22] Cleopatra thinks of it as a "noble act" ("Methinks I hear / Antony call: I see him rouse himself / To praise my noble act" [V.ii.282–4]), just as Dolabella thinks of it as a dread performance ("thyself art coming," he tells Caesar, "To see perform'd the dreaded act which thou / So sought'st to hinder" [V.ii.330–2].)

But if Cleopatra performs her death rather than just undergoing it, this performance must be understood within a context, must itself be seen as a counterperformance to the one that Caesar seeks to stage. For every aspect of it can be seen as the opposite, the transformation of what Caesar himself would stage Cleopatra as. Antony predicts that Caesar will stage her as a whore, "the greatest spot / Of all thy sex; most monster-like, be shown" (IV.xii.35–6). Cleopatra is obsessed with this fear. She tells Charmian:

> The quick comedians
> Extemporally will stage us, and present
> Our Alexandrian revels: Antony
> Shall be brought drunken forth, and I shall see
> Some squeaking Cleopatra boy my greatness
> I' th' posture of a whore.

> (V.ii.216–21)

Where Caesar would stage her as a whore, she stages herself as a wife ("Husband, I come!" [V.ii.287]), not Antony's spurned mistress, but his legitimate wife, not only a wife but a mother ("Peace, peace!" she says of

the asp, "Dost thou not see my baby at my breast" [V.ii.308–9]). Where
Caesar's triumph would demote her in class, turn her into the varletry she
is shown to, her own performance insists that she is a queen ("Show me
my women, like a queen; go fetch / My best attires ... Bring our crown
and all" [V.ii.227–32]). Where all the descriptions of Caesar's triumph
depict Cleopatra as being stripped of physical volition, "hoisted" to the
"shouting varletry," "pinioned" at Caesar's court, "uplifted" to the view
of mechanic slaves and made to "drink their vapor," where Caesar would
stage her as powerless even over her own body, Cleopatra's final performance of herself insists on her as a goddess. She is Isis, with a serpent at her
breast. She is Venus, with the power not only to command her own body,
but the power to evoke an erotic response from nature itself. "I am again
for Cydnus / To meet Mark Antony" she says (V.ii.228–9). But Enobarbus has already told us that at Cydnus "her own person / ... beggar'd all
description" (II.ii.197–8), that she overpictured that "Venus where we see
/ The fancy outwork nature" (II.ii.200–1), that her sails were so perfumed
that the "winds were love-sick with them" (II.ii.194) and her oars so kept
stroke to the tune of flutes that the water was "amorous" for her strokes.
Where Caesar would present her as powerless over even her own body,
Cleopatra's final presentation of herself is not just a performance, but a
masque, staging her not merely as a queen but as a goddess with erotic
power over the whole natural universe.

What is at stake in Cleopatra's prerogative to stage her own death,
then, is in fact the capacity to define what she is, to represent her life, to
name what she is. But this is not "merely" a matter of representation. Or
rather, representation itself is not merely a matter of presenting an image
or reflection or copy of what already "is." The last act of *Antony and
Cleopatra* devolves into a virtual competition between Caesar and Cleopatra about who will get the final performance, who will get the prerogative to stage her. Caesar grows increasingly desperate about this. He tells
Proculeius: "Give her what comforts / The quality of her passion shall
require / Lest in her greatness, by some mortal stroke / She do defeat us"
(V.i.62–5). "For her life in Rome / Would be eternal in our triumph"
(V.ii.65–6). He means of course that her life in Rome would make his
triumph eternal, but the slip suggests the power her very image has.

The whole last act of the play can be seen as a series of performances
and counterperformances: Proculeius puts on an elaborate performance
of Caesar's generosity ("you shall find / A conqueror that will pray in aid
for kindness / Where he for grace is kneel'd to" [V.ii.26–8]), and Cleopatra puts on an elaborate counterperformance of her own obedience: "I
hourly learn / A doctrine of obedience, and would gladly / Look him i' th'
face" (V.ii.30–2); Caesar arrives and offers an elaborate act about seeing

the injuries Cleopatra has dealt him as mere accidents. Cleopatra presents an elaborate counterperformance in which she suggests that he offers a better rationale for her weakness than she can beg for herself. In the exchange with Seleucis, Cleopatra holds back her inventory and pretends to be interested in money, in order to convince Caesar she's planning to stay alive, and Caesar pretends to think her wise for doing so. But all these are secondary to and, in a sense, prologues to the real struggle, the struggle between the triumph Caesar wants to stage and the counterper-formance Cleopatra does stage of her own death.

But in what kind of world would the prerogative to stage oneself be of such crucial importance? In a world in which things lack or are believed to lack an independent existence apart from their own theatricalizations. And this is exactly the view of reality to which virtually everyone in *Antony and Cleopatra* subscribes. Why do so many people in this world conceive of themselves or each other or reality itself in theatrical terms? (Cleopatra conceiving of political action as theatrical action, Caesar telling Antony to "Take in that kingdom, and enfranchise that / *Perform't*, or else we damn thee" [I.i.23–4, italics mine], Cleopatra conceiving of reality itself as a script ["I'll seem the fool I am not, Antony / Will be himself"], Dolabella thinking of even his news as a performance, "I have perform'd / Your pleasure and my promise" [V.ii.203–4]). Thidias defines himself as Caesar's actor, "One that but performs / The bidding of the fullest man, and worthiest / To have command obey'd" (III.xiii.86–8). Scarus thinks of Antony's turning tail at sea as an "action" of shame.

More to the point, why do people in this world so frequently want things acted out? "Speak to me home," Antony tells the messenger from Rome, "mince not the general tongue. . . / Rail thou in Fulvia's phrase" (I.ii.105–7). He wants the criticisms of him in Rome acted out. Caesar and Charmian and Cleopatra all express a much more profound expectation that the universe will offer a theatrical manifestation for its deepest occurrences: "The breaking of so great a thing should make / A greater crack" says Caesar at Antony's death, anxious that the death could occur without a visible and theatrical manifestation in the world (V.i.14–15). "The round world / Should have shook lions into civil streets / And citizens to their dens" (V.i.15–17). Charmian too expects the universe to register visibly Cleopatra's death, expects nature to act out her grief: "Dissolve, thick cloud, and rain, that I may say / The gods themselves do weep!" (V.ii.299–300). Cleopatra too wants the asp to articulate what an ass Caesar is:

> Come, thou mortal wretch,
> [To an asp, which she applies to her breast]
> With thy sharp teeth this knot intrinsicate

Of life at once untie. Poor venomous fool,
Be angry, and dispatch. O, couldst thou speak,
That I might hear thee call great Caesar ass
Unpolicied!

(V.ii.303–8)

Why do people in this world so frequently need and expect and want things acted out? Cleopatra railing at the messenger for not dressing and playing the part of a fury if harm has come to Antony, Caesar chiding Octavia for coming without theatrical effect: an army for an usher, the neighs of horses to tell of her approach, the trees bearing men. In fact, the belief at the heart of this world is the one Caesar articulates when he tells Octavia she has "prevented / the ostentation of our love; which, left unshown / Is often left unloved," the same belief Proculeius articulates when he tells Cleopatra "Do not abuse my master's bounty by / Th' undoing of yourself. Let the world see / His nobleness well-acted, which your death / Will never let come forth" (V.ii.43–6). The belief at the heart of this world is that things simply fail to exist at all apart from their own theatricalizations, not only power or identity, but masculinity, love, nobleness itself.

The play's "defense" of theatre, then, is made not on any moral ground, lies not in any capacity to salvage theatre from the critiques both the play and the period supply, but on what are virtually ontological grounds: if things fail to exist apart from their own theatricalizations, then what is enacted is simply more "real" than what is not, theatricality simply the constitutive condition of existence itself. How does such a claim differ from the claim that in the Renaissance there were "selves and a sense that they could be fashioned" or the claim that "the public sphere, the realm of the gaze constitutes reality as a theatrical space?"[23] What is finally so disturbing about *Antony and Cleopatra* is that while this is a world that believes *things in general* fail to exist apart from their own theatricalizations, it seems to be *masculinity in particular*, masculinity more than anything else, that needs to be enacted and compulsively re-enacted in order to exist. Why does no one ever seem to regard femininity as contingent, as something that has to be maintained or enacted or upheld in order to exist? Perhaps because the woman is always the *feared* thing, the thing one is in danger of regressing or slipping into, nobody ever thinks of femininity as *needing* to be staged.

But in light of this it is striking that it *is* the woman, Cleopatra, not Antony or Caesar who gets to stage herself: her "triumph" in staging her death is not just the capacity to "represent" her self in an abstract sense as if that self already existed, but the capacity to create that self, to constitute it. In performing her death, she creates a self.

Does the play then celebrate the very female theatricality that the tracts abhor, celebrate it in the full recognition of its effeminizing, even fatal power to dissolve those men it is aimed at? Our impulse to say yes is tempered not only by the fact that it is Caesar who inherits the world, but by the recognition that this particular performance costs Cleopatra her life.

Perhaps Shakespeare is not so much celebrating the power of female theatricality as he is mourning its loss: for the cost of Cleopatra's last performance is, indeed, her life. And at what more timely moment would Shakespeare mourn such a loss than at one in which his own world has passed from the hands of a woman monarch, whose theatricality swept its populace into itself in a rhetoric of love, to the hands of a male king who, though he, like Caesar, spoke the rhetoric of universal peace, took his theatricality indoors to the world of court masques where it would not be achieved "in the public eye"?[24]

What we have seen in *Troilus and Cressida* and *Antony and Cleopatra* is Shakespeare imagining the world the anti-theatricalists fear, a world in which men really can be transformed into women. In *Troilus and Cressida* he identifies the cost of preventing this transformation: to be men, men will have to "act" like men, will have to "perform" their masculinity, and to do this they will have to remain in a perpetual state of war. In *Antony and Cleopatra*, Shakespeare suggests that this is finally impossible, shows us the process of this particular performance breaking down. What we shall see as we turn to *Epicoene* is Jonson imagining the world the anti-theatricalists demand: a world built around the premise that "signs" lead to things, that certainty is possible. Jonson's critique of anti-theatricality takes a very different form from Shakespeare's, then, for in making the flight from androgyny, or what he calls the "epicene," a type or example of all flights from uncertainty, he suggests that anti-theatricality is about as viable as trying to rid the world of ambiguity itself.

4   Theatre as other: Jonson's *Epicoene*

Much has been written about Jonson's anti-theatricality, but what critics have failed to do is reconcile that anti-theatricality with what has been called a "subversive hankering" for theatre on Jonson's part. The most thorough attempt to produce a unified vision of Jonson on theatre, for instance, ends with the conclusion that Jonson was ambivalent: "Alongside the well articulated anti-theatricalism, that is, there lurks a less acknowledged but nonetheless potent theatricalism." This critic argues that Jonson's energy and "equilibrium" spring precisely from the "uneasy synthesis" between a "formal anti-theatricalism" and a "subversive hankering" after the arts of show and illusion.[1]

The problem with a picture of Jonson that posits a conscious ("formal") anti-theatricalism and an unconscious ("less acknowledged") theatricalism is that it fails to take into account the strenuous critiques of anti-theatricality that emerge in Jonson's late plays – his "*anti*-anti-theatricality." Such a position therefore fails to arrive at an understanding of the way Jonson himself finally mediated between these two opposite positions. In part, this reflects a canonical bias, for discussions of anti-theatricality in Jonson generally take their terms either from *Volpone* or the poems.[2] But perhaps such a failure springs as well from the *kind* of anti-theatricality that critics have identified.[3] In their response to the moral and philosophical currents in Jonson's work, even the most intelligent analyses have ignored the ways Jonson's hostility to the stage replicates the gender anxieties that dominate popular anti-theatrical tracts.[4]

One play, in particular, offers an opportunity to revise this picture. Built on the key tropes of popular anti-theatricality – homophobia, effeminization and androgyny – Jonson's *Epicoene or the Silent Woman* thematizes the stage convention which gave rise to anti-theatrical hysteria, the convention of boys playing women. But because the play also contains an anti-theatrical figure, one who is continually at pains to "bar his doors" against theatre, and because this figure is the object of the play's relentless criticism, *Epicoene* also provides an instance of Jonson's anti-anti-theatricality.

Jonson mediates between these two positions through the notion of masque.[5] Dauphine's apparent ability to restore sexual difference at the end of the play – his revelation of Epicoene as a boy – suggests a masque-like power to banish the chaos typical of the anti-masque, a chaos this play envisions specifically as androgyny. (In the words of one critic, "Nearly everyone in the play is epicene in some way.")[6] But Dauphine's restoration is itself precarious, not only because of the many androgynous characters who remain at the end, but because of the dialectic the play has already established about androgyny itself. *Epicoene* presents two radically different accounts of the "epicene." The first, which blames theatre for the "epicene," argues that "epiceneness," androgyny, is accidental, and implies an easy solution to the problem: remove the costume and it is possible to have back an essential male. The second account, which argues that rather than being accidental, the epicene is inherent in life itself, inherent in a world of time, offers no solution and, in fact, takes refuge in the notion of costume as an escape.[7] The first account corresponds to Jonson's anti-theatricality, the second to his anti-anti-theatricality. Jonson attempts to mediate between these two positions in the play's final masque-like gesture, but the success of the masque is at best precarious, and it is this second account rather than the first which prevails at the end of the play.

A leg or an eye: Jonson's anti-theatricality

Epicoene begins by articulating the pair of anxieties at the heart of the anti-theatrical attack: the fear of effeminization and the fear that theatre is an excuse for homosexuality. Describing his trips to the "College" of mannish women in the play, Clerimont's boy says that Lady Haughty forces him to dress as a girl:

The gentlewomen play with me and throw me o' the bed, and carry me in to my lady, and she kisses me with her oiled face, and puts a peruke o' my head, and asks me an' I will wear her gown, and I say no; and then she hits me a blow o' the ear and calls me innocent, and lets me go. (I.i.13–17)[8]

The story articulates the two fears at the heart of the anti-theatrical attack, for it argues both that men can be effeminized (the boy is not only dressed as a girl, but made passive, the object of the lady's blows and kisses alike), and second that costume is merely a pretext for homosexuality. It is only as a girl that Lady Haughty wants to fondle the boy, and the evocation of female homoerotic play calls attention to the possibilities for

male homoeroticism beneath the costume. For Lady Haughty is played by
a boy dressed as a woman, and Clerimont's boy, if we follow out the logic
of the anecdote, is played by a boy dressed as a boy, and subsequently
dressed (by Lady Haughty) as a girl. The anecdote is implicitly anti-
theatrical, then, for it invokes the Elizabethan stage convention which
provided a focus for anti-theatrical hysteria, the convention of boys
wearing women's costume. In this anecdote it is the "actor" – the boy put
into the costume – who is effeminized, softened by the experience. But as
we shall see, by the end of the play, it is the spectator, Morose, who is
nearly subjected to violent emasculation by the performance in front of
him.[9]

Implicitly, then, the play begins by arguing that women effeminize
men.[10] Repeating the boy's anecdote a moment later, Clerimont tells
Truewit that "no man can be admitted" to the college, "but the boy
here." The Collegiates will not admit a man, but they will admit a boy, a
compromised partialized version of a man. And even then the boy must
be turned into a girl. What the anecdote, taken with this gloss, suggests is
that women cope with the idea of an "other" – a sexual other – by
partializing and reducing it, by turning this "other" into a version of the
self. In the process, the other, the man, is deprived of his masculinity. The
play begins, then, by establishing an analogy between women and theatre
as partializing, effeminizing forces.[11] (As we shall see, this analogy will be
strengthened throughout the course of the play. In this instance, the
theatre, the costume, the peruke and the gown, are the instruments of the
effeminization and the woman is the perpetrator, though this relationship
will be reversed by the end of the play.)

The play begins, then, by taking a very clear point of view toward the
issue of "epiceneness." The epicene is a function of externals, specifically
the externals of theatre and women. Effeminization and hence androgyny
are things which are imposed from outside, though this suggests that they
are also things which can be taken away. This logic, however, reaffirms
the notion of the "essential" male – the boy beneath the costume – for it
suggests that, were it not for the effeminizing woman or effeminizing
costume, the man would be whole, fully male.

This logic is extended throughout the play. The idea that the man
would be whole, but for the theatre or woman that tries to diminish him,
is suggested first through a set of fantasies about dismemberment. Initially, the argument is that women dismember men, though the play finally
acknowledges this claim as a kind of smokescreen and admits that the real
impulse to dismember originates within theatre itself.

Haranguing Morose about his intended marriage, Truewit argues that
what women really want is to dismember men:

Alas, Sir, do you ever think to find a chaste wife in these times? Now? When there are so many masques, plays, Puritan preachings, mad folks, and other strange sights to be seen daily, private and public? If you had lived in King Ethelred's time, sir, or Edward the Confessor's, you might, perhaps, have found in some cold country hamlet then, a dull frosty wench would have been contented with one man; now they will as soon be pleased with one leg or one eye. (II.ii.27–34)

Though the moral of the story – the literal message – is that a woman will not be content with one man, the passage ends on the disconcerting images of the leg and the eye, disembodied. What the woman really wants, the passage insinuates, is the dismantled limb, the man reduced to a part, a leg or an eye. Without the woman, the man would be whole. This notion is taken a step farther when Morose wants to get out of his marriage: "Would I could redeem it [the marriage] with the loss of an eye, nephew, a hand, or any other member" (IV.iv.7–8). "Marry, God forbid, sir," says Dauphine, "that you should geld yourself to anger your wife" (IV.iv.9–10). Again, though the literal message is that to be free of a woman a man must give up a limb, the subliminal message is that the cost of marriage, of contact with a woman, is castration. In fact, the association of women with dismemberment does seem to be somewhat justified, for when we see the Collegiates with Dauphine, they do immediately reduce him to a set of members or parts. Centaure: "I could love a man for such a nose!" (IV.vi.33), Mavis: "Or such a leg" (IV.vi.34). Centaure: "He has an exceeding good eye" (IV.vi.35). Mentally dismembering him, the Collegiates construe Dauphine entirely as a set of parts. Like Lady Haughty with Clerimont's boy, they are able to "admit" only the idea of a partialized other.

The play then assembles a good deal of evidence to support the idea that effeminization and the consequent "epiceneness" it causes are the fault of women. But if we look closely, the real impulse to dismember is contained within theatre itself. Thus the theatrical Truewit stages around Daw and La Foole – first feeding their grudges and then pretending to placate them – revolves around the persistent theme of dismemberment:

TRUEWIT: Well, I'll try if he will be appeased with a leg or an arm; if not, you must die once.
DAW: I would be loth to lose my right arm, for writing madrigals.
TRUEWIT: Why, if he will be satisfied with a thumb or a little finger, all's one to me. You must think I'll do my best. (IV.v.107–112)

Truewit's insistent characterization of what he is doing as theatre ("Here will I act such a tragicomedy between the Guelphs and the Ghibellines, Daw and La Foole ... You two shall be the chorus behind the arras, and whip out between the acts and speak" [IV.v.27–30]) argues that theatre per se is being identified with this impulse toward dismemberment, this very real capacity to diminish the spectator. Later Truewit will claim he has bargained La Foole down to "your upper lip, and six o' your fore-teeth" (IV.v.238), "I brought him down to your two butter teeth, and them he would have" (IV.v.241–2). The bodily parts Daw will have to forfeit get smaller and smaller, as if Daw himself were being equated with a smaller and smaller part, but the theme of the theatrical persistently comes back to the fantasy of dismemberment.

But if the impulse toward dismemberment is merely thematized within the theatrical, one might argue, then theatre still contains – in the sense of limiting and sealing off – potentially destructive impulses. It is at this point in *Epicoene* that the destructive impulses threaten to break through the theatrical container and become real. For Dauphine, behind the scenes, suggests not merely "acting" the scene of Daw's dismemberment, but dismembering him in fact:

TRUEWIT: He will let me do nothing, man he does all afore me; he offers me his left arm.

CLERIMONT: His left wing, for a Jack Daw.

DAUPHINE: Take it, by all means.

TRUEWIT: How! Maim a man forever for a jest? What a conscience hast thou!

DAUPHINE: 'Tis no loss to him; he has no employment for his arms but to eat spoon-meat. Besides, as good maim his body as his reputation. (IV.v.115–23)

This is where Jonson advances a specifically anti-theatrical argument, for he shows us a theatre which boasts for itself the function of "curing" the distempered spectator (Clerimont: "Otter's wine has swelled their humours above a spring tide" [IV.iv.150–1]. Truewit: "If I do not make 'em keep the peace for this remnant of the day, if not of the year, I have failed once" [IV.v.30–2]) but which he reveals to contain a much more destructive set of impulses than the ones it is purporting to cure.[12] By widening the gap between theatre's claim for itself and the violent impulses which theatre can barely contain, and by casting these impulses in the very terms in which the anti-theatrical tracts cast them, Jonson implicates *Epicoene* in a deep and pervasive anti-theatricality, the anti-theatricality of the popular tracts.

Thus whenever theatre claims for itself the virtue of cure, Jonson reveals its intention of diminishing and dismembering the spectator, of literally invading the spectator's body boundaries. This is most farcically the case when Epicoene proposes to "cure" her husband Morose of his madness by reading him Pliny and Paracelsus, Greene's *Groat's Worth of Wit* and Bacon's *The Sick Man's Salve*, for even this theatrical involves an implied threat to Morose's body: "Lay hold on him," Epicoene says, "for God's sake. What shall I do? Who's his physician, can you tell, that knows the state of his body best, that I might send for him?" (IV.iv.42–4).

But it is most spectacularly so in the theatrical of "searching" that constitutes the play's climax. In this scene, Jonson validates all the anxieties of the anti-theatrical tracts. For it is theatre, in the form of Cutbeard and Otter as Canon and Divine, that makes Morose profess his own impotence, confess that he is "manifestam frigiditatem" (manifestly impotent) and "prorsus inutilis ad thorum" (utterly useless for the marriage bed): "Utterly unabled in nature, by reason of frigidity, to perform the duties or any the least office of a husband" (V.iv.42–3).[13] Symbolically, Morose is emasculated by being made to renounce his masculinity. (He does not merely say that he is impotent, but that he is not a man: "I am no man, ladies" [V.iv.40].) Physically, he is threatened with emasculation, for this is another moment when the theatrical impulse toward dismemberment threatens to break through the pretense of curing Morose of his marriage and become real. This is the moment the women threaten to "search" him:

EPICOENE: Tut, a device, a device, this, it smells rankly. A mere comment of his own.
TRUEWIT: Why, if you suspect that, ladies, you may have him searched.
DAW: As the custom is, by a jury of physicians.
LA FOOLE: Yes, faith, 'twill be brave.
MOROSE: O me, must I undergo that!
MRS. OTTER: No, let women search him madam: we can do it ourselves.
MOROSE: Out on me, worse! (V.iv.48–57)

The play opened with Clerimont's boy's anecdote which made women the perpetrators of effeminization and theatrical costume the instrument. This scene reverses the hierarchy, for now it is Truewit's theatrical impulse to castrate the spectator which sweeps women into it. The castration itself – the "searching" – is cast as theatre, as spectacle. (Hence La Foole's "Yes, faith, 'twill be brave.") This scene affirms the fear at the heart of the anti-theatrical tracts, for it shows theatre seeking to emasculate the spectator. It is no coincidence, then, that the scene titillates the other anxiety that anti-theatrical tracts pair with effeminization, the fear of homosexuality: through theatre Morose has married a boy.

But if theatre is what effeminizes the male spectator, then were it not for the theatre he would be a "real" male. In other words, the loss of gender is the fault of theatre, the epiceneness imposed from outside, and if the theatre is expelled, the epiceneness can be expelled as well. The anxiety about effeminization is not incompatible with – in fact, supports – the belief in an "essential" male. The boy would be a boy but for the costume the woman puts him in. The man would be whole and potent but for the theatre that tries to dismember and castrate him. These scenes, then, not only share a pronounced anti-theatricality, but also affirm the play's initial attitude toward the epicene. The cause of the effeminization – and hence the loss of gender – is always outside the self. This is the premise behind the anti-theatricalism which always needs to focus on expelling externals. It is also the premise behind Clerimont's song – "but to be neat" – and defense of nature, which insistently presuppose a "real" beneath the artifice. These scenes, behind their fear of external threats, all preserve a buried idea of the "real" or essential male beneath the costume.

But the play also contains within it a very different explanation of the epicene, according to which the "real" is itself epicene, according to which the epicene is not something imposed from outside, but something inherent in nature, and particularly in time itself. Arguing for the propriety of artifice in I.i, Truewit says,

> I once followed a rude fellow into a chamber, where the poor madam, for haste, and troubled, snatched at her peruke to cover her baldness and put it on the wrong way.
> CLERIMONT: O prodigy! (I.i.116–20)

This moment of the perception of the baldness beneath the peruke is also a moment of androgyny, a recognition of the epicene. The baldness is "prodigious" (monstrous) precisely because it signals the loss of sexual difference, and in a deeper sense, the loss of all difference. The bald woman is neither one thing nor another, neither man nor woman, and in this sense her epiceneness becomes a type or figure for all the ambiguity in the play which is simply the consequence of living in a world of time. To this version of the epicene – which is not conferred by anything external and which cannot be expelled by expelling theatre – there is no solution, but only flight from knowledge, willed blindness.

The play then establishes a dialectic between the idea that the epicene is imposed from outside and can be expelled (the anti-theatrical position typified by Clerimont's boy's story) and the competing idea that the epicene is inherent in a world of time, and that attempts to "expel" it are futile. In the scenes which focus on Morose, Jonson advances this second position, which is *anti*-anti-theatrical. For Morose, too, is in flight from time, in flight from the idea of the thing which is neither one thing nor another. In these scenes, then, the "epicene" becomes not simply literal androgyny, but all those things which are neither one thing nor another, those things which constitute the experience of uncertainty itself.

But with your leg: Jonson's anti-anti-theatricality

At the heart of Morose's fascination with silence is the fantasy of absolute power, imaged in the figure of the Turk who "exceed[s] all the potentates of the earth ... most of his charges and directions given by signs, and with silence" (II.i.27–30). The operative word here is "signs," for Morose's attempt to create a system of "signs," to rid language of all ambiguity, is his attempt to flee the epicene inherent in life itself. What is at stake in the reduction of language from a system of sounds to a system of signs is the attempt to convert language from something connotative – sounds being variable and capable of affect as well as change – to something denotative. "Is it not possible that thou shouldst answer me by signs, and I apprehend thee, fellow?" (II.i.4–5) Morose asks the Mute. Thus the "sign" for agreement with any proposition that Morose has put forth is the Mute's "leg." ("But with your leg, your answer, unless it be otherwise" [II.i.11–12].) The attempt here is to create a world of absolute certainty, a world in which each sound shall mean only and exactly and always what contract has arranged it shall mean: "How long will it be ere Cutbeard come?" Morose asks the Mute, "Stay; if an hour, hold up your whole hand; if half an hour, two fingers; if a quarter, one" (II.i.19–21). Part of the fantasy of absolute power, then, consists in being the one with the prerogative to set the contract. (For it is a characteristic of this system that the speaker gets the prerogative to frame all propositions and the listener only the chance to affirm or deny them.) But an even greater part of the fantasy of power consists in the sensation of certainty itself.

Now the interesting question is what creates such a need for certainty in the first place. And like Truewit in flight from the recognition of the baldness under the peruke, the answer is the same. Morose is in flight from the intimation of that thing which eliminates all difference, that great producer of the "epicene," the idea of death. The room Morose creates for himself ("And you have fastened on a thick quilt or flock-bed on the outside of the door, that if they knock with their daggers or with brickbats, they can make no noise?" [II.i.9–11]) suggests quite clearly that noise is experienced as a threat, an invasion, almost a kind of rape, something which can enter the body itself. ("Bar my doors! Bar my doors!...O, the sea breaks in upon me! Another flood! An inundation!" Morose says [III.v.28 and III.vi.2–3]. "They have rent my roof, walls and all my windores asunder with their brazen throates" [IV.ii.121–2] he cries when the Collegiates come.) And, in fact, their arrival does constitute an invasion, nearly a rape. But even before their arrival, if we look at the kinds of "noise" Morose seeks to eliminate, we shall see that he is in flight from all those things which bring up the idea of death itself.

To begin with, Morose seems only to seek to eliminate innocent noises, the knowledge of music, for instance. ("A trumpet should fright him terribly, or the hautboys," Truewit says [I.i.145]. "Out of his senses," says Clerimont, "The waits of the city have a pension of him not to come near that ward" [I.i.146–7].) He seeks, that is, to eliminate all sounds that are not strictly referential, that cannot be pinned down to mean one thing or another, but are instead "epicene," connotative or affective. He seeks as well to eliminate the knowledge of trade. He has "been upon divers treaties with the fish-wives and orange-women, and articles propounded between them" (I.i.135–6). "A brazier is not suffered to dwell in the parish, nor an armorer" (I.i.141–2). It might be argued that the knowledge of trade has little to do with the knowledge of death, but in fact the idea of poverty – in this case the evidence that there are people who have to work in order to get money – brings up the idea of powerlessness. And Morose is in flight from all things which suggest the limits of his own power, and in such a way bring up reminders of the ultimate limit of that power, death. His flight is the retreat into self, into the fantasy of the omnipotent self. "All discourses but mine own afflict me," he says, "they seem harsh, impertinent, and irksome" (II.i.3–4).[14] By constructing a universe peopled only by his own utterances, he tries to create a world which is all self, a world in which the only knowledge he has to tolerate is the knowledge of the self. Like anti-theatricalists he is obsessed with the idea of an "absolute" self. [15] To this end, he seeks to eliminate reminders of all form of "other." If we take as indicative his own classification of female "speech" as the sign, for instance of female sexuality – "You can speak then. . .O immodesty! a manifest woman!" (III.iv.30–7) – he seeks to eliminate the knowledge of anyone sexually "other" than himself. (He deals with sexual otherness in the same way the Collegiates do, by looking for a compromised version of the "other," by turning the "other" into a version of the self.) More significantly, Morose flees the knowledge of a secular "other," a power or authority outside his control. In the Queen's time, Clerimont says, when the bells presumably stood for coronations and progresses, rather than sickness, "he was wont to go out of town every Saturday at ten o'clock or on holyday eves" (I.i.164–5) to avoid them.

But the most powerful form of an "other" that Morose tries to exclude is the knowledge of death itself:

But now, by reason of the sickness, the perpetuity of ringing has made him devise a room with double walls and treble ceilings, the windows close shut and caulked, and there he lives by candlelight. (I.i.164–8)

What Morose seeks to exclude in the "noise" of the plague bells is the knowledge of death, the knowledge of time. This is the most powerful form of an "other," the other which cannot be partialized or reduced or turned into a version of the self. This is implicit even in his very attempt to prevent Dauphine from "reigning" over him: "this night I will get an heir and thrust him out of my blood like a stranger; he would be knighted, forsooth, and thought by that means *to reign over me*" (II.v.87–9, italics mine). For it is a refusal to accept the transitoriness of his own reign, to accept the existence of time in the world, as if by barring Dauphine from a succession, he could insure his own permanence. His flight into a world of self, then, like his preoccupation with a language of "signs," is an attempt to bring about the sensation of certainty by reducing the idea of death. Jonson suggests that, taken to its logical extreme, this flight constitutes solipsism, and, what is more, that it reveals the precariousness of the "self" underneath: what the persistent fantasy of an "other" who can invade one's boundaries suggests is that the boundaries are precarious to begin with, as the images of holes and orifices, windows and mouths, imply.

Now the belief in the capacity of signs to guarantee absolute certainty is of course the belief at the heart of the period's anti-theatricalism. As we have seen, tracts against the stage were obsessed with the idea of a one-to-one correspondence between "sign" and thing. The frantic defense of the Deuteronomic code is built on an explicit theory of signs:

The law of God very straightly forbids men to put on women's garments, garments are set downe for signes distinctive betwene sexe and sexe, to take unto us those garments that are manifest signes of another sexe, is to falsify, forge and adulterate, contrarie to the expresse rule of the words of God.[16]

For Gosson, in being the "sign" of the gender beneath it, the clothing is the proof that we live in a referential universe in which direct knowledge is possible. "Outward shew" must represent that "which is within," he says. And oddly enough, for Munday, the actor offers a similar guarantee. For although Munday complains about the actor's hypocrisy and deceit, what he really believes is that the role the actor plays is the exact reflection of what he is: "For who can better plaie the ruffin than a verie ruffin? who better the lover, than they who make it a common exercise?"[17] The assumption here – completely at odds with the attack on theatre as lies – is that actors play those parts which display what they are. "Are they not notoriouslie knowen to be those men in their life abroad as they are on the stage?"[18] For Munday, the actor, despite his perverse insistence on "acting," is really only a part of a greater plan, a pervasive system of correspondences that makes it possible for us to know things.

Jonson casts anti-theatricality itself then – the obsession with reducing the world to a manageable system of "signs" – as a flight from reality itself, a flight from the inevitability of death. (For it is not only Morose's obsession with "signs" that marks him as an anti-theatricalist, but his frantic attempts to "bar his door" against all signs of theatre: music, wedding masques, epithalamia, revelry in general.) In casting the anti-theatrical preoccupation with signs and certainty as a flight from reality, Jonson himself exhibits a profound anti-anti-theatricality. Not only, Jonson suggests, does such a flight, taken to its logical conclusion, constitute willed solipsism, anti-theatricality itself a kind of "narrow dark room," but ultimately, as in the puppet show in *Bartholomew Fair*, the attempt to create a world of pure reference destroys the very possibility of referentiality at all. For Morose's insistence on eliminating all ambiguity leads to the impossibility of detecting ambiguity, as well as the impossibility of detecting paradox, contradiction, uncertainty and lies. In organizing language, for instance, so that the prerogative to frame all propositions falls to the speaker and only the prerogative to affirm or deny falls to the listener, Morose loses all the information that facial expressions, tones of voice, mannerisms and hesitancies can provide about lies, and is continually forced to hypothesize the sincerity of the speaker, a hypothesis which is quite frequently unwarranted.[19] "This I conceive, Cutbeard," he keeps saying without any evidence for it being the case, "you have been pre-acquainted with her birth, education and qualities, *or else* you would not prefer her to my acceptance" (italics mine). It is the "or else" Morose has no way of verifying, since, among other things, there is no way for a listener to affirm part of a proposition without affirming all of it. Jonson suggests, then, that the attempt to eliminate ambiguity, "epiceneness," makes real knowledge impossible, makes it impossible to know the "thing" behind the "sign." Thus, when Morose talks about trying Epicoene further, or says that he is satisfied with her outward appearance but now must "try her within" (II.v.18), the point is that he cannot possibly know her within. It never occurs to him to suspect duplicity, let alone the fact that she is a boy.

Jonson's anti-anti-theatricality is based less on any moral agenda, then, than it is on an epistemology, and, more to the point, the pragmatic critique that epistemology generates: Morose's anti-theatricality leaves him defenseless in an ambiguous and epicene world. Where Clerimont's boy's story suggests the epicene is superficial and that if one pulls off the costume, one will find a real boy, the scenes of the play which focus on Morose suggest that the epicene is inevitable, that the world itself is epicene, and that systems which try to reduce the anxiety this causes lose their ability to interpret the world. By banishing the ambiguity in language Morose loses the ability to understand signifiers outside his own system, like the word "Epicoene." By banishing theatre, he loses the ability to detect what is theatre, fails to recognize he is in a theatre, and that in Renaissance theatres, women are played by boys.

For into this world of rigorous denial come Truewit and Dauphine, the theatrical forces in the play, bringing proof of the existence of the ultimate "other," death itself. Dressed as a post from court, a secular other (beyond Morose's control) and carrying a noose, Truewit arrives, inviting Morose to die, arguing that marriage is death:

Marry, your friends do wonder, sir, the Thames being so near, wherein you may drown so handsomely; or London bridge at a low fall, with a fine leap, to hurry you down the stream; or such a delicate steeple i' the town, as Bow, to vault from; or, a braver height as Paul's; or, if you affected to do it nearer home and a shorter way, an excellent garret-windore into the street; or a beam in the said garret, with this halter [he shows him a halter], which they have sent, and desire that you would sooner commit your grave head to this knot than to the wedlock noose; or take a little sublimate, and go out of the world like a rat, or, a fly, as one said, with straw i' your arse: any way rather than to follow this goblin Matrimony. (II.ii.17–27)

The invitation to die is one which Dauphine will repeat in seriousness at the end of the play when he tells Morose, "Now you may go in and rest, be as private as you will, sir. I'll not trouble you till you trouble me with your funeral, which I care not how soon it come" (V.iv.191–3). Though they come with all the obvious signs of revelry, with horns and venison and reproaches to Morose for forgetting a wedding masque and epithalamium, they come bringing exactly the dour knowledge Morose has been trying to flee, the knowledge of death. What does it mean that theatre is cast as "other" in this play, as that which finally destroys the fantasy of absolute self?[20] The destruction of solipsism alone would seem to accord it the status of truth, though throughout the play it has systematically sought to deceive and delude.

This seems to create a kind of logical impasse, for if theatre offers an invitation to die and anti-theatricality itself is only a futile flight from the acceptance of death, then the play offers us a set of almost equally grim alternatives. If theatre is presented as dismemberment and anti-theatricality as willed blindness, what positive value governs this relentless critique? If both halves of the opposition, theatre and anti-theatricality, receive such bleak censure, perhaps the opposition between them is more apparent than real. But to what third thing would they be opposed? Perhaps if theatre seeks to deceive the spectator and anti-theatricality is self-deceiving, they are opposed to some third thing which can deliver knowledge, restore truth. What I am about to suggest is that that "third thing" is masque. Jonson invokes the notion of masque to reconcile two antithetical positions. And as an idea, the notion of masque does offer such a reconciliation. But as an event, in the world of the play, the masque's efficacy is highly problematic.

Off with her peruke: masques and masks

Into the epicene world of *Epicoene* steps Dauphine, pulling off Epicoene's peruke and revealing a boy:

Then here is your release, sir; (He takes off EPICOENE's peruke) You have married a boy: a gentleman's son that I have brought up this half year at my great charges, and for this composition which I have now made with you. What say you, Master Doctor? This is *justum impedimentum*, I hope, *error personae*? (V.iv.181–5)

Unlike all the other scenes of theatre in the play, which disguise and deceive, this one reveals. Unlike the other scenes of theatre which effeminize, this one restores the idea of an essential male under the costume. In stripping Epicoene of his artifice and revealing him to be a boy, Dauphine reaffirms the idea of the "real self," restores the very idea of the real. In banishing the epicene, Dauphine's final gesture reaffirms the premise the play began with, that all that was needed to get back the essential male was to banish theatre, to take off the disguise, though after all we have seen this seems like an alarming simplification.

Jonson ends the play with a flourish, a paradoxical reassertion of the very anti-theatrical bias it began with. Jonson ends the play with a flourish and Dauphine ends the play with a kind of masque. His revelation of Epicoene as a boy implies the masque hero's capacity to banish chaos and discord. "From the very beginning the resolution of discord . . . was a defining feature of the [masque] form for Jonson," says Stephen Orgel.[21] It is not simply the tangled plot which Dauphine seems to untangle by removing Epicoene's wig, but the substance of the discord, the loss of sexual difference, the "epiceneness" itself. And if Dauphine is a kind of disenfranchised king, barred by Morose (lest he reign over him) from a succession, Dauphine wins back his kingdom through his extraordinary ability to transform discord, the discord he himself has created. The play ends with a promise to undo even the factionalism and heal the marital strife which dominate its world, a promise to restore the missing "princess." ("Tom Otter, your Princess shall be reconciled to you" [V.iv.195–6].) Dauphine's revelation of Epicoene as a boy enacts his ability to publicly discover the "real" behind the artifice, the power to "find out" which (Orgel argues) Bacon claimed illustrated the monarch's control over his environment: "it is the glory of God to conceal a thing, but it is the glory of the king to find a thing out."[22]

Finally Dauphine alone has the ability to step outside and manipulate the fiction at the heart of the play, the fiction of Morose's marriage. Orgel argues that "the characters in Jonsonian antimasques, played by professional actors, are nearly always unaware that there are spectators," whereas the attribute of the hero is his awareness of the fiction. "The figure who is capable of stepping outside or violating the conventions of his form is by nature invincible."[23] Dauphine's uniqueness in the world of the play is his ability to step outside the fiction which no one else knows is a fiction. This, too, suggests the masque hero's power, suggests that (potentially) Dauphine's final revelation of Epicoene as a boy involves a masque-like assertion of certainty.

It is no coincidence that the masque which Jonson composed closest in time to *Epicoene*, *The Masque of Queens*, conceives of discord in terms highly similar to *Epicoene*. Like the dismembering Collegiates in *Epicoene*, the hag witches in *The Masque of Queens* are "masculine" and "hermaphroditical" women, emblems of female rage, violent dismemberers of men. Midway through the anti-masque, the witches recount their various dismemberments, the bodies they have dismantled:

> Under a cradle I did creep
> By day, and when the child was asleep
> At night, I sucked the breath and rose
> And plucked the nodding nurse by the nose

says the fifth hag, and the sixth and seventh answer respectively:

> I had a dagger: what did I do with that?
> Killed an infant to have his fat

and:

> A murderer yonder was hung in chains
> The sun and the wind had shrunk his veins:
> I bit off a sinew, I clipped his hair,
> I brought off his rags that danced i' the air.[24]

The content of the discord that Jonson is trying to transform in both works consists in a particularly garish vision of women as violent, as androgynous, as dismemberers of men. In *Epicoene* he replaces the vision with the reassuring idea of the essential male, in *The Masque of Queens* with the vision of the Queens themselves, paragons of female virtue.

But the two texts have a significance to each other beyond the fact that they envision discord in the same "epicene" terms. Both reveal a working-through of the same artistic problem – a problem that is philosophical and psychological as well as artistic –though they approach this problem from exactly the opposite points of view. Orgel has argued that *The Masque of Queens* represents a crucial transitional moment in Jonson's development, specifically in Jonson's ability to integrate important elements of theatre into the masque form ("when Jonson adapted the traditional *antic-masque*, the grotesque or acrobatic entertainment, to his own purposes as an *antimasque*, 'a foil of false masque' to *The Masque of Queens*, the world of theatre became firmly established within the ethical and dramatic structure of the form as well.")[25] Unlike its early predecessor, *The Masque of Blackness*, *The Masque of Queens* has the potential for a dramatic conflict, is built "not around a paradoxical abstraction, but around a group of figures capable of entering into a dramatic conflict while retaining their symbolic value."[26] This construction involves a crucial ability to reconcile the theatrical elements implicit in a "dramatic conflict" with the imperatives of anti-theatricality which are built into the very notion of the masque, such imperatives as the fact that "Masquers are not actors ... [for] playing a part ... constitutes ... a lie, a denial of the true self."[27] In *The Masque of Queens*, Jonson learns to accommodate the imperatives of anti-theatricality inherent in the masque to an increasingly theatrical structure. In *Epicoene* he reconciles the tension between theatre and anti-theatricality through the idea of the masque itself. What the two texts taken together suggest is the very great importance of this moment in Jonson's theatrical career (usually grudgingly acknowledged to imply an increasing "tolerance" of theatre) both in his development *of* the masque form, and in his *use* of the masque as a means of transforming anti-theatricality. The fact that both texts do envision discord in terms of androgyny and epiceneness points to the very great degree to which Jonson shared, though ultimately tamed, the anxieties about gender and the self which filled the tracts of his contemporaries.

But perhaps even more interesting is the sense in which both texts fail to effect the transformations their endings imply. *The Masque of Queens* occupies a unique position in Jonson's canon of masques because it creates a set of *dramatis personae* and the potential for a dramatic situation which it then fails to resolve dramatically. Orgel says:

In *The Masque of Queens*, an antimasque of witches had been banished by the "sound of loud Musique...with which not only the Hagges themselves, but theyr Hell into which they ranne, quite vanished" and evil had been destroyed by the mere imminence of good. In *Oberon* the shift from antimasque to masque takes place not through a momentary confrontation, but through the gradual ordering of chaos, a creative act. No mere character can bridge the gap between the witches' hell and the queens' heaven. But Silenus possesses "all gravitie, and profound knowledge, of most secret mysteries" and he is able to join together the satyrs and the faery prince.[28]

Another way of putting this would be to say that from a *dramatic* standpoint, the dispelling of discord in *The Masque of Queens* is insufficiently motivated, contrived:

No progression from antimasque to masque can take place through dramatic means, for drama implies interaction and conflict. But the world of witches does not conflict with the world of the queens; on the contrary, it negates and contradicts it. So the very essence of drama is here unavailable to Jonson: his antagonists, absolute good and absolute evil, cannot by their very natures confront each other on a stage and resolve their discord.[29]

The witches and their disorder are dispelled not by a dramatic necessity but by a sound of music and a note in the text. Similarly, the banishing of the epicene in *Epicoene* has a forced quality, seems insufficiently motivated. If Epicoene is a "real" boy, La Foole is still a "precious mannikin" and the Collegiates still masculine and hermaphroditical. The real quality of epiceneness lingers behind. Nor is it easy to believe that Tom Otter's "princess" will really be reconcil'd, that this locus of female rage will be wholly transformed. And nothing has been done about what the play has already suggested is the true cause of "epiceneness" in the world, time itself. Morose is banished not to prosper, but to die.

A tension exists in *Epicoene* between Dauphine's masque-like assertion of certainty in his revelation of Epicoene as a boy and the many discordant elements the play leaves unresolved. That tension would have been heightened – and the masque-like assertion steadily ironized – by the actual performance conditions of *Epicoene*.[30] For if Epicoene is revealed to be "really" a boy, all the remaining women on stage are also played by boys and hence are "really" still epicene. Though the play's final revelation of Epicoene as a boy calls attention to its own staging, it also reminds us that the world of the stage itself finally remains epicene. In this sense, too, the play reminds us that the androgyny which has dominated its world will never be dispelled.

Epicoene was performed by The Children of the Queen's Revels. To picture the effect, we have to imagine a cast of actors at least some of whose voices have not yet broken.[31] Knowing the company who would perform the play, knowing both the ways in which an all-male company would aggravate the sense of the epicene at the end of the play and the ways in which a company comprised partly of child actors would make farcical and disjunctive Morose's growing concern with age and death, Jonson must have known that Dauphine's "restoration" of Epicoene as a boy would, at least on stage, have insistently pointed to its own failure. It would take the real Restoration and a radically different set of performance conditions – first women playing women and finally women playing even the boy Epicoene[32] – before Dryden could see in the play the restoration of certainty which Dauphine's masque-like ending potentially implies.[33]

5 The "nothing" under the puppet's costume: Jonson's suppression of Marlowe in *Bartholomew Fair*

Somewhere in the middle of the puppet show at the end of Act V of *Bartholomew Fair*, the Puritan Busy attacks the puppet Dionysius with one of the period's stock attacks against theatre: "My main argument against you," he says, "is that you are an abomination, for the male among you putteth on the apparel of the female and the female of the male" (V.v.86–8). The puppet, who is more skilled in "such controversies" than the Puritan, lifts up his skirt and says, "It is your old stale argument against the players, but it will not hold against the puppets; for we have neither male nor female among us" (V.v.91–3).[1] The moment, like the puppet himself, is a naked and disconcerting one; for underneath the puppet's clothing there is nothing there.

In a metaphorical sense, the issue of whether there is anything "there" "underneath" or "beyond" the costume is absolutely central to Jonson's play, for notwithstanding all its own attacks on theatre, *Bartholomew Fair* relentlessly raises the question of whether there is anything or anyone who stands outside theatre. But the "nothing" beneath the puppet's costume raises a "culture-specific" question as well: Busy's "argument," taken from Deuteronomy, that the "male putteth on the apparel of the female and the female of the male" provided a focus for the fears of Jonson's own tract-writing contemporaries as they attacked the stage; provided a focus in particular for the fear that the female costumes of the period would effeminize the boy actors who wore them.

But the puppet's response to the Puritan is not to defend theatre, not to argue that gender is safe from costume, but to present a world devoid of gender to begin with. The puppet enacts not the loss or collapse of gender which the anti-theatricalists fear, but its radical and given absence. What is Jonson's attitude toward this absence? And what does it have to do with the particular play the puppets perform, a "modernized" version of *Hero and Leander*? The puppet presents a world devoid not only of sexual difference but of the very possibility of erotic experience itself. Given this, why is it Marlowe's intensely erotic poem to which the anti-theatricalist must be reconciled?

There are, of course, two biographical myths of Marlowe which might account for Jonson's use of *Hero and Leander*. Francis Meres, writing in 1598, says, "As *Iodelle*, a French tragical poet, being an Epicure and an Atheist, made a pitifull end: so our tragicall poet *Marlow* for his Epicurisme and Atheisme had a tragicall death. . ."[2] This is the myth of Marlowe as atheist, as homosexual, as member of the school of night, the Marlowe killed by a serving man, the Marlowe who somehow stood outside the eerie fringes of normative belief and practice, the Marlowe whose life as well as whose work Stephen Greenblatt has called a flaunting of "society's cherished orthodoxies."[3]

There is no direct evidence to suggest that Jonson thought of Marlowe in this way. In *Discoveries*, he speaks contemptuously of those dramatists who "fly from all humanity, with the Tamerlanes and Tamerchams of the late age, which had nothing in them but the scenical strutting and furious vociferation," but he has nothing to say about Marlowe the man himself.[4] But even if Jonson had thought of Marlowe in this way, the association would still not explain why he chose to "modernize" Marlowe's poem instead of one of those "vociferous" plays like *Tamburlaine* or *The Jew of Malta* which are so clearly about "aliens" and strangers.[5] Had Jonson been trying to identify the figure of the "alien" flaunting "society's cherished orthodoxies" with the figure of the vagabond playwright, unsavory and "epicurean," he would have found a much more likely emblem for such an association in one of Marlowe's plays than in *Hero and Leander*. He does not, then, invoke Marlowe out of his own antitheatricality, the way an anti-theatricalist of the period might have done, to characterize the stage itself as prodigal, unorthodox, homosexual.

There is another biographical myth pointing in a very different direction, which seems to provide more fertile ground for speculation. This is the myth of Marlowe as shepherd, the lyric poet cut down in the prime of life after writing a handful of lyrics and *Hero and Leander* (or, as some critics would have it, before finishing *Hero and Leander*, Marlowe's "fragment").[6] Richard Carew, writing in 1595, compares Marlowe to Catullus: "Will you reade *Virgill*? take the *Earll of Surrey: Catullus? Shakespeare* and *Marlowe's* fragment. . ."[7] Oddly enough this myth too gathers momentum from stories of Marlowe's death, for it treats that death as the proof of his poetic excellence, as if his poetry itself were too good to survive in the world. Meres writes, "As the poet *Lycophron* was shot to death by a certain rival of his: so *Christopher Marlow* was stabd to death by a bawdy Servingman, a rival of his in his lewde love."[8] Though it is "lewde love" the rival is a rival in, the comparison to Lycophron implies the existence of a poetic rival as well, and the passage may well suggest an origin of the legend of Kyd's professional jealousy as a motive for the murder.[9]

This myth of Marlowe as shepherd, lyric poet, seems to provide a much more fruitful basis for understanding Jonson's use of *Hero and Leander*: the puppet show is about the way that the modern stage also slaughters pure poetry, of which *Hero and Leander* is the most obvious emblem. "Nothing in our age . . . is more preposterous than the running judgments upon poetry and poets," says Jonson in *Discoveries*. ". . . This false opinion grows strong against the best men . . . The puppets are seen now in despite of the players."[10] Thus in *Bartholomew Fair*'s puppet show, Marlowe's "mighty line" has been reduced to rhyming doggerel. The supernatural and unseen have been turned into the merely bawdy (Cupid metamorphosed into a "drawer"). Hero has been transformed into a whore whose favors can be won by fresh herring and sack, and love itself has been reduced to lust: when his three pints of sherry fail to "flaw" Hero, Cupid puts "love" (an aphrodisiac?) into her sack. We might argue then that Jonson chooses *Hero and Leander* as an emblem of the various ideals the stage debases. This argument would be consonant with the way that several critics have reconciled the whole issue of Jonson's anti-theatricalism with his career as a playwright: Jonson believed in the play as a literary text, an ontological entity discrete from the institution of theatre which repeatedly degraded it.[11] *Hero and Leander* is the emblem and ideal of that tradition which theatre degrades.

The problem with this position lies in what it fails to account for – the very moments Jonson has cut from the poem, the Neptune sequence, for instance, in which the sea god drags Leander to the ocean floor and nearly drowns him in his overwhelming homosexual embrace. If *Hero and Leander* embodies a set of ideals, why has it been necessary not merely to parody such moments but to suppress them entirely? It will not be enough then to consider the various biographical myths of Marlowe. We will have to look more closely at *Hero and Leander* itself. To account for Jonson's use of the poem, we will have to be able to account for the very moments he excised, all of which seem to register an intense anxiety about the issue of sexuality. In fact, it will turn out to be not just the Neptune episode that Jonson makes the puppets leave out of the play, but everything in the poem bearing on Leander's ambiguous sexuality, his golden tresses that were never shorn, his transvestite-like appearance, everything in fact related to the issue of his effeminacy. The question is, then, who would have been provoked by such material? Whose needs would such excisions have served? That the anti-theatrical tracts of the period display a strikingly similar set of anxieties seems to chart a logical path for such an inquiry: Why is it that Jonson has cut from *Hero and Leander* everything potentially objectionable to an anti-theatricalist? To answer such a question we will first have to look more closely at *Hero and Leander* and then at the intensely connected set of anxieties – amounting almost to a structural homology – that it shares with the general suspicion of theatre during the period.[12]

The first homology that *Hero and Leander* shares with the anti-theatrical tracts of the period is a belief in the capacity of homosexual passion to swallow and engulf, to utterly annihilate individual identity, and a related belief in the tendency of heterosexual desire to lead automatically to homosexuality. The poem betrays a "Pandora's box" notion of the self in which desire begets worse desire and worse desire leads inevitably to violence, a notion of the self in which "appetence" accelerates not in "steps" but in inevitable and degenerative "leaps." "From pyping to playing, from play to pleasure, from pleasure to slouth, from slouth to sleepe, from sleepe to sinne, from sinne to death, from death to the Divel," says Stephen Gosson in an analogous moment in *School of Abuse*.[13] In *Hero and Leander*, these allied beliefs are articulated at several moments throughout the poem, but nowhere so powerfully as in the Neptune episode. We need, then, to look both at this episode itself as well as its placement in the poem between Leander's first and second nights with Hero.

From the very beginning of *Hero and Leander*, Marlowe's speaker argues strenuously that there is a kind of violence built into the structure of desire itself, though this argument raises continual questions about what kind of desire it is that is so dangerous, and though the argument itself is always in curious tension with the speaker's praise of the lover's physical beauty. Thus beside the claim that "lovely fair was Hero" (I.45) is the intimation of a fatal violence embedded in that loveliness: "Her kirtle blue, whereon was many a stain / Made with the blood of wretched lovers slain" (I.15–16).[14] Beside the claim that "far above the loveliest Hero shined" (I.103) is the intimation that the perception of this loveliness is the perception of death itself. ("And as in fury of a dreadful fight, / Their fellows being slain or put to flight, / Poor soldiers stand with fear of death dead-strooken / So at her presence all surprised and tooken" (I.119–22). The sight of Hero is like the sight of the dead. Words like "fury," "fight," "slain," "death," "dead-strooken" all insist upon this.

Similarly, the praise of Leander's beauty moves from the implicitly to the explicitly violent. That his hair is like the golden fleece (I.55–8) implicitly recalls the violence of Medea's desire, her witchcraft, murders, suicide, the poisoned dress. That Leander's posture is as straight as Circe's wand recalls another kind of violent magic in Circe's power to transform those men who desired her into swine. But the explicit characterization of desire in terms of violence comes in the identification of Leander with Pelops:

> Jove might have sipped out nectar from his [Leander's] hand.
> Even as delicious meat is to the taste,
> So was his neck in touching, and surpassed
> The white of Pelops' shoulder.

(I.62–5)

By identifying Leander's hand with the cup from which the gods drink, the lines begin by merely associating Leander with Ganymede, the homosexual lover of Jove with whom Leander will become specifically identified later in the poem. The nuzzling of the hand is a sexual image, but not a violent one. But as the lines progress, the nuzzling turns into an almost uncontainable cannibalistic rage: Leander's neck becomes identified first with "delicious meat" and then with the white of Pelops' shoulder, the shoulder literally devoured when served up to the gods by Pelops' father, the shoulder that had to be reassembled by Mercury. Beneath the encomiums of Leander's beauty, then, is the image of the cannibalistic feast, a kind of warning about what beauty has the capacity to provoke.

But what kind of beauty is it that has the capacity to provoke this level of violence? There is a curious lack of symmetry between the two opening catalogues of praise. The list of those who might have flown to Hero contains only Cupid (who mistakes her for his mother) and some bees (who mistake her for honey). She is loved only by mistake, only for those things which she is not, but at which she is good, better than nature, at imitating. But the catalogue of those who might have loved Leander is more exact, detailed, though he too provokes a kind of epistemological crisis, seeming to be that which he is not. ("Some swore he was a maid in man's attire" [I.83].) As Hero is the most beautiful of women, so Leander is the most beautiful of men. As men would die to possess Hero, so, we expect to be told, would women die to possess Leander. But except for the initial reference to Cynthia, who "wished his arms might be her sphere" (I.59) – a sphere that Neptune, not Cynthia, ultimately enjoys – all of those who yearn for Leander are men. It is not only the "vent'rous" (and male) "youth of Greece" who would have been "allured" by Leander's "dangling tresses," not only Jove who would have "sipped out nectar from his hand" but a host of male others. Leander's distinctiveness lies in the response he provokes not in women, but in other men:

> Had wild Hippolytus Leander seen,
> Enamored of his beauty he had been;
> His presence made the rudest peasant melt,
> That in the vast uplandish country dwelt.

The barbarous Thracian soldier, moved with nought
Was moved with him, and for his favour sought.
Some swore he was a maid in man's attire,
For in his looks were all that men desire

(I.77–84)

We might account for the violence implicit in Hero's beauty, then, by arguing that the violence conceals a more vital energy, conceals the fact that the real sexual energy of the poem is homoerotic. The speaker imagines a corpse when he speaks of Hero, because behind the corpse is the fantasy of Leander. The violence is a screen for the deeper desire. The violence contains a kind of rage which is itself defensive. Thus the final ensnaring of Hero is depicted not merely in terms of the traditional simile of the limed bird, but rather in terms of the bird's neck being wrung: "Even as a bird, which in our hands we wring / . . . She trembling strove" (II.289–91). The problem with this explanation of violence is that it does not account for the mounting violence in the descriptions of male beauty, nor, more importantly, for the poem's most profound acknowledgement of the capacity of desire to violently destroy, a capacity that is rendered as specifically homosexual.

Imagistically, the pinnacle of the violence implicit in desire comes in the description of the walls of the church of Venus on which one might see "the gods in sundry shapes, / Committing heady riots, incests, rapes" (I.143–4). But dramatically, the pinnacle of this violence comes in the Neptune episode in the moment when Neptune, enflamed by Leander's beauty, drags him down to the ocean floor. This moment is at once the poem's most concrete and graphic (i.e. not metaphorized) depiction of sex – "he watched his arms, and as they opened wide / At every stroke, betwixt them would he slide / And steal a kiss . . . / And there pry / Upon his breast, his thigh and every limb" (II.183–9) – and at the same time the moment where sexual desire most nearly kills: "for under water he was almost dead" (II.170). The passion itself is depicted as a threat to life: "therefore on him [Neptune] seized. / Leander strived, the waves about him wound, / And pulled him to the bottom" (II.158–60). At the heart of the poem, then, is a belief in sexual desire as engulfing, as annihilating, as literally having the capacity to drown and destroy the self, and this desire is envisioned as specifically homosexual. (Significantly, this desire poses a supreme threat both to individual identity and to gender: Leander is mistaken for Ganymede and believes he is mistaken for a woman: "I am no woman, I" [II.190].)

But it is crucial to note the moment at which the encounter with Neptune takes place: Neptune's watery seduction occurs directly after the first night Hero and Leander spend together ("He asked, she gave, and nothing was denied" [II.25].)[15] More exactly, it takes place after Leander has felt the stirrings of a desire for Hero that is specifically sexual: "The more she strived, / The more a gentle pleasing heat revived" (II.67–8). More exactly, it takes place after Leander has had the intimations of a knowledge that is specifically sexual. Till now he has vaguely suspected that some "amorous rite" or other were "neglected," but after that "pleasing heat," he knows "all that elders know" (II.69).[16] Perhaps it is equally important that the Neptune episode takes place after Leander revolts against authority in the form of his own father, the one natural (human) parent who appears in the poem. (Because "none but gods have power their love to hide" [II.131], Leander's father knows exactly where he has been and "for the same mildly rebuked his son" [II.137].) It is at this point that Leander jumps into the Hellespont and is overwhelmed by Neptune's waves pulling and prying at his thighs and "other limbs."

The poem imagines a kind of inevitable progression from illicit heterosexual desire to illicit homosexual desire, from trespassing against authority to being overwhelmed by the turbulence of natural forces outside one's control, a progression from criminal desires within the self to tempestuous and uncontrollable forces without, from criminal (though normative) heterosexual desires to nearly fatal homosexual ones. The Neptune episode presents both a kind of moral argument and a psychological one: morally, the episode itself can be seen like the sun in "purple weeds / And red for anger that he [Leander] stayed so long" (II.89). It is as if the moment authority is violated, the moment the father's rule is broken, all the turbulence and violence of authority's retaliatory rage burst through in the form of Neptune's billows.[17] In one way, the Neptune episode suggests that the power of forbidden impulses *is* so intense that it can summon up gods. Psychologically the episode argues that to arouse one kind of sexual desire is to arouse all kinds of desire: when Leander gives in to a forbidden passion for Hero, he quite literally opens the floodgates to an even more forbidden kind of passion – homosexual passion, imaged as Neptune's waves.

But all of this is exactly what Jonson has cut from the text. Gone is the homosexual embrace at the bottom of the ocean, the embrace so powerful it has the capacity to annihilate distinctions of gender and identity, the capacity to annihilate life itself. Gone is the whole argument about the relationship of that homosexual embrace to the heterosexual desire that preceded it, the vision of sexuality as an endless chain in which desire leads to worse desire, worse desire to violence. Gone is the fatal androgyny that had the capacity to titillate that homosexuality, drawing not only Neptune to Leander but hypothetical Joves, Hippolytuses, rude peasants and barbarous Thracians. Instead of the volatile effeminacy which can stir up the Hellespont itself, we have only Leatherhead's ominous prediction that we shall see what Leander "doth lack." But what Leander "doth lack" seems to be what all the puppets lack, which is gender itself.

But in the service of what needs – and whose – does Jonson cut this material? To say that Marlowe's poem shares with the anti-theatrical tracts of the period an intense anxiety about the danger of homosexuality is to state the obvious. John Rainolds compares the homosexual response engendered by boys in women's clothing to the kiss of poisonous spiders: "if they doe but touch men onely with their mouth, they put them to wonderfull paine and make them madde: so beautiful boyes by kissing doe sting and powre secretly in a kinde of poyson..."[18] But to cite the homologous belief in the dangers of homosexuality is only part of the story. For what is more telling is the way that poem and tracts both envision this annihilating homosexual experience as the inevitable extension of heterosexual desire. At the heart of the anti-theatrical "psychology" of homosexuality is a profound contradiction, and it is as if to settle the contradiction anti-theatricalists organized the experience of desire itself as a degenerative chain.

At the heart of the anti-theatrical "position" is the conviction that the person with allusions to both sexes will elicit the really powerful homosexual response by providing a screen and a pretext for homosexual impulses to mask themselves behind. The putting on of women's clothing may kindle "sparkles of lust," warns Rainolds cautiously.[19] Ever graphic, William Prynne insists that dressing like women is always the necessary stimulant to homosexuality: the "male priests of Venus" always oblige their companions the "passive beastly sodomites of Florida" by going clad in women's clothing, the "better to elliciate, countenance, act and colour their unnaturall execrable uncleanesse."[20] What this conviction implies of course is that the heterosexual titillation is pretext and the homosexual response what is "real." What this spectator is "really" attracted to when he looks at the stage is a man.

But on the other hand anti-theatrical tracts betray the much more profound fear that even the man will dissolve into a woman. Consider Prynne's description of the warrior in women's clothing who does "degenerate" into a woman, shedding not only his trophy for a needle and thread, but developing a shrill voice and an "extenuated" spirit,[21] or Prynne's depiction of the Incubi who "dissect" their boys to transform them as "neere as might be into women."[22] This claim depends on the premise that underneath the clothing, locked away within the male body itself, is a woman, waiting for the appropriate attire and the removal of those extra "virilities" which would allow her to assume her proper shape.

At the heart of the anti-theatrical "psychology" of homosexuality, then, is a profound contradiction about what is provoking the sexual response in the first place – man or woman. And it is as if to mediate this conflict that anti-theatricalists organized the experience of desire itself chronologically: the spectator begins by getting excited at the theatre, and ends by having sex with the man. For very different reasons, then, the tracts of the period, like Marlowe's poem, envision desire itself as a degenerative chain. At the end of the chain there is always something violent, something fatal, whether the fatality takes the form of Rainolds' poisonous spiders or Prynne's "dissections" or whether it takes the simpler form of Gosson's associations of pleasure with death.

We could say then that *Hero and Leander* shares with the tracts a set of intense anxieties about the capacity of desire to destroy masculinity, an anxiety maintained by the fear that what is really under the clothing is a "maid in man's attire," a female self. But what is striking about *Hero and Leander* is the actual lack of anxiety that this idea seems to generate. This is a world apparently where masculine and feminine are not mutually exclusive but complementary poles of the self.[23] The vision of the maid beneath the man's clothing is not a source of anxiety but a source of erotic power. Leander's ability to titillate homosexual responses is in fact at the root of his civilizing power. He makes the "rudest" peasant melt, moves the "barbarous" Thracian soldier. Even Leander's brush with a perilous homosexuality which nearly drowns him becomes the transition between his first (but quite clearly unconsummated) night with Hero ("She fled / And seeming lavish, saved her maidenhead") and the consummation of his sexual desire, his entrance into the "orchard of the Hesperides." Disturbingly, like the liminal moment in certain separation rituals, the poem suggests that it is the ritual of being dragged to the bottom, being striven against, being made passive and feminine that allows the consummation to take place.[24] The poem contains the threat and excitement of homosexuality within a vision of consummated heterosexual desire. In acknowledgement of the bloody kirtle, the bird's wrung neck, the cannibalistic feast, the moment at the bottom of the ocean, the poem argues that violence is an inevitable component of the erotic itself. The poem's vision is both homologous *and* intensely threatening to the world of the tracts.

This would seem to provide an answer, if not to the first, then to the second question raised by the puppet show: why *Hero and Leander*? Why is it this poem the anti-theatricalist must be reconciled to? In theory, the answer should be that the anti-theatricalist must be reconciled to *Hero and Leander* because the poem stages precisely the anxieties that would agitate him the most. This would be true, in fact, if it were Marlowe's

Hero and Leander Busy were watching – consider the Neptune episode "staged," if such a thing could be imagined. But in fact in Littlewit's version of *Hero and Leander* the material most provocative to an anti-theatricalist is exactly what has been cut from the play. There is nothing left for Busy to be converted to – the text itself has already been "converted."[25] The puppet's "modernized" version of *Hero and Leander* is Jonson's vision of what a world would be like in which theatre had already accommodated itself to anti-theatricality. And Littlewit is Jonson's vision of the playwright who does the accommodating – the playwright who equilibrates and compromises his very art to soothe and protect the anxieties of his severest critics.

To say this is to insist that the same anxieties which pervade Renaissance anti-theatrical tracts also agitate the spectators who constitute Littlewit's immediate world and audience. But what evidence is there that this is so? What I would suggest is that the eruptions of sexual violence that punctuate the play from time to time betray these anxieties, though it is true that characters also articulate them more directly. If I am right, then *Bartholomew Fair* also occupies a "homologous" relation to the tracts, although clearly that "relation" will be somewhat different from the one that Marlowe's poem occupies.

One of the most expressive articulations of violence in *Bartholomew Fair* is Quarlous' lengthy speech on widow hunting which compares sex with an old woman to entering a tomb with a torch:

Thou must visit 'em, as thou wouldst do a tomb, with a torch, or three handfuls of link, flaming hot, and so thou mayst hap to make 'em feel thee, and after, come to inherit according to thy inches. (I.iii.68–71)

What the speech argues is that one must scald the woman – violently brand her as Quarlous in fact brands Ursula with her own scalding pan – in order to make her feel one's presence as a man. But behind this violence against women lies a deeper fear about the woman's own capacity to weaken the man:

A sweet course for a man to waste the brand of life for, to be still raking himself a fortune in an old woman's embers; we shall ha' thee, after thou hast been but a month married to one of 'em, look like the quartan ague and the black jaundice met in a face, and walk as if thou hadst borrowed legs of a spinner, and voice of a cricket. (I.iii.71–6)

The woman has the capacity to reduce the man to sickness. Quarlous articulates even more vividly apropos of Ursula the way the woman can dissolve the man's identity itself. He compares sex with Ursula to "falling into a whole shire of butter" (II.v.90). "He that would venture for't, I assure him, might sink into her and be drowned a week ere any friend he had could find where he were" (II.v.86–8).

It may be objected that Quarlous only articulates this fear apropos of Ursula, not apropos of "generic woman," but in fact "generic woman" is exactly what Ursula is identified with: she identifies herself with Eve, the first woman, with a kind of ur-female self: "I am all fire and fat, Nightingale; I shall e'en melt away to the first woman, a rib again" (II.ii.48–9). Grown monstrous, an emblem of desire run amok, this female "ur-self" with the capacity to dissolve male identity is figured externally in the form of Ursula rather than as something underneath the costume.[26] In a much grosser form, then, the lines articulate the same fears about sexuality – about its capacity to dissolve and drown – that Marlowe articulates in the Neptune episode, though of course Quarlous articulates them about sex with a woman, not sex with a man.

But if Quarlous associates sex with Ursula with a figurative loss of male identity, Edgeworth associates homosexuality with literal emasculation. Describing Wasp's fascination with Captain Jordan's decoy or "circling" boy, Edgeworth alludes to:

One Val Cutting, that helps Captain Jordan to roar, a circling boy; with whom your Numps is so taken that you may strip him of his clothes, if you will. I'll undertake to geld him for you, if you had but a surgeon, ready, to sear him. (IV.iii.106–10)

The passage makes "searing" and "gelding" almost the logical consequence of homosexual pleasure, and at the same time it *reacts* to homosexuality with the violent fantasy of searing and gelding. Like Quarlous, then, Edgeworth's response to a threatening sexuality is one of violence.[27]

Where Marlowe's speaker manages ideas of dissolution and effeminization through a strategy of containment – he contains the threats of homosexuality and violence within a vision of consummated heterosexual desire – speakers like Quarlous and Edgeworth manage anxieties about effeminization and dismemberment through fantasies of reciprocal violence. Given such a constituency, it seems a small wonder that Littlewit strips from his puppet show everything that could agitate his spectators. He has suppressed even the recognition of a violence implicit in sexuality itself. Gone is the bloody kirtle, the cannibalistic feast, the devoured shoulder, the moment on the bottom of the ocean floor. Instead, the violence of the puppet show is the random, sanitized, almost motiveless violence of puppets hitting each other over the head with pots. ("O my haunches," says Hero when Damon and Pythias kick her in the ass [V.iv.301]. "O my head," says Leatherhead as the puppet Cole hits him over the head. "Pink his guts, Pythias," says the puppet Damon when Leatherhead calls them both whore-masters [V.iv.237]. "Leander ... stand'st thou still like a sot / And not offer'st to break both their heads with a pot?" [V.iv.302–3]) By systematically dissociating violence from desire, Littlewit erases all traces of a violent origin – an implicit violence – in sexuality itself. We could say then that where *Hero and Leander* transforms the anxieties at stake in the tracts, Littlewit's puppet show simply excises them.

Jonson makes Littlewit "modernize" *Hero and Leander*, then, in order to indicate what a world would be like which accommodated itself to anti-theatricality. But how will his evocation of this world help account for the "nothing" under the puppet's costume? A crucial analogy exists between the "nothing" under the puppet's costume and the excisions in Marlowe's text. Both the puppet and the poem have been gelded, emasculated, stripped of their seductive power to provoke dangerous responses. Both represent the supreme fantasy of sanitization. The puppet cannot be implicated in the world of sexuality, not because he is superior to it but simply because he lacks the equipment. He stands outside the world of erotic desire not because he is able to resist its temptations but simply because he lacks the capacity to perform its actions. In this sense the sexless puppet is the logical "solution" to a view of the self in which the will has been rendered inoperative, pyping does lead to pleasure, pleasure to sloth, and sloth to death, a world in which sexuality is simply a degenerative chain. The puppet, as much as Marlowe's mangled text, is Jonson's vision of a world which has met the demands of the anti-theatricalist.

But if this is so, what is the puppet's power over the anti-theatricalist? Why is he able to disarm him, to arrest his attacks on the stage? ("I am confuted ... Let [the play] go on" [V.v.101–4].) Perhaps part of his disquieting power lies in the fact that it is impossible to think about the radical absence of gender without immediately imagining the gender that is supposed to be there, impossible to imagine the absence of genitals without imagining both the genitals themselves and the fact of their removal. Paradoxically, then, the puppet evokes just the thoughts of castration his genderlessness ought to forestall.

But even this does not exhaust the image of the "nothing" under the puppet's clothing. (Nor does it exhaust the wish for there to be "something" there, a wish that has been oddly replicated in even the stage history of the play. For at least one important production insisted on staging the scene using glove puppets, putting a "thing," a hand, under the puppet's costume, when clearly the only way for there to be literally nothing under the costume would be to use marionettes.)[28] There is still something puzzling, indecipherable, something about the image capable of producing a vague alarm, fascination but also a kind of vertigo. Taken metaphorically, if there is really "nothing" under the puppet's costume, then this "nothing" constitutes the supreme challenge to the notion of referentiality itself.

In the world the anti-theatricalists long for (and profess to believe in) the woman's costume will be the exact "sign" and symbol of her female genitals, and word will correspond directly to thing: "garments are set down for signes distinctive betwene sexe and sexe," says Gosson, "to take unto us those garments that are manifest signes of another sexe is to falsify, forge and adulterate, contrarie to the expresse rule of the words of God."[29] This is a supremely knowable world with a predictable set of correspondences and therefore a predictable set of rules for interpretation. In the world presented by Renaissance boy actors, the woman's costume will be the inversion, the reversed sign of the boy's genitals, and word will refer to the exact opposite of "thing." This is a more problematic world than the first one, since it requires an active reversal on the part of the interpreter, but it is still a world in which a predictable set of correspondences can be drawn. But in the world the puppet presents to Busy, there is no such relationship between sign and thing because there is no "thing" under the sign, no genital under the costume for the sign to refer to. This is what makes the "nothing" under the costume so frightening: the moment which should be the play's starkest moment of revelation, the stripping of symbol from "thing," is the play's least naked moment because there is no "thing" to reveal. This is part of the power the puppet has over the anti-theatricalist. He forecloses the very possibility of meaning and therefore of knowledge itself.

The puppet does this in a world whose center contains an extraordinarily powerful belief in direct knowledge, in certainty: "I, Adam Overdo, am resolved ... [to] make mine own discoveries" (II.i.35–6). Despite constant misinterpretation, Overdo does make a "discovery" (though it is not the one he expected to make) and this implies the existence of a "thing" to be discovered. What makes *Bartholomew Fair* so tremendously difficult is that, in a sense, it seems to endorse both positions, both the position that direct knowledge, "discovery" is possible, and the position that it is not because there is no "thing" to discover. For again and again, Jonson arouses, only to frustrate, the expectation that he will define an alternative to theatre – produce something "real" that stands outside or under or apart from the costume.

The play begins with an indictment of theatre, in the analogy it establishes between theatre and prostitution, an analogy it establishes through Littlewit, the play's playwright who in busily costuming his wife for Quarlous to kiss is immediately established as a pimp ("She may call you an apple-John, if you use this" [I.iii.51]).[30] (Later he will turn his wife over to the real pimps, just as he will prostitute the text of *Hero and Leander*, making it only "a little easy and modern for the times" [V.iii.111–12]).

But by establishing this analogy between prostitution and theatre, Jonson raises the expectation that he will ultimately define an alternative. The play will define a moral center and that moral center will produce something "a-theatrical": someone or something *not* involved in a kind of theatre, since if that which is corrupt is implicitly theatrical, that which is to be free of corruption will have to be a-theatrical. It is this expectation, that there is anything which is not theatrical, which Jonson repeatedly arouses and disappoints. He arouses it first by making us think the *anti-*theatrical will stand apart from theatre. For a moment it looks as if Busy will do this, defining himself as he does in strict opposition to theatre (he has even quit his trade as baker because the cakes worked their way into morris dances). But the anti-theatrical turns out to be just another guise of the theatrical: Busy goes to the fair to set up a rival theatre to preach.

Jonson raises, only to frustrate, a similar expectation that he will provide an instance of something or someone not implicated in theatre in Acts II and III as well, though these acts establish an analogy not between theatre and prostitution but between theatre and theft: both the theft of the marriage license and the theft of Cokes' purse are explicitly cast as kinds of theatre: "We had wonderful ill luck to miss this prologue o' the purse," says Quarlous, "but the best is we shall have five acts of him ere night" (III.ii.1–2). Edgewood too calls his agreement to steal the wedding license an "act" which is "nothing without a witness" (IV.iii.102–3).[31] Again, the criminalization of theatre and the theatricalization of crime lead us to expect the play to define an alternative which in not being criminal will not be theatrical.

But here too Jonson frustrates the expectation he raises, for the "alternative," the anti-theatricalist Justice Overdo, come to weed out the fair's "enormities" (the tracts of the period made the word virtually synonymous with theatre),[32] not only arrives in costume, but articulates the most pervasive faith in theatre in the play, the faith that if one could simply shed one's public identity, one could gain access to direct, unmediated knowledge:

For alas, as we are public persons, what do we know? Nay, what can we know? We hear with other men's ears; we see with other men's eyes. A foolish constable or a sleepy watchman is all our information . . . I, Adam Overdo, am resolved therefore to spare spy-money hereafter, and make mine own discoveries. (II.i.25–36)

Now what makes *Bartholomew Fair* so problematic is that in a sense Jonson validates Overdo's fantasy: he does make his own discovery, he does detect an enormity, though it is not the one he expected to find. ("If this [Trouble-All's madness] be true, this is my greatest disaster!" [IV.i.56]). Not only is anti-theatricality simply another guise of theatre, but the play seems to endorse the proposition that Overdo's theatricality yields for him direct knowledge, unmediated truth. How is it that knowledge is possible, when the play has refused to yield an alternative to costume, to show, to disguise, a "thing" apart from the costume? The answer lies in what it is Overdo "knows," something at once completely interior and subjective (his own enormity) and something (uniquely) ontologically real.

For it is in Trouble-All paradoxically that the play finally does produce an index to the ontologically "real," something which is not only not merely theatre, but which can be told from theatre: though Overdo may be unable to distinguish between the "real" Trouble-All and Quarlous disguised as Trouble-All, the play itself never doubts that there is a difference. It never argues that costume is constitutive, that (in that sense) everything is "theatre," that whoever wears the Trouble-All costume or behaves like Trouble-All "becomes" Trouble-All. Paradoxically, it is through the play's madman that Jonson affirms both the ontologically real and the possibility for certain knowledge, ours if not Overdo's: there *is* something under the costume even if that something happens to be mad.[33]

But if the play finally affirms the existence of a knowable "thing" under the costume, what is the status of the "nothing" under the puppet's clothing with its attendant challenge to referentiality? The puppet's "nothing" remains Jonson's vision of a hypothetical world. Such a world, Jonson argues, stripping itself of everything objectionable, would ultimately destroy the possibility of reference itself, the tenet which, ironically, those anti-theatricalists it strips away to accommodate profess most dearly to cherish.

The problem with these anti-theatricalists lies in the contradiction between what they do profess and what clearly motivates them. Tracts like Gosson's *Playes Confuted* certainly profess to believe in a world where signs "refer," but what is clearly much more vital to their view of the world is the idea that signs "behave" – hypnotizing, coercing, compelling, effecting. Nowhere is this more vivid than in Gosson's own account of a performance of *Bacchus and Ariadne*:

When Bacchus rose up ... the beholders rose up ... When they sware, the company sware, when they departed to bedde; the company presently was set on fire, they that were married posted home to their wives; they that were single, vowed very solemly, to be wedded.[34]

Here, the representation, the "sign," doesn't refer, it seduces, coercing the spectator to go home and imitate it in scrupulous detail. And what is crucial to this anecdote is its belief that the seduction is embedded – like the pull within a magnet – in the representation itself. Tracts like Munday's *Third Blaste* insist that male spectators compulsively repeat the love speeches they hear on stage to manipulate the concealed hearts, "the conceits of the minde," of women.[35] But Munday never entertains the possibility of the seduction taking place within the concealed heart itself. The seduction is always the property of language. It is this rhetorical view of the world which underlies the claims about reference anti-theatricalists profess.

It is this discrepancy which Jonson exposes through his depiction of an audience at the puppet show. From the very beginning, Leatherhead warns Cokes that what he will see is in effect only rhetoric ("Indeed, I am the mouth of 'em all" [V.iii.74]), only illusion ("Betwene you and I, sir, we do but make show" [V.iv.253]). But notwithstanding the puppeteer's persistent tendency to strip the play of its ability to cast an illusion, Cokes insists on seeing the puppets not as representations but as real: "I am in love with the actors already, and I'll be allied to them presently" (V.iii.121–2). "I warrant thee, I will not hurt her, fellow; what, dost think me uncivil? I pray thee be not jealous; I am toward a wife" (V.iv.5–7).

Where the tracts betray the belief that the dynamic for seduction is contained (like a seed or a kernel) within the structure of language itself, Jonson argues that even if language strips itself of all seductive power, there will still be a spectator capable of being seduced. In this sense, Marlowe's *Hero and Leander* constitutes a transitional text: homologous to the tracts in its own deep suspiciousness of language, the poem nevertheless argues that seduction takes place in some quintessentially private sphere outside the province of language itself.[36] Though Leander is a rhetorician, an "orator," a "bold sharp sophister," involved in the most strenuous verbal efforts to make Hero yield up her virginity, Marlowe suggests that Hero's seduction has already taken place in the privacy of the mind, before Leander ever began to speak: "These arguments he used, and many more / Wherewith she yielded what was won before" (I.330–1). The seduction has already taken place somewhere else before its own embodiment in language.

Jonson takes this argument one step farther in his depiction of Cokes, who is "seduced" not by anything he sees on stage but simply by his own gullibility, his own desire to believe that the puppets are real. We have, then, an answer to the third question, the question of Jonson's "attitude." Jonson's portrait of Busy interrupting the puppets to cry "abomination" suggests that no matter how much theatre sanitizes itself, the anti-theatricalists will always find abominations. Differently, and perhaps more to the point, Jonson's depiction of Cokes at the puppet show argues that no matter how much theatre excises, there will always be a spectator somewhere who is seducible. Jonson suggests that even if theatre could accommodate itself to the anxieties of the anti-theatricalists, it would still not solve the problem of the gullible spectator. Jonson transfers the capacity for seduction from theatre, from language, from the province of representation itself to the irreducible gullibility of this spectator.

But if this is so, does this mean that for Jonson the power of theatre inheres only in the spectator? For Jonson in *Bartholomew Fair*, the answer is yes. The "Caveat to Cutpurses," Win's staged pregnancy urges in order to get into the fair, Quarlous' disguise as a madman, all depend on the gullibility of their various spectators. But this very gullibility and the viciousness of Jonson's satire of it imply that ideally theatre might resonate with very different powers, and clearly some of these powers would consist in what has been stripped from Marlowe's poem, the capacity for erotic experience itself. Marlowe's is a world in which the vision of the maid beneath the man's clothing is not a source of anxiety or weakness or monstrosity but of erotic power, and a world in which erotic power is not conceived as threatening or inimical to the self but as conducive to it. This is a world in which beauty is so compelling and desire so intense that it ultimately must express itself as violence through the images of blood and cannibalistic delight.

The capacity for truly erotic experience is precisely what is missing from *Bartholomew Fair*. It is not that the play is devoid of all sexuality but that it is the sterile sexuality of chamber pots and tired prostitutes, the substitutive sexuality of Ursula's mountainous fat, a sexuality devoid of eroticism and hope. Even Grace, the one character in the play who declares that she must marry for love – although the syntax of her declaration makes the love sound a little coerced: "I must have a husband I must love" (IV.iii.13–14) – even Grace enters into a marriage that is utterly arbitrary. And in place of the violence of the bloody kirtle, the cannibalistic feast, the violence *Bartholomew Fair* offers is the violence of the whore Alice bursting through the tent to beat Overdo's wife for taking away her trade:

A mischief on you, they are such as you are that undo us, and take our trade from us, with your tuft taffeta haunches. ... The poor common whores can ha' no traffic for the privy rich ones; your caps and hoods of velvet call away our customers and lick the fat from us. (IV.v.61–2 and 64–6)

In place of the poem's ability to imply that the dark violence of blood and orality is so deeply embedded in the structure of desire itself as to be inextricable from beauty, *Bartholomew Fair* offers only substitutive and compensatory expressions of violence, the scalding pan, the vapours game which erupts into fights, Ramping Alice's outburst. Sexuality in this play is thoroughly mercantilized.

In his bitterness, then, Jonson acknowledges an uneasy analogy between his own sterility and the anti-theatricalists he so viciously attacks. But at the same time, *Bartholomew Fair* articulates a nostalgia for precisely the erotic experiences that terrified anti-theatricalists like Munday and Gosson. Unlike *Antony and Cleopatra*, which registers its nostalgia, even its erotic nostalgia, in politicized terms, in terms of kings and queens, this play registers a private nostalgia for a world in which erotic experience is still possible. Perhaps this is why Jonson is able to invoke in the Induction of the play a spectator diametrically opposed to the one envisioned by the anti-theatricalists, a spectator whose will and reason are intact. Perhaps this is why he is able to invoke (if only as an ideal to whom the actual spectator is compared) a spectator capable of exercising judgment.[37] Jonson can envision a reasonable spectator because there is no longer anything to be seduced by. The puppet show is in every way about the issue of reduction. The puppets are reduced. The text is reduced. The gods within the text are reduced. Everything "other" in the poem is reduced to a version of the self – the self of the spectator watching the puppet show. Perhaps, then, nostalgia is also a means of reduction, since it allows Jonson to reduce to manageable proportions the erotic experiences he presented – and therefore presumably imaginatively experienced – as rapes and dismemberments in earlier plays like *Volpone* and *Epicoene*. At least in *Epicoene* the Collegiates' violent searching of Morose, with its threat of castration, provided some pleasure, and at least there was something there to be castrated. In the comparable moment in *Bartholomew Fair*, the revelation of the "nothing" under the puppet's costume, Jonson suggests that the erotic itself has finally been successfully stripped from the world.

What we shall see in King James' *Daemonologie* is just the opposite state of affairs; there no such reduction is possible. There, the danger of the erotic is experienced in horrific, giantized terms. There the rapes and dismemberments of *Epicoene* have become a virtual property of the physical – or at least external – universe itself. For *Daemonologie* culminates in a series of "sperm-stealing" fantasies in which spirits get into the male body and drain out its essence, its very nature.

If Jonson acknowledges both his affinity with anti-theatricality and the sterility this affinity implies, no such acknowledgement is possible for the texts about magic we are about to consider. They do not seek to "come to terms" with the anxieties of the tracts in the way Shakespeare and Jonson do. Rather, they confirm that these fears were operative and important on a larger scale than a look at the history of the stage would lead us to expect.

6   Magic as theatre, theatre as magic: *Daemonologie* and the problem of "entresse"

Midway through *Daemonologie*, James' 1597 handbook on witches, Epistemon, the book's spokesman for its author, describes a scene that could come right out of an anti-theatrical tract. At the instruction of the devil, he says, witches learn "how to make Pictures of waxe or clay" which destroy the persons they represent, causing them to be "continuallie melted or dryed awaie" by sickness (p. 44).[1] Epistemon's vision of the witches destroying their victims by image magic is animated by the same fear at the heart of attacks against the stage, the fear that representations can actually alter the things they are only supposed to represent. In fact, the fear that costumes can alter the boy actors who wear them is just a special case or localized instance of this fear, and the exactness with which the anxiety about costume corresponds to the description of the witches at work at their craft suggests how completely anti-theatrical tracts as a class are animated by a belief in magic itself.[2]

In fact, it turns out that the scene Epistemon describes is framed by a disclaimer – the witches cannot really do what he has said they could. Neither the wax itself nor the pictures they create has any inherent power ("that instrumente of waxe [has] no vertue in that turne doing" [p. 46]). Rather, the scene itself is all part of a carefully scripted illusion, a charade orchestrated by Satan. As a spirit, it is he who has the capacity to "weaken and scatter the spirites of life" of a given patient, destroying the digestion and sucking out the humors of the body. He times this event to coincide with the wax images that the witches are busily melting in order to make it look like the witchcraft itself is responsible. Behind the vision of magic *as* magic is another one of Satan as a consummate theatricalist, a charlatan, a kind of creaky, if clever, illusionist and a fraud. What we have here then is *almost* the fear at the heart of anti-theatricality, the fear that copies can alter the things they are merely supposed to represent. But this fear is framed by a disavowal. It is as if the text dangles the vision of a supremely powerful set of representations in front of us for a moment and then takes it back as if to say they were only illusions – mere theatre.

The assumption that magic is basically a kind of theatre is embedded not only in the story I have just cited, but in the central conceit of *Daemonologie*, the conceit of Satan as "God's Ape." The difference between God's miracles and Satan's, says Epistemon, is that what God makes appear in miracles "is so in effect," whereas Satan, "God's Ape," can only counterfeit miracles. Implicit in this notion of Satan as ape is an ontology in which magic itself is only a copy or imitation. Magic is, in effect, only mere theatre and therefore has no inherent power.

But if the text claims that magic has no inherent power, it fears something very different indeed, fears that magic has a constitutive power over the body – or at least over the male body – itself. *Daemonologie* culminates in a series of "sperm-stealing" fantasies in which spirits break into the male body and steal out its "nature," its very essence. How can we account for this fear, which not only belies James' explicit insistence that magic has no inherent power but seems to imply that through magic men can be made into women? Neither Renaissance anatomies nor the critics who reproduce them are of any apparent help here, but rather complicate the situation. For while extraordinary stories exist in which women, in the presence of great heat or exertion, turn into men, no equivalent metamorphosis is ever possible the other way around. "Such transformations...seem to work only up the great chain of being," says Thomas Laqueur.[3] The explanation, then, must lie either in the nature of the text's conception of theatricality itself or in some fundamental, if unacknowledged, assumption being made about the human body. What I will ultimately suggest is that both things are true. Though the text claims that magic is mere theatre, like anti-theatrical tracts, its real fear is that theatre itself is constitutive.[4] But in a sense, this is possible because of the notion of the human body which is already at work in the text. It is possible for *Daemonologie* to culminate in a vision of dissolving masculinity because beneath this vision is a conception of the human body as already in some profound sense female.

Why would a text that insists that magic is mere theatre seem to believe in the capacity of magic to reconstitute masculinity itself? Let us examine the possibility that within the dismissal of magic as mere theatre lies a conception of theatre itself as having a constitutive power.

Most frequently the power accorded to Satan's theatricality in this text is the power to deceive, although even this power is severely circumscribed. The book is, in effect, a virtual encyclopedia of Satan's roles. Thus he can appear as a disembodied voice or a man walking solitary in a field in order to seduce a prospective witch who is herself walking or lying "pansing" in bed. He can appear as a good spirit, "genius bonus," for the sole purpose of deluding men into believing that there are good spirits. In the days of papistry, for instance, he used to appear regularly in the shape of "Brownie," a rough man who did no particular overt damage, but materialized for the specific purpose of deluding Christians into believing that the enemy of God was a spirit of light. Satan has a whole litany of shapes he appears in to magicians and necromancers, and in fact the skill of these workers in the black arts is measured precisely by the kind of shape they can compel him to appear in. To the "baser sorte," he will appear only in the "likenes of a dog, a Catte, an Ape, or such-like other beast; or else to answere by a voyce onlie" (p. 19). To more skilled magicians, the "most curious sorte," he will appear "in a dead bodie ... a continuall attender, in forme of a Page," or (for portability's sake) "ether in a tablet or a ring ... which they may easely carrie about with them" (p. 20).

Taxonomies themselves say something about what a text takes to be important, and the classification of magicians according to the shapes they can get Satan to assume seems to accord a certain power to theatricality. But, at least initially, Epistemon is careful to circumscribe the limits of this power by making delusion a function of the moral state of the spectator. In scripture we are told that Satan transforms himself into an angel of light. And indeed God allows him to do this, licenses, as it were, his theatricality, because Christian knowledge offers a kind of insurance policy against the deceptions that Satan perpetuates. His disguise as the spirit of Samuel, for instance, caused no particular "inconvenience" to the prophets, because God only allows those who deceive themselves to be deluded. By making confusion a function of the moral status of the spectator, the text manages to protect two ideas which would normally seem to contradict each other: the possibility of an almost limitless theatricality and the simultaneous possibility of knowledge, even of certainty, for the virtuous.

Since only those who first deceive themselves can be deceived, it comes as no surprise that, among the population of those susceptible, necromancers and magicians, witches and sorcerers constitute a formidable clientele. And the particular deception that Satan perpetrates upon this population is the belief that the arts he trains them in have actual power, a power to work palpable change. Thus he makes the men to whom he teaches the "devilles rudiments" believe that "knitting roun-trees ... turning ... the riddle, or doing ... innumerable thinges by wordes" work change through their own power, even though, as the text asserts again and again, it is "not by anie inherent vertue in these vaine wordes and freites" but only "by the power of the Devill for deceaving men" (p. 12). Similarly, he makes conjurors believe that the circles they draw to raise spirits have a power "inseparablie tyed or inherent" in them. His quintessential performance is, in effect, the capacity to persuade his disciples he hands them actual power, so that they believe themselves commanders when they actually serve.

But if it is Satan's skill to make it seem as if magic has an actual power, the refrain of the text is that it does not. Necromancers have no actual power, but power only by pact with Satan ("*ex pacto* allanerlie" [p. 9]). The power of the devil's rudiments consists not in any power in these tricks themselves but only in the power of the devil for deceiving people. More emphatically than anything else, the conjuror's circles and rites have no inherent power. The very "ground" which Epistemon tells Philomathes they must lay in talking about conjuring is:

that it is no power inherent in the circles, or in the holines of the names of God blasphemouslie used: nor in whatsoever rites or ceremonies at that time used, that either can raise any infernall spirit, or yet limitat him perforce within or without these circles. (pp. 16–17)

None of these "meanes" which the Devil teaches "can of them selves help any thing to these turnes," says Epistemon, for Satan is merely God's ape (p. 44).

This notion gets its most elaborate and extended expression at the center of the book, in Book II, chapter 3, in the vision of magic as a mirror world, a replica, an imitation, a copy, a fake. This vision is based on an elaborate set of correspondences between Satan's mode of adoration and God's. As God's worshippers convene for services, so do Satan's. As God's are marked by the seal of baptism, so Satan's are marked with his seal, the devil's mark. As God's worshippers convene in churches, so Satan draws his followers together in churches. As God speaks by oracles, so does Satan. As God has churches sanctified to his service with altars, priests, sacrifices, ceremonies and prayers, so does Satan. In all of these things, Satan tries to "counterfeit," and the vision of magic that proceeds from this counterfeiting is of a mirror or replica. Far from having inherent power, magic is itself an imitation. Ontologically it has no status.

So far there is nothing in this vision of things to suggest a conception of theatre that would account for the constitutive power magic seems to have later on in the book, and yet there are curious lapses, moments when the claims that magic has no inherent power seem to wear thin. Epistemon says that none of the formal properties of magic have any inherent power, not the conjuror's circles, not the names used, nor any of the rites whatsoever.

But if there is no power inherent in the formal properties of magic, why are some of these things more indispensable than others? Why must there always be more than one conjuror? "Then laying this ground, as I have said, these conjurationes must have few or mo in number of the persones conjurers (alwaies passing the singuler number)," says Epistemon. "Two principall thinges cannot well in that errand be wanted: holie-water (whereby the Devill mockes the *Papistes*) and some present of a living thing unto him" (p. 17). If the details have no inherent power, are, in effect mere formalism, why must some of them always be there? Why must there always be more than one person present? Why must there *always* be holy water and some present of a living thing? And why, above all, if the circles have no constitutive power, is the conjuror lost forever if he steps a jot over the circle's line? Epistemon says:

if they have missed one iote of all their rites; or if any of their feete once slyd over the circle through terror of his feareful apparition, he...carries them with him bodie and soule. (p. 18)

Although the claim is that the circle has no inherent power, it is as if it functions in fact as a place of safety, a protection, as if it *constitutes* that safety. The text insists that the circles are powerless, but acts as if they were in fact constitutive.

In these moments, magic itself seems to be endowed with constitutive power. But there are other moments in the text, which seem to challenge the ontological foundations of a world in which representations themselves are only copies and the things they represent are "real." In a passage on whether the Devil actually has foreknowledge, Epistemon says that while Satan is "worldlie wise" and can gauge things by a kind of probability model, taught by continual experience, since he has been around since the beginning of the universe, he cannot know things directly, cannot know "anie thing by loking upon God as in a mirrour (as the good Angels doe)" (pp. 4–5). In this curious moment in which God becomes the mirror (the reflected thing, the imitation) and the created beings (the angels) become "real," the ontology on which a view of magic as imitation depends crumbles. If the problem with the conjuror's circles is that what is supposed to be merely a prop, merely theatre, seems to assume a constitutive power, the problem here is that the text seems to register a curious vertigo in which the very categories of "real" and imitation become reversed.

But perhaps the most serious strain on the idea of magic as imitation comes in the very vision of Satan as ape, the vision of magic itself as an extraordinary set of correspondences. In the middle of detailing the analogies between God's world and Satan's, Epistemon gets to the witch's mode of adoration, the kissing of what he politely refers to as Satan's "hinder partes":

Yea, their forme of adoration [is] the kissing of his hinder partes. Which though it seeme ridiculous, yet may it likewise be true, seeing we read that in *Calicute*, he appearing in forme of a *Goate*-buck, hath publicklie that un-honest homage done unto him, by everie one of the people. (p. 37)

Contained (though barely) within the set of correspondences is essentially an ass-kissing fantasy. What is striking about this is not the fantasy itself, a stock trope of Renaissance witch lore, but the way in which the text has to normalize it, has to work though a machinery of correspondences in order to "contain" and disguise its sexual energy. The sexual and farcical content of the material is accounted for and thus normalized by being the last in a set of extended correspondences:

So ambitious is [Satan] and greedie of honor (which procured his fall) that he will even imitate God in that parte, where it is said, that *Moyses* could see but *the hinder partes of God, for the brightnesse of his glorie.* (p. 37)

As Moses could only look at God from behind for the brightness of his glory, so witches must kiss Satan's "hinder partes." So out of keeping is the moment both with the Biblical passage it draws on and with the correspondences in the chapter, that it suggests the strain or pressure the correspondences themselves are under, that the very idea of magic as a mirror world or imitation is under. But what would the source of this strain be? We might hypothesize that just as the localized correspondence with Moses works to contain the fantasy of kissing Satan's "hinder partes," so the larger claim that magic is an imitation – the vision of magic as a whole set of correspondences – works to defend against a larger sexual threat. But what would this threat be? What I am going to suggest is that the threat is of something getting into the body and changing its very gender. But to see this we have to look at the ass-kissing fantasy in context, since it is only one moment in what turns out to be a kind of seduction narrative, a story about the nature of desire itself.[5]

At the beginning of this narrative, witches are associated in only the most general way with desire. They are knowable, distinguishable, that is, from melancholics, by their eating and drinking, their inclination to pleasure, some of them "fatte or corpulent in their bodies," most of them "given over to the pleasures of the flesh...all kind of merrines, both lawfull and unlawfull" (p. 30), in contrast to melancholics who are lean, pale and constantly offering up *gratis* the kinds of confessions that have to be extorted from witches. Witches are, at the beginning, then, associated in only the most general terms with appetite, but as the narrative progresses, this appetite becomes increasingly sexualized, increasingly specific.

Even before he meets a prospective witch, Satan manipulates her affections by promising either wealth or revenge, these being the two things witches crave most ("for such of them as are in great miserie and povertie, he ... [promises] greate riches and worldlie commoditie. Such as though riche, yet burnes in a desperat desire of revenge, hee allures them by promises to get their turne satisfied to their hartes contentment" [p. 32]). But we are told that even an enemy as crafty as Satan cannot assail a victim or win over a prospective witch unless he gains what the text calls "entresse":

It is to be noted nowe, that that olde and craftie enemie of ours, assailes none, though touched with any of these two extremities, except he first find an entresse reddy for him. (p. 32)

What is this "entresse" and how does the Devil gain it? It seems at first to be a kind of moral or metaphorical notion implying access to the soul. But as the text progresses it becomes increasingly literal and physical, an "entresse" into the human body itself. And the process by which the devil gains it falls into a series of recognizable, highly codified stages.

Even before meeting the witch, Satan manipulates her despair by "feeding [her] craftely in [her] humour" while he waits for the proper time to discover himself. He appears to her only when she is alone, preferably "pansing" in her bed or else walking solitary in a field. He appears either as a man or a disembodied voice and sets what the text specifically refers to as a second "tryist." At this second tryst he gets the witch to "addict" herself to his service, "discovers what he is unto [her]," gets her to renounce God and baptism and "gives [her] his marke upon some secreit plaice of [her] bodie, which remains soare unhealed" (p. 33). What is the nature of this mark? It causes an "intollerable dolour that they feele in that place, where he hath marked them [and] serves to waken them, and not to let them rest" (p. 33). The mark is an eroticized place (in some texts the devil marks them with his tongue), a sexually charged area that keeps them up at night and causes a "dolour."[6] It also serves as an epistemological marker (both to James to recognize the witch, and to the witch herself as proof of the way Satan can hurt or help her). At the third meeting Satan always makes a show to keep his promise.

What we have here is a seduction narrative. It is for the most part a narrative of heterosexual seduction, since we find out subsequently that twenty out of every twenty-one witches are female. It begins with the witch alone or in bed, moves to a touch so potent it creates a kind of localized burning as if the mark itself were a displacement or distillation of all the sexuality of the encounter. But this narrative itself is only part of a larger story about desire, for in the next chapter we get the vision of those witches kissing Satan's "hinder partes." What this is is a vision of foreplay, a narrative about the progression of desire itself. And if it is the story of how Satan gains "entresse," what we logically expect to follow is some kind of literal "entresse," some moment of penetration, the logical conclusion to a heterosexual seduction, the male (the devil) penetrating the woman.

What we get, though, is not any penetration of bodies, but a weird preoccupation with whether witches can penetrate houses, solid walls. What we get is not a vision of a man penetrating a woman, Satan penetrating a witch, but a vision of the witch, the woman in the act of penetrating. In response to Philomathes' question about how witches get to their "conventions," Epistemon names three ways they claim to travel: 1) natural riding or sailing, which he believes are both possible, 2) being invisibly carried on the wind, which is also possible, though it runs the risk of extinguishing the witch's breath, and 3) flying through solid walls in the shapes of small beasts and chickens. "For some of them sayeth," says Epistemon:

That being transformed in the likenesse of a little beaste or foule, they will come and pearce through whatsoever house or Church, though all ordinarie passages be closed, by whatsoever open, the aire may enter in at. (p. 39)

Though the text goes to great lengths to establish that witches can't penetrate solid walls (it would be too much like transubstantiation; it's as much in the nature of a solid body to have substance as it is in the nature of a spiritual one to lack it; when Peter got out of prison he did so because the door opened, not because he penetrated a solid wall) these reasons are never sufficient to exhaust the anxiety that in fact witches can penetrate solid walls. The anxiety that such acts of penetration are possible keeps coming back in different forms.

In fact, as soon as Epistemon has eliminated the possibility of witches penetrating solid walls, the anxiety recurs in the form of whether *spirits* can penetrate solid walls. In the chapter on house-haunting spirits, Philomathes asks:

But by what way or passage can these Spirites enter in these houses, seeing they alledge that they will enter, Doore and Window being steiked? (p. 58)

There are two answers to this question: they can assume a dead body, at which point they can get up and open the door or window, or they can "enter as a spirite onelie," in which case any place large enough for air is good enough for them. The issue of "entresse" has become explicitly physical. "They will choose the passage for their entresse, according to the forme that they are in at that time" (pp. 58–9).

But no sooner have we dealt with how spirits get into locked houses, than we are confronted with the question of how they get "into" the human body, the fear that it feels as if the text has been gravitating toward all along. In the chapter on succubi and incubi, the spirits "more monstrous nor al the rest" (p. 66), Epistemon talks about the two ways the devil may enter and have sex with humans. He can borrow "a dead bodie and so visiblie, and as it seemes unto them naturallie as a man [converse] with them" (p. 67) or he can enter "onelie as a spirit...they not graithlie seeing anie shape or feeling anie thing" (p. 67). In other words, the two ways are the ways he can enter a locked house: the text articulates a tacit analogy between houses and bodies, envisions the body itself as a site of invasion, porous to "entresse."

What keeps threatening the claim that magic has no inherent power is this fear of "entresse" or penetration itself. For what begins as a narrative of seduction culminates in a vision of rape. This is the vision of desire in this text, the progression it implies. Like Marlowe's vision of "appetence" or desire moving not in gradated steps but in leaps and bounds, like Gosson's vision of desire moving from "pleasure to slouth, slouth to sleepe, sleepe to sinne, sinne to death," in James' narrative of desire, eating and drinking, touching and kissing, result in the invasion of the body itself. It is as if Marlowe's vision ended with Leander on the ocean floor, drowning in Neptune's embrace.

But it is not just that the text envisions a rape, but that this rape itself is imagined to have a constitutive power: the capacity to dissolve masculinity itself. For it is not just that Satan gets into the human body, but what he does when he gets there that makes this experience both threatening and transformative. What he does when he gets into the male body is to take out its sperm, what the text calls its "nature" ("For if [Satan] steale out the nature of a quick person, it cannot be so quicklie carryed, but it will both tine the strength and heate by the way" [p. 67]).[7] And in doing this he steals what it is that makes the man male in the first place, his very essence, his gender itself.

That the sperm is what makes the man male is made clear in the explanation of why succubi and incubi themselves have no inherent gender, but take on their gender only through action, only in response to whom they "converse" with. Epistemon says:

And whereas yee inquire if these spirites be divided in sexes or not, I thinke the rules of Philosophie may easelie resolve a man of the contrarie: For it is a sure principle of that arte, that nothing can be divided in sexes except such living bodies as must have a naturall seede to genere by. But we know spirites hath no seede proper to themselves, nor yet can they gender one with an other. (pp. 67–8).

If the reason that succubi and incubi have no inherent gender is because they have no "seed" and what they do to male human bodies is to steal that seed, then at stake in the fear of "entresse" is the fear of simply having one's gender stolen, as if that gender were localized and reified in the seed itself.

In theory such a fantasy might extend to women as well. Galenic anatomy had a powerful hold on the Renaissance, and Galen offered a two-seed theory of conception: both men and women had sperm and that sperm required sufficient heat to "seminate." Indeed there are echoes of such an anatomy in the very claim that to be divisible into sexes one must have a seed, as there are in the passage's obsessive attention to cold sperm, the loss of heat necessary for what Epistemon calls the "agitation" requisite for procreation. But though in theory the fantasy might extend to women, what is striking about *Daemonologie* in practice is the way it is *only* concerned with the theft of male sperm. Epistemon's example makes this clear. "By two meanes this great kinde of abuse might possibly be performed," he says:

The one, when the Devill onelie as a spirite, and stealing out the sperme of a dead bodie, abuses *them* that way, *they* not graithlie seeing anie shape or feeling anie thing, but that which he so convayes in that part. (p. 67) (italics mine)

Who are the "they" and "them" of this passage that get abused with the sperm? Epistemon specifies their gender a moment later when he says: "as we read of a Monasterie of Nunnes which were burnt for their being that way abused" (p. 67). As it is the Nunnes who are "that way abused," it is clear it is the men from whom the sperm is being stolen. And it is the anxiety that it can be stolen that it is figured again and again throughout the text. What is interesting is the way the sperm is actually necessary for the abuse, even though we are told that it cannot create conception.

For again and again we are told that conception cannot take place, that whatever way the devil goes about things, his sperm is always too cold. If he steals the sperm out of a living person, it loses heat, and if he occupies a "dead bodie as his lodging" – the phrase again makes explicit the association between bodies and houses – the sperm must be cold because of its "participation" with the dead body itself (p. 67). Cold sperm "can work nothing in generation." In a teleology of heat, this is one of the ways that the text insists that Satan is merely an imitation. "For the Devilles parte therein, is but the naked carrying or expelling of that substance" (p. 68). It is in its incapacity to produce new life that magic is most profoundly a copy, in this way that the text insists most profoundly that Satan is an "ape." He can imitate a birth by substituting some "monstrous barne brought from some other place" at a childbirth which is already in progress, but he cannot create an actual birth, cannot bring about new life.

But this ape, this imitation incapable of effecting conception, can bring about an equally momentous change by draining the man's gender itself. And in this respect magic acquires a constitutive power, a power envisioned in just the opposite way from that of the pictures of wax we began with. For if the fear that witches can transform their victims through wax pictures is circumscribed by the disclaimer that they cannot, here the disclaimer that Satan is only an imitation is undermined by the fear that he can reconstitute gender itself. Beneath the text's dismissal of magic as "mere" theatricality is a vision of that theatricality as capable of radical, constitutive change.

In one sense this vision is only the logical extension of the text's view of succubi and incubi as supremely "theatrical" in the first place. As things which take on their genders through action "according to the difference of the sexes that they conversed with," succubi and incubi represent theatricality at its most radical and constitutive: for them action literally determines gender. But in another sense the belief that magic can reconstitute gender is a function of the text's attitudes toward both masculinity and the human body itself. On the one hand, it imagines masculinity as so precarious, so localized and reified in the sperm that it can be made portable and carried away. On the other, it envisions the body itself in terms usually relegated to the female body during the period.[8] In the analogy between bodies and houses which comes to dominate the last two thirds of the text, even the male body is depicted in terms usually reserved for the female body during the Renaissance. Like a house, the body is experienced as porous and always open to invasion, imagined as a collection of orifices and holes. It is possible for James' treatise to culminate in a vision of dissolving masculinity, because beneath this vision is one of the body as already in some sense female.

To trace this narrative of "entresse" is to see that *Daemonologie* exhibits the same fear that tracts against the stage do, the fear that what is supposed to be merely representation can alter and dissolve masculinity itself. We would expect *Daemonologie* to manage this fear in the same way that pamphlet attacks do, then, by turning to some system which guaranteed certainty. In fact, *Daemonologie* seeks to do just that: in its insistence that only those who delude themselves can be deceived by Satan, in its insistence that it is possible to know a witch from a melancholic, in its insistence that it is possible to tell a true confession from a false one, it seeks to guarantee certainty. But as the text progresses, this certainty crumbles: confessions about out-of-the-body travel, for instance, are neither true or false, but a product of the witch's delusion. But if there is a category of confession which is neither truth nor lie, then it is no longer possible to have certainty that a confession is true even if it is extorted through torture.

Daemonologie is so riddled with contradictions about what can be known that it finally offers no systematic epistemology.[9] But if we turn to *Newes from Scotland*, a text that suggests the way the king put his beliefs into practice, we see the same mechanism at work as we do in pamphlet attacks against the stage, the attempt to contain a growing terror about the constitutive power of representations by turning to a dogmatic epistemology, a system of signs. In *Newes from Scotland* that "sign" is not clothing, but the devil's mark "discovered" on the witch's body, the mark that is supposed to guarantee the witch is a witch.

7 Magic as theatre, theatre as magic: the case of *Newes from Scotland*

Midway through the anonymous pamphlet *Newes from Scotland*, the pamphleteer explains the epistemology of the devil's mark: "It hath latelye beene found," he tells us, "that the Devill dooth generallye marke [witches] with a privie marke ... and generally so long as the marke is not seene to those which search them [the witches] ... will never confesse."[1] The devil's mark is a sign, both to the examiners that the witch is a witch and to the witch herself that she will have to confess. As a sign, it is also the hallmark of the same epistemology embraced by anti-theatricalists like Stephen Gosson, when he calls costume a "signe distinctive" between the sexes.[2] As we have seen, this is an epistemology governed by a faith in a one-to-one correspondence between each "signe" and the thing it stands for, and it is the exclusivity of that correspondence, its one-to-one nature, that makes knowledge possible.

But just as Gosson's claim that costume is the "signe" of the gender beneath is belied by the deeper fear that costume can actually alter the gender it stands for, so in *Newes from Scotland* the epistemology of the devil's mark betrays a deeper fear. At the heart of the text is the fear that, rather than representing the things they are supposed to stand for, signs can actually alter them. What *Newes from Scotland* shares with the anti-theatrical tracts of the period is the frightening vision that representations can actually make the things they stand for mimic them – a vision of a kind of mimesis in reverse. And it is in response to this fear that the examiners (at James' bidding) must insist on the epistemology of the devil's mark, and the text must assert that they are right to do so.

But while this may explain the preoccupation with the devil's mark and even the violence necessary to "discover" it, it will not explain the steady escalation of that violence throughout the text. *Newes from Scotland* presents three case histories: that of the witch Geillis Duncane who has to be "searched" before the devil's mark is found on her throat, that of the witch Agnis Sampson who has to be shaved before the devil's mark is found on her genitals, and that of John Cunningham, alias Doctor Fian, whose body is eventually destroyed after it fails to yield a devil's mark.

120

Why do the examiners in *Newes from Scotland* grow increasingly violent with each witch they deal with? Why does the devil's mark offer up more and more resistance to being found? What I am going to suggest in the pages which follow is that each witch's magic offers a deeper threat than the last to the philosophical underpinnings of reality as the examiners construct it. The more the confessions they hear threaten the premise of an essentialist world – the premise that reality can only be depicted, not altered, by the signs that represent it – the more James and the examiners need to construct a universe governed by the opposite logic, a logic in which signs point infallibly to the things they refer to without affecting them, the logic of a universe in which certainty feels possible.[3]

What is the stated purpose of *Newes from Scotland?* The pamphlet's stated intention is to discredit a false rumor of discovery, a false account of a "poore Pedler travailing to the towne of Trenent [who] by a wonderfull manner . . . was in a moment convayed at midnight, from Scotland to Burdeux in Fraunce", and then returned to Scotland, where he discovered the witches and ultimately brought them to King James' attention. All of this is "moste false," says the pamphleteer (p. 5). And just to satisfy the few "honest mindes" left who desire the truth, he will provide the real story of discovery, which was all the king's. In other words, the text begins by having to discredit one way of knowing things (the peddler's) in order to establish another (the king's), begins by having to discredit one epistemology in order to establish the legitimacy of another. Even the preface, then, establishes the way the king's epistemology is in competition with other things.

In the case of the first witch treated, the witch Geillis Duncane, the thing that the king's epistemology is in competition with is not presented specifically as knowledge, but as power (though ultimately these imply each other). Geillis Duncane is a maidservant who works for the bailiff David Seaton, and there are two notable facts about her. The first is that like the poor peddler in the preface, she disappears mysteriously overnight, and the second is that she displays inexplicable healing powers. The bailiff is suspicious of these powers and begins to question her to determine whether they are legal or not. But his questions lead nowhere, so he has her "searched," and the searching soon reveals a devil's mark on her throat, and Duncane confesses to being a witch.

What does this story show? What is the story it tells? First of all, Duncane, like the peddler of the preface, is poor. More importantly, she occupies a position with respect to her master that is analogous to the position the peddler occupies to the king: by position, that is, she is powerless, weak, lacking in social status, occupies the role of dependent or child to parent. But if this is so by position, by her actions, she seems to demonstrate remarkable and incomprehensible powers. And when those powers cannot be rationally explained and accounted for, she must be rendered powerless.[4]

But it is the form this reduction of power takes that interests me. For the story this first anecdote tells is the story of the triumph of a naive epistemology over the unknowable: Geillis Duncane is searched. The devil's mark is found on her throat. The mark is itself both the "sign" and the means of establishing a more familiar system of knowledge, and it makes possible an explanation of where Duncane's powers came from: they came from Satan, and once this has been established the powers themselves are rendered dysfunctional. The function of the naive epistemology is to render powerless what was before unknowable. And what I shall argue in the next section is that it requires more violence and more energy to strip the next witch, Agnis Sampson – also called Agnis Tompson – of her powers, because these powers are conceived of as more intensely threatening. (The very ambiguity over this witch's name suggests the difficulty of establishing a one-to-one correspondence between sign and thing – the text alternately refers to her as Agnis Sampson and Agnis Tompson as if the two were interchangeable.)[5]

Where Geillis Duncane had only to be searched before the devil's mark was located, Agnis Sampson must be shaved, as if the removal of clothing no longer insured nakedness, but part of the body itself had to be removed and dismantled to arrive at real nakedness, the truth. It is as if the truth itself, the thing to be known, were offering more and more resistance to its knowers. And the sign that finally points to that truth has moved; knowledge itself become sexualized: unlike Duncane, whose mark was in the "fore crag" of her throat, Agnis Sampson's is on her genitals. To view the devil's mark then is (here) inevitably to look at its bearer sexually. And it is not just the examiners that look at that bearer, but the king as well, at whose behest they do the examining.

Why does the devil's mark offer up more resistance to being found in this anecdote? Why has it moved to a genital? Let us see if there is anything in the confession that follows to account for these changes. In fact what we find is precisely the fear that costume activated in the minds of the anti-theatricalists, the fear that representations that can alter the things they are merely supposed to represent. We will see this when we look at the discrete acts of witchcraft themselves, but before we can look at them, we need to look at the context they take place in, which is a narrative with a very clear underlying story of seduction.

We are told that about 200 witches were in the habit of meeting off the coast of North Barrick in Lowthian for Allhollon, and sailing off to sea in boats called "Riddles" or "Cives."[6] At first, the vision is one of generalized revelry involving "flaggons of wine," "making merrie [dance and] singing all with one voice" (p. 13). There is a theatrical element to all this which the king appreciates, and in fact wants re-enacted. For when he is told that Geillis Duncane played the "Jew's Trump," James has Geillis brought back and makes her perform for everyone. We shall return to this aspect of the interaction, for just as the mood of the moment – the apparent pleasure it offers – seems bizarrely at odds with the moments of torture which precede and follow it, so its theatrical nature is at odds with what we shall see is the basically anti-theatrical bias of the text, as well as the examiners the text depicts and the king whose wishes they execute. It may seem odd in light of the work that has been done on James' own theatricality to characterize James as having an anti-theatrical bias, but as we have already seen in *Daemonologie* he had a pervasive fear of a malevolent theatricality outside the self, a theatricality with the power to unman and unfashion. His odd moments of theatrical delight, then, with Geillis Duncane, must be framed by this sense which we have already seen him manifest.

It is, in fact, the song that the witches sing that identifies the narrative that follows as one of seduction. For established witches sing to prospective witches to come away with them. They try to "seduce" them in the most literal sense of the word, to lead them away:

> Commer goe ye before, commer goe ye,
> Gif ye will not goe before, commer let me.
>
> (p. 14)

The song is a seduction song between witches, but it is also a stage, a rung on the ladder of a larger seduction narrative, one in which though the characters change, the action moves inescapably from flirtation (singing and kissing) to intercourse. At the next stage of this narrative, the witches will kiss Satan's buttocks: in penance for their tardiness, he puts his buttocks over the pulpit barre and makes them kiss.

If the early stages of this seduction narrative, the songs and buttock kissing, constitute something like foreplay, they produce the expectation that what will come next is a moment of consummation. But it is precisely at the moment we expect consummation that what we get instead is a threat to consummation: not the witch's consummation, but the king's. In response to James' dismissal of the witches all as a pack of "extreame lyars," Sampson tells James that she would hate to have him think of her that way and to prove that he is wrong, she will tell him exactly what he said to the Queen on their wedding night. The words themselves are never repeated by the text, but apparently James believes her, for he swears that all the devils in hell couldn't have known what she knew.

Now it is true that in itself the witch's presence doesn't prevent the king from consummating his marriage, but it does suggest very strongly a potential threat to that consummation. We know from other sources that the king did believe witches sought to sabotage his marriage. We know from *Daemonologie* that he thought witches in general had the power to cause impotence as well as the ability to summon spirits who could get into the body and steal out its sperm. In fact, the cultural association between witchcraft and impotence was so old and basic, so widespread, that the inquisitor's manual *Malleus Maleficarum* had, in 1486, used the capacity of witches to cause impotence as an example, to prove that the devil worked through witches rather than on his own. The witch's presence hovering around the king's bed on his wedding night, then, immediately suggests a vision of impotence and failure, the same vision which underlies Gosson's claim that theatre effeminates the mind, or William Prynne's vision of boys with "dissected...virilities." If we think of this moment as one of a series of sexual moments in which, though the characters change, the overall narrative is one of seduction, it is at this point in the process that the momentum suddenly stops. A moment later, we hear of an attempt to sink the ship bearing the king's wedding gift to the queen as well – rich jewels and treasures. One of the formal aspects of the wedding consummation, then, is actually impaired.

At the heart of the narrative, then, just as in *Daemonologie*, where the moment of consummation is supposed to be, is a threat to consummation. A rite of passage is threatened exactly at its moment of fulfillment. But surrounding this threatened moment is a completed seduction narrative: the witches that begin by singing "Gif ye will not goe before, commer let me," and continue by kissing the devil's buttocks, end by sleeping with him: he uses them carnally, though to their "little pleasure," since his sperm is so cold.

As a narrative, then, the story successfully envisions a moment of sexual consummation. But the consummation is not the king's. The narrative imagines a consummation only by containing at its center the opposite vision, a vision of paralyzing impotence. The central moment and the larger narrative it takes place in are casually superimposed upon each other without any recognition of their capacity to disrupt each other. It is as if the cost of the devil's sexual consummation is the impotence of the king.

In a sense, we are back to the story of the poor peddler whose "discovery" the text begins by discrediting. There, in order to establish the legitimacy of the king's knowledge, the epistemology of the devil's mark, the text had to discredit a rival epistemology, a rival way of knowing things. Here, since the implicit argument is that the cost of demonic sexuality is the king's potency, that demonic sexuality will surely have to be destroyed before the king's potency can be insured. Perhaps this begins to explain why Agnis Sampson must not simply be "searched," but shaved, why the devil's mark must be on her genitals and that part must be made into public spectacle, publicly viewed. Because the king's virility in particular is threatened by this particular witch, it is not just enough to make the witch powerless, she must be made sexually power-less. The first similarity that *Newes from Scotland* shares with the anti-theatrical tracts, then, is a fear of impotence itself. Where anti-theatrical tracts react by attacking theatre, *Newes from Scotland* reacts by attacking the witches conceived of as causing it. But as we shall see, it is not simply the issue of impotence but what that impotence means in the context of other threats posed by magic that is at issue.

But the threats to the king's virility are not the only threats implied by this narrative. For the first overt act of witchcraft contained within it constitutes not merely a threat to the king's potency, but a threat to the king's life. (". . . She is the onlye woman," the pamphleteer says, "who by the Divels perswasion should have entended and put in execution the Kings Maiesties death in this manner" [pp. 15–16].) In a sense, this confession is the culmination of a series of patricidal bewitchings in *Newes from Scotland*: "Ewphame Meealrean ... who conspired and perfourmed the death of her Godfather ... Barbara Naper [who bewitched] to death Archibalde, last Earle of Angus" (p. 11). What we have here is the last of a series of women who offer threats to older men in positions of paternal and legal responsibility, in a sense the logical cul-mination of the "poore Pedler" whose very existence constituted a threat to the king's power to "find things out."[7]

But it is the means of her witchcraft, its mechanics, which offer the real threat, not only to the king's person but to the very ontology on which the devil's mark depends. For the principles of this magic threaten the logic not only of referentiality itself but of the world it presupposes, a world in which representations are merely the barometers or imitations of the things they represent, not capable of changing their actual natures. At the heart of this magic is the idea that, rather than imitating the things they represent, copies can make the things they represent mimic them.

We are told that Agnis, now Tompson again, took a black toad, hung it up by its heels for three days and collected its venom in an oyster shell. And that she "kept the same venome close covered untill she should obtaine any parte or peece of foule linnen cloth, that had appertained to

the Kings Maiestie, as shirt, handkercher, napkin, or any other thing"
(p. 16). Now it looks as if she merely wanted to poison the king. And
there is a certain symmetry to this – as Geillis Duncane's powers revolve
around healing, the powers here revolve around harming, medicine in
reverse, medicine as revenge. But in fact, this is not the case. For at no
point is it necessary for the king to actually put the poisoned shirt on for
the magic to work. Rather, like the roasted pictures in *Daemonologie*
which have the power to sicken the subjects they represent, the principle
underlying this magic is that the part shall contaminate the whole, the
representation contaminate the thing represented. This is both contagious magic (what has touched the king, in being altered can alter the
king) and sympathetic magic (what stands for the king, in being altered
can alter the king):[8]

if she had obtained any one peece of linnen cloth which the King had worne and
fouled, she had bewitched him to death, and put him to such extraordinary paines,
as if he had been lying upon sharpe thornes and endes of Needles. (p. 16)

We are far from a mimetic world in which copies merely mimic or imitate
the things they represent. This is *Daemonologie*'s world of roasted pictures, the vision it tries to disclaim. This is a world in which mimesis can
somehow work backwards, slide into retrogress, a world in which, rather
than mimicking the things they represent, representations can somehow
make the things they represent mimic them: the king can be made to
imitate the shirt dipped in poison, the shirt that is both a "part" of him
and a representation of him, and in this way he can be put to "such
extraordinary paines."

In its profound fear that representations can actually alter the things
they represent, *Newes from Scotland* shares its deepest affinity with the
anti-theatrical tracts of the period. For just as Gosson fears the capacity
of female impersonation to make the impersonator into the thing im-
personated, and Stubbes fears the power of costume to literally "adulterate" the gender beneath it, and Prynne fears the power of women's
clothing to make the warrior "degenerate" into a woman with his veiled
face, so here the fear is that the representation, the shirt dipped in poison,
can reconstitute and diminish – even kill – the king it stands for.

But there is more. If Sampson's first overt act of witchcraft threatens
the ontological foundations of the devil's mark, threatens a vision of
reality in which things remain fixed and secure from the representations
that are only supposed to depict them, Sampson's second overt act of
witchcraft threatens that epistemology itself in which signs are supposed
to lead inevitably to knowledge. She confesses that while the king was in
Denmark, she took a cat, christened it and "afterward bound to each

parte of that Cat, the cheefest partes of a dead man and severall ioynts of his bodie" and that the following night the cat was thrown into the sea (pp. 16–17). The effect was to raise a localized tempest which, leaving other parts of the water untouched, sank the boat carrying the king's "sundrye Iewelles and riche giftes" to the queen.

What is the principle of magic at work here? Is the dead cat a representation of the king and the dead man's joints a representation of what the witches wish for him? Does the cat represent the ship to be sunk and the dead man's joints what it means to be disembodied, taken apart? Or is the cat with human joints attached simply an image of unholy mixture, in that sense an image of the tempest itself which will mix water and land, ship and sea? Finally, this is unknowable. The relation between representation and thing represented, representation and thing to be damaged, cannot be specified. There is no definite relationship between sign and thing, and this makes knowledge impossible.

It may seem contradictory to turn to a confession at all to explain the rising hostility of torture, for if the confession follows the torture, how can it provide a rationale for it? But to pose the problem this way is misleading. The very fact that for the Renaissance, as *Daemonologie* itself indicates, confessions extorted under torture were more "valid" and hence more valued than voluntary confessions suggests, in a general way, that for the period valid confessions are always in some sense collaborative efforts, always in some sense responsive to the needs of the examiners who extract them.[9] In a more specific way, the testimony of the next prisoner examined, the sorcerer John Cunningham (alias Dr. Fian), suggests that the confessions witches offered tried to meet the specifications of their examiners, told, in effect, the stories the examiners needed to hear. Fian ultimately says that what he said and did in his testimony "was onely done and sayde for feare of paynes which he had endured" (p. 28), and thus suggests in fact that the confessions are collective fantasies. From this point of view such collective fantasies may very well explain the violence they both seek to forestall and ultimately end up precipitating.

One would think that little could surpass a threat to kill the king, but if the intensity of torture used is any measure of the threat experienced, there is something about Fian that more profoundly threatens the court than either of the testimonies which has preceded it. On the surface, this is difficult to understand, since the object of Fian's magic is an anonymous village girl, where the object of Sampson's magic is the king himself. But the challenge Fian's magic – and Fian himself – pose to the philosophic underpinnings of reality, as the examiners construct it, offers an even more profound threat than the magic of Agnis Sampson.[10]

If the story of Geillis Duncane illustrates the restoration of a naive epistemology through simple "searching" and the story of Agnis Sampson illustrates the restoration of that epistemology only at the cost of shaving and greater violence, the story of John Cunningham, alias Dr. Fian, illustrates the failure to successfully reinstate that epistemology at all, and the attendant breakdown of the text into violence. Why must the torture exponentially increase in Fian's case?

From the very beginning, Fian's confession is more difficult to wrest from him than the confessions of either of the preceding witches. If there is an "it," a truth being hidden, that truth is more resistant to pressure and consequently elicits a level of violence which exceeds anything either of the previous witches have been subject to. Though the text says Fian is used with "accustomed paine," it also boasts that he is put to "the most severe and cruell paine in the world," namely the bootes. It describes in ascending order a series of torments:

First, by the thrawing of his head with a roape, wherat he would confesse nothing.

Secondly, he was perswaded by faire means to confesse his follies, but that would prevaile as little.

Lastly, he was put to the most severe and cruell paine in the world, called the bootes. (p. 18)

But even this is insufficient, the torture ineffective; after Fian has received "three strokes," he is asked "if he would confesse his damnable acts and wicked life" but "his tung would not serve him to speak" (p. 19).

Normally, this is the moment the examiners would have the witch searched for a devil's mark. She would confess and the torture would end. But there is no mention of a devil's mark at this point in Fian's case, and the court thus seems deprived of its usual means of stripping the unknown of its power.[11] We might hypothesize, then, that it is the absence of any kind of epistemological marker that drives the examiners crazy and that leads to an increase in torture. But in fact the burden of the "sign" that the examiners must find is simply transferred from the devil's mark to a set of charmed pins: the fact that Fian's "tung would not serve him to speak" turns out to be a physical condition ("the rest of the witches willed to search his tung, under which was found two pinnes thrust up into the head, whereupon the witches did laye, 'Now is the Charme stinted,' and shewed that those charmed Pinnes were the cause he could not confesse any thing" [p. 19].) When the pins fall out Fian spontaneously confesses. Although there is no devil's mark, then, the notion of a "thing" which offers incontrovertible proof of witchcraft has simply come back in a new form. It cannot be solely the absence of an epistemological marker, then, that leads to an increase in torture, although the very movement from mark to pins, a movement from lesser to greater physicality, shows the increased need for a definitive "sign," definitive evidence, as if a mark were no longer physical enough to provide the necessary reassurance.

But if Fian's body ultimately does offer up a form of evidence as compelling as the devil's mark, why does Fian himself still elicit such violence? What is there about Fian's story that is so threatening to the examiners? The question is particularly puzzling, since at least initially his story does not threaten but entertain. For initially the story itself takes the form not of narrative which even ostensibly separates speaker from auditor, but of a theatrical performance which elicits the king's "great admiration." Admitting that he bewitched a certain gentleman, a rival of his for a girl living in Saltpans, Fian actually brings the gentleman to court to reproduce for his majesty the lunatic fit he threw the gentleman into every twenty-four hours:

he caused the Gentleman to be brought before the Kinges Maiestie, which was upon the xxiiij day of December last, and being in his Maiesties Chamber, suddenly he gave a great scritch and fell into a madnes, sometime bending himselfe, and sometime capring so directly up, that his head did touch the seeling of the Chamber. (pp. 20–1)

The gentleman demonstrates all the classical signs of possession, capers about the room, has to be forcibly restrained till his fury passes, shows the strength of ten men, and afterwards, when asked where he's been, says he's been soundly sleeping: all of this to his majesty's "great admiration." The performance offers a temporary hiatus, then, a brief moment of merriment in between the scenes of torture which precede and follow it, and throughout this hiatus the threat of Fian's magic seems suspended in the king's obvious delight, just as for the moment the court's own powers of retaliation are suspended. For the moment, Fian's powers are in the service of satisfying the court rather than terrifying it.

But when Fian turns to the heart of his narrative, to the part no longer susceptible to theatricalization before the court, the energies he provokes in his audience are no longer ones of admiration, and can no longer be similarly suspended. What is it about this narrative – and about the part in particular that cannot be acted out before the court and king – that is so enraging?

The heart of the narrative revolves around Fian's attempts to bewitch and seduce the girl herself, a seduction which apparently depends on the theft of three pubic hairs. "It happened," the pamphleteer tells us, that "this gentlewoman being unmarried, had a brother who went to schoole with [Fian]" (p. 21), whom Fian commissioned to obtain "three haires of his sisters privities" (p. 21). The brother sets out on his mission with a piece of conjured paper, but God who knows the secrets of all hearts prevents him from succeeding. The girl, asleep in her bed, "suddenlye [cries] out to her mother, declaring that her brother would not suffer her to sleepe" (p. 22). The mother, immediately suspecting Fian's intentions, substitutes three hairs from the udder of a cow (or more specifically a heifer that has not "gone to the Bull," or "borne Calfe") for the girl's hairs (p. 23). And Fian, thinking the hairs are the girl's hairs, wreaks his art on them, and is immediately followed into the church by the heifer they belong to, who begins to paw all over him:

But the Doctor had no sooner doone his intent to them, but presentlye the Hayfer or Cow whose haires they were indeed, came unto the doore of the Church wherein the Schoolemaister was, into the which the Hayfer went, and made towards the Schoolemaister, leaping and dauncing upon him, and following him foorth of the church. (p. 23)

The principle which governs Fian's magic – revealed after the fact in the mother's subversion of it – is the principle at work in Agnis Sampson's bewitched shirt, or for that matter, in Prynne's fears that costumes effeminize the men who wear them, the principle that representations can make the things they represent mimic them, the possibility of a frightening mimesis in reverse. Thus we know when the cow is controlled by what is done to its hairs that the girl would have done the same thing (the hairs being both a part and a representation of the thing they come from), though we know this only in retrospect, and only indirectly, by implication. The first threat to the court's construction of reality, the first frightening possibility built into Fian's confession, then offers a direct threat to the ontological foundations of the devil's mark, for it suggests that, rather than merely designating the things they stand for, representations can change them.

But this in itself would not explain why Fian's narrative is more threatening than Sampson's, nor is it in fact the only thing that is threatening about Fian's narrative. For it is not only the capacity of the magic to control the girl that is threatening, but the capacity of that magic to generate new acts of magic, the way Fian's conjuring triggers the mother's conjuring, the way his substitution of pubic hair for the girl triggers her substitution of cow hair for pubic hair. The capacity to wreak magic on three pubic hairs is threatening not only because of what it can do to the girl whom they stand for and come from, but because of its capacity to engender subsequent acts of the same kind. It is the way the process of substitution itself gets out of control, the way substitutions beget more substitutions, representations more representations. This is the same world Gosson envisions when he pictures the spectators of Bacchus and Ariadne "posting home to their wives" or rushing off to be wedded, a world in which imitation itself begets compulsive imitation, as if magic itself were a degenerative chain, the end of that chain bestiality itself. (Fian ends up in the arms of a heifer, just as Gosson's male spectators end up as "braying colts.") If the epistemology of the devil's mark implies a world in which, ontologically at least, signs are only the copies or barometers of the things they stand for, we are as far from that world as possible in a world in which each representation can not only alter the thing it is a copy of but give rise to another representation.

But this in itself seems problematic. For if court and text share an anti-theatrical bias, if the root of the anxiety generated by confessions of witchcraft is the capacity of images to unfashion the things they represent, the capacity of images to beget new images, why are the theatrical moments within the text not merely tolerated but lauded? Why do the actual spectacles provoke not rage, but pleasure? We might hypothesize that either such spectacles meet some actual need on the part of the court, or else they somehow fall outside the realm of what the court thinks of as representation itself. As we shall see, both possibilities are the case. For the "need" such performances meet is the need for certainty itself.

When the sister cries out in the night, what we expect the mother to suspect is that her brother is trying to molest her. But what she suspects instead is Dr. Fian's "entention," the theft of three pubic hairs as part of a local bewitching process. What this seems to envision is a community of shared assumptions in which sisters who cry out at night are normally evidence of brothers trying to steal pubic hairs for local conjurors. Why is this the mother's first suspicion? Because she herself is a witch. There is no one in this narrative, victim or victimizer, who is not a possible or probable witch, no one who is not in some way implicated in witchcraft. To remain consistent, the narrative has to keep positing more witches, witches to put pins in Fian's mouth, witches to sing the lay to remove the charm, witch-mothers to know that their daughters are being bewitched, witch-like conjurors to do the bewitching. Like a dream with doubling in it, a dream in which the threat keeps multiplying, the proliferation itself is a sign of the stress the narrative's logic is under. In describing this family in which a protective mother who's concerned about her daughter being molested just happens to be a witch herself, the text seems inadvertently to normalize the crime of witchcraft itself.

But what is the central premise of the narrative's logic? It is the notion of "discovery" itself, the belief that good can be distinguished from evil, and that in so doing, evil can be limited. But what is disconcerting about the mother's discovery is the way it contaminates and undermines the convention of discovery itself. Were it not for the mother's witchcraft, she would offer a perfect homology for what the king himself is doing: God will not suffer evil to go undiscovered, so the sorcerer must be found out.

The mother is the instrument of that discovery, but by the lights of this court, she is such an unclean instrument that she poses an even more profound threat to the very premise of the text than the poor peddler whose "discovery" the text begins by discrediting. Here, the very epistemology capable of discovering evil is contaminated by evil; the mechanism for discovering witchcraft is witchcraft itself. We expect that for witchcraft to be discovered is for witchcraft to be limited. But just the opposite is the case: for witchcraft to be discovered is for witchcraft to engender more witchcraft. The story poses the ultimate threat to the epistemology of the devil's mark, for worse than suggesting that truth is unavailable, it suggests that truth is impotent, no longer has the capacity to strip witchcraft itself of its power, and it is in response to this that the court must desperately insist on the epistemology of the devil's mark, to try to restore the mimetic world it stands for.

But this time this is what the court is unable to do. Fian is committed to prison and seems genuinely repentant. He renounces the devil and vows to "leade the life of a Christian." He seems "newly connected towards God," but the next day he claims that the devil appeared to him in a black robe with a white wand to see if he remained loyal (p. 25). Fian says, "Avoide Satan, avoide," whereupon Satan threatens to claim him at death and vanishes, breaking his white wand. Fian continues in solitary, calling on God and seeming to "have care of his owne soule" (p. 26), but that night he breaks out of prison and flees back to the Saltpans, where he is tracked down by the king and brought back to be re-examined.

But this time the doctor will confess to nothing, whereupon the king assumes he's entered into a new league with the devil and immediately has his body searched, assuming that "hee had beene agayne newly marked" (p. 27). But though they search him again and again, they are unable to find any mark ("for the which hee was narrowly searched, but it coulde not in anie wise bee founde" [p. 27]). And now the need for certainty is practically unmanageable: first his nails are pulled out and under every one is thrust in two needles. Then he is put to the torment of the bootes again. Then both his legs are crushed and beaten "as small as might bee, and the bones and flesh so brused, that the bloud and marrowe spouted forth in great abundance, whereby they were made unserviceable for ever" (p. 28). The body must be unrecognizable *as* a body. But even after this torture Fian will not confess. What drives the examiners crazy is the discrepancy between his previous written testimony and his refusal to give oral testimony now – in fact it is not only that he will not confirm what he said before, but that he specifically discredits it ("utterly denied all that which he had before avouched" [p. 28]), claims only to have said what he said to avoid torture ("and would saie nothing thereunto but this, that

what hee had done and sayde before, was onely done and sayde for feare
of paynes which he had endured" [p. 28]).

In these final scenes Fian becomes *like* his own magic or like Sampson's
magic or like anyone's magic in that his examiners cannot establish a
one-to-one correspondence between his own separate testimonies, cannot
turn him into something knowable. The violence into which the text then
degenerates is a barometer to the rage (and implicit fear) this causes: he is
strangled and then burnt as if the body must be destroyed again and again
to eradicate the contradictions it has embodied.

To say this, then, is to point to the "need" that Fian's spectacle serves.
For at such moments, paradoxically, theatre itself becomes a means of
authenticating testimony, like Sampson's capacity to repeat the king's
words on his wedding night. Such performances are understood not as
representations, but (oddly) as pieces of historical evidence. At such
moments theatre itself attains the status of a "sign," becomes not a
representation capable of unfashioning an original, but a sign that such
an unfashioning has already taken place.

It is in this way, then, that the performances themselves become not
only compatible with, but actually in the service of, the deeply anti-
theatrical bias of the court. And it is in this way that, paradoxically, when
Fian arrives at the part of the story that simply cannot be theatricalized,
the need for a sign recurs with increased vigor and rage.

No naive epistemology can be made to triumph in Fian's case, no
referential world restored, and the violence that breaks out is the measure
of the need to do so. Fian himself, then, is the case that tests (and proves)
the hypothesis. The rage that is contained (though barely) in Duncane's
searching and Sampson's shaving, and suspended (briefly) in Fian's
ability to provide performances which authenticate his story, is unleashed
by his inconsistencies, the refusal of his body to provide a devil's mark
and the refusal of his various testimonies to provide a one-to-one set of
correspondences.

Epilogue

What we have seen in *Newes from Scotland* is the operative fear of anti-theatricality elevated to its logical conclusion, the fear that representations have the power to alter the things they should only be able to represent. But this fear has now been escalated so that it can only be assuaged by torture. What we witness in *Newes from Scotland* is a mechanism we have seen before, the progression from strategy to more radical strategy to ward off a terrifying idea: with each successive witch the examiners interrogate, they reach for more and more extreme means to ward off what they fear, and each of these "means" expresses itself as a more rigorous form of torment – searching, shaving, the "bootes."

In a sense we have seen something like this in key scenes in Shakespeare: Troilus, in the scene on the walls, reaching for more and more radical means to defend against the idea of Cressida betraying him (the denial of ocular evidence, the "splitting" of Cressida into two Cressidas, the use of radical doubt itself) although in fact these are less defenses against the outward phenomena Troilus watches than they are against his own mounting rage. Antony too turns to more and more desperate measures to ward off the idea of his own effeminization: first to displacement (it is the land that is "ashamed," not Antony, and Caesar not Antony who wore his sword like a dancer) then to denial ("I am Antony yet," he rages) and finally to the whipping of Thidias to convince himself that it is Thidias (not Antony) who is the "boy," Thidias who should have been born a daughter. Indeed we witness something similar in anti-theatrical tracts themselves. In their attempts to manage a contradictory sense of self they first project conflicting ideas of monstrosity and indeterminacy onto the figure of the androgynous actor who seems to lack an inherent gender, then turn to the construction of an epistemology of signs to quell the idea that there are things without inherent genders, then turn to the essentialism necessary to maintain such an epistemology, and finally to the dogmatism necessary to protect essentialism itself from the logical strains it is under. In all of these texts what we see is a progression:

134

as each defense fails, a more radical one must be erected until the defenses themselves become so elaborate that they ultimately break down under the weight of the idea they are designed to ward off.

But we could establish a cultural continuum that worked on the same principle. If the fears at the root of a culture revolved around a constellation of embedded ideas (that representations had the power to alter the things they were only supposed to represent, the more specific version of this fear that costumes had the power to alter the male body itself, the fear this presupposes that there is no essential male body) then one way of dealing with these fears would be to attack the stage, to focus one's anxieties on the institution that specialized in representations, the institution whose existence could in a sense be said to provide a rationale for such anxieties. But what would happen when there was no established institution to provide such a focus – say, in the wilds of Scotland? What would happen when there was no overt institution to focus one's anxieties on would be precisely what happens at the moments in Fian's narrative which can't, by definition, be theatricalized. If only to provide a rationale, the mind would have to invent some version of theatre: a witch with the capacity to create similar representations. And then one might have to torture the witch to make her relinquish her power. And when this failed, reach for more radical tortures until a leg became unrecognizable as a leg.

What I am suggesting is that the torture that erupts in *Newes from Scotland* is just such a "radical defense," part of a cultural continuum that begins with anxiety about the stage (an anxiety that is in some sense safely "contained" just by being anxiety about the stage). I do not mean to suggest that all torture springs from such anxieties or even that all torture of witches in Renaissance England does, but that the torture of the witches "examined" by James in this text represents an extreme case of the same fears shared by Gosson and Prynne.

Where does theatre itself fit into such a picture, into what I have called a cultural continuum? Theatre can become a rationale for anxiety but it can also express anxiety or pass its anxieties onto its own spectators. Shakespeare provides a portrait of theatre doing just that in his depiction of Ulysses who deals with the anxieties of effeminization he and everyone else in the play articulate by creating rage in his spectators, and who deals with the horrified vision of mixture he articulates in the degree speech by engendering just this perception of mixture in Troilus in the scene on the walls. His scenes of theatre pass on to others the anxieties he cannot manage. And in fact, as we have seen, *Troilus and Cressida* itself behaves in the same way, managing its anxieties by fomenting aggression and doubt in its own interpreters.

But an alternative model for managing anxiety would lie in a kind of "working out" of fears through their embodiment in drama itself, a kind of perpetual rehearsal. Like Cleopatra rehearsing her own death to gain mastery, Shakespeare and Jonson rehearse through their plays the attacks of their own attackers, the anxieties of their culture.

Notes

1 All quotations from *Antony and Cleopatra* are taken from *The Riverside Shakespeare*, textual ed. G. Blakemore Evans (Boston: Houghton Mifflin Co., 1974). Cleopatra staging a scene which sends Antony to his suicide epitomizes a fear articulated both in tracts and in plays about the threat theatre poses to its spectator. For the classic study of the opposite fear, the threat posed *by* the spectator and the attendant need to "obliviate him, to deny his presence," see Michael Fried's powerful and exhaustive *Absorption and Theatricality: Painting and Beholder in the Age of Diderot* (Berkeley: University of California Press, 1980), especially p. 103.

2 Stephen Gosson, *The School of Abuse* (1579; rpt. London: The Shakespeare Society, 1841), p. 22, and *Playes Confuted in five Actions*, in Arthur F. Kinney, *Markets of Bawdrie: The Dramatic Criticism of Stephen Gosson*, Salzburg Studies in Literature, No. 4 (Salzburg: Institut für Englische Sprache und Literatur, 1974), p. 181.

3 For a discussion of the way Thomas Greene and Jonas Barish take their terms from *Volpone* and the poems, see chapter 4, notes 1–3.

4 See Jonas Barish, "Jonson and the Loathed Stage," *The Anti-theatrical Prejudice* (Berkeley: University of California Press, 1981), p. 135 for the claim that "Jonson himself would not have countenanced the suggestion that he was attacking theatre in its essence" but would have seen himself as attacking the accidentals of theatre as something publicly performed.

5 For a different version of the way that rehearsal can be a means of conquering (by first absorbing) what is alien, see Steven Mullaney's fascinating "The Rehearsal of Cultures" in his *The Place of the Stage: License, Play and Power in Renaissance England* (University of Chicago Press, 1988), pp. 60–87, especially pp. 68–74.

6 Gosson, *School of Abuse*, p. 19 and Phillip Stubbes, *The Anatomie of Abuses* (1583; rpt. Netherlands: Da Capo Press, 1972), sig. F5$^\text{V}$.

7 *Playes Confuted*, p. 175.

8 See Stephen Orgel, *The Illusion of Power: Political Theatre in the English Renaissance* (Berkeley: University of California Press, 1975), p. 42.

9 See Stephen Greenblatt, "Invisible Bullets; Renaissance Authority and its Subversion," *Glyph 8: The Johns Hopkins Textual Studies* (Baltimore: The Johns Hopkins University Press, 1981), p. 57, and Jonathan Goldberg, *James 1 and the Politics of Literature: Jonson, Shakespeare, Donne, and their*

Contemporaries (Baltimore: The Johns Hopkins University Press, 1983), p. 149.

10 See *Discipline and Punish*, trans. Alan Sheridan (New York: Vintage Books, 1979), p. 26. For Leonard Tennenhouse's reworking of Foucault, see *Power on Display* (New York: Methuen, 1986), especially pp. 14–15 and 120–2.

11 See "Invisible Bullets," p. 56, and p. 1 of *Renaissance Self-fashioning* for the initial claim that in the Renaissance there were "selves, and a sense that they could be fashioned" (Greenblatt, *Renaissance Self-Fashioning* [University of Chicago Press, 1980]).

12 See *James 1 and the Politics of Literature*, p. 151.

13 In a series of fascinating and influential essays, Louis Montrose describes Elizabeth's deployment of her virginity in staging her power. (See "'Eliza, Queene of shepeardes,' and the Pastoral of Power," *English Literary Renaissance*, 10 [1980], 153–82, for instance, for the claim that Elizabeth's hyperbole "renders the marginal states of virginity and poverty as sources of power" [p. 156].) But even in Montrose, deployments of gender are essentially in the service of staging power, which is always the thing conceived of as being performed.

   As numerous critics have suggested, Montrose's later work sees gender and power as more mutually constitutive, but since this later work is less explicitly about theatricalization, it doesn't really imagine gender as existing only in the performance of itself and is thus somewhat tangential to my discussion. (See, for instance, "*A Midsummer Night's Dream* and the Shaping Fantasies of Elizabethan Culture: Gender and Power and Form," in *Rewriting the Renaissance*, ed. Margaret W. Ferguson, Maureen Quilligan and Nancy J. Vickers [Chicago University Press, 1986], pp. 65–87, and "The Work of Gender in the Discourse of Discovery," *Representations*, 33 [1991], 1–41, for arguments particularly sensitive to the compensatory nature of patriarchal forms.)

14 See Judith Butler, *Gender Trouble: Feminism and the Subversion of Identity* (New York: Routledge, 1990) for the following claim: "That the gendered body is performative suggests it has no ontological status apart from the various acts which consistute its reality" (p. 136). See pp. 140–1 for the claim about the possibilities of transformation.

15 My argument differs from many feminist critiques of New Historicism in that most feminist critics who have taken New Historicism to task for paying insufficient attention to the issue of gender have done so primarily by pointing to the discrepancy between "theory" and practice. Thus Marguerite Waller accuses Greenblatt of perpetrating the very colonialist practices he describes. Carol Neely says New Historicism has not taken its own admonitions to historicize seriously enough, and Lynda Boose says that, while "the New Historicist manifesto insists in theory on granting equal status to both the literary and the social text," in practice the literary work is inevitably seen as being historically determined.

   In this attention to the disparity between theory and practice, feminist critiques of New Historicism are not atypical, for most critiques of New Historicism, even when they look like critiques of theory, are really about disparities within the practice. The one notable exception, the one critic to try to isolate something within the "theory" which necessitates the limitations of the practice, is Walter Cohen, who has suggested that the New Historicist assumption that any two things in a culture are related, the belief in "arbitrary connectedness," leads to a synecdoche in which certain texts – like the gynecological ones utilized by Greenblatt in "Fiction and Friction" – come to stand for a whole culture. Like Cohen, my attempt is to understand what in the theory results in the practice. Specifically I seek to identify what in the theory is not being acknowledged, but being passed over in silence: the powerlessness implicit in the epistemology that New Historicism's ontology of power dictates.

For important and valuable feminist critiques of New Historicism, see Carol Thomas Neely, "Constructing the Subject: Feminist Practice and the New Renaissance Discourses," *English Literary Renaissance*, 18 (1988), 5–18, and Lynda Boose's brilliant "The Family in Shakespeare Studies; or – Studies in the Family of Shakespeareans; or – the Politics of Politics," *Renaissance Quarterly*, 40 (1987), 707–42. For other important and valuable critiques of New Historicism, see Valerie Traub's introduction to *Desire and Anxiety* (London: Routledge, 1992); Jean E. Howard, "The New Historicism in Renaissance Studies," *English Literary Renaissance*, 16 (1986), 13–43; Peter Erickson, "Rewriting the Renaissance, Rewriting Ourselves," *Shakespeare Quarterly*, 38 (1987), 327–37; and Edward Pechter, "New Historicism and its Discontents: Politicizing Renaissance Drama," *PMLA*, 102 (1987), 292–302. For crucial work that seeks to compare the limitations of feminism, cultural materialism and New Historicism see Walter Cohen, "Political Criticism of Shakespeare," in *Shakespeare Reproduced: The Text in History and Ideology*, ed. Jean Howard and Marion O'Connor (New York: Methuen, 1987) pp. 18–46. For a response to and critique of feminist critiques of New Historicism and cultural materialism, see Jonathan Dollimore, "Shakespeare, Cultural Materialism, Feminism and Marxist Humanism," *New Literary History*, 21 (1990), 471–93. For Waller's critique of Greenblatt, see Marguerite Waller, "Academic Tootsie: The Denial of Difference and the Difference it Makes," *Diacritics*, 17 (1987), 2–20.

16 In my analysis of the fear that the self is really female, I differ first from those feminist critics who read female transvestism as offering at least a glimpse of an acknowledgement, from a culture accustomed to grounding discussions of gender in the language of essentialism, that femininity is constructed, and second from critics like Stephen Greenblatt who see the transvestite theatre in England as the verifiable sign of the culture's anatomical belief that (teleologically) there is only one gender, a male one. My position is closer to that of Stephen Orgel, who says about Renaissance beliefs about anatomy, "The frightening part . . . for the Renaissance mind, however, is precisely the fantasy of its reversal, the conviction that men can turn into – or be turned into – women; or perhaps more exactly, can be turned *back* into women. . ." The texts I treat exhibit the fear that femininity is neither constructed nor a superficial condition susceptible to giving way to a "real" masculinity, but rather the underlying or default position that masculinity is always in danger of slipping into. In its analysis of a *fear*, my argument is compatible with feminist accounts of the recognition of the constructed nature of gender in the

Renaissance, since it is necessary to reconstruct the logic of a culture's misogyny to understand the nature of resistance offered to it.

For the insistence that transvestism should not be read at all for what it reveals about beliefs about the "real" gender beneath the costume, but as a third kind, see Margorie Garber's *Vested Interests* (New York: Harper, 1992) pp. 1–40. For the opposite claim that homosexuality is not "transvestite masquerade," and that not "all homoeroticism in Renaissance drama is ... legible through considerations of cross-dressing" (p. 110) see Jonathan Goldberg, *Sodometries* (Stanford University Press: 1992, pp. 105–41). Goldberg argues that *Edward II* voices "a different kind of male/male desire" (116) and that "the sodomy inextricable from friendship in this play" is not the sodomy of transvestism. But in his attempt to disassociate the sodomy of Marlowe's play from transvestism, Goldberg categorically contests an association between sodomy and transvestism in anti-theatrical tracts and ascribes to the critics the misogyny and paranoia of the tracts.

For important treatments of transvestism (on the stage, off the stage and in stories performed on stage, male and female) which emphasize the constructed nature of femininity in particular, see Linda Woodbridge's early treatment of *Haec Vir* in *Women and the English Renaissance* (Chicago: University of Illinois Press, 1984), pp. 140–51, especially p. 149; Kathleen McLuskie's "The Act, the Role, and the Actor: Boy Actresses on the Elizabethan Stage," *New Theatre Quarterly* 3 (1987), 120–30; and Jean Howard's important "Cross-dressing, The Theatre, and Gender Struggle in Early Modern England," *Shakespeare Quarterly*, 29 (1988), 418–40. For Stephen Greenblatt's claim, see "Fiction and Friction" in *Reconstructing Individualism*, ed. Thomas C. Heller, Morton Sosna and David E. Wellbery (Stanford University Press, 1986), pp. 30–52 (discussed in the notes to Chapter 6). For Stephen Orgel's critique of the claim, see "Nobody's Perfect: or, Why Did The English Stage Take Boys for Women?" *South Atlantic Quarterly*, 88:1 (1989), 7–30.

I   MEN IN WOMEN'S CLOTHING

1 Stephen Gosson, *The School of Abuse* (1579; rpt. London: The Shakespeare Society, 1841), p. 19.

2 Phillip Stubbes, *The Anatomie of Abuses* (1583; rpt. Netherlands: Da Capo Press, 1972), sig. F5^V.

3 William Prynne, *Histrio-mastix: The Player's Scourge or Actor's Tragedy* (New York: Garland Publishing, 1974), p. 197.

4 Until 1986, almost all explanations of anti-theatricality began by proposing a model of the fixed self as the operative force behind hostility to the stage. (See notes 5, 6 and 9 for a summary of the kinds of selves proposed.) A few exceptions did not propose models of the self but offered instead political explanations. See, for instance, William Ringler's discussion of the tension between the city authorities of London and the Crown: "though the Mayor and Alderman were able to hinder playing, they were not able to suppress it. The royal government supported the actors, and without its assistance the London authorities could not institute effective action" (William Ringler, *Stephen Gosson, a Biographical and Critical Study* [Princeton University Press,

1942], p. 80). What both kinds of explanations failed to account for is the increasing fear of effeminization which comes to dominate anti-theatrical tracts.

The question of how to account for this fear raises an important methodological issue. Though anxieties about gender clearly have political and religious implications as well as the implications about the self which I detail, the difficulty in offering a political explanation lies in establishing a strict correlation between the details of the tracts themselves and any one political situation or gross change in politics or religion which occurred between 1579 and 1642. Any attempt to correlate anxieties about gender with large-scale changes in religious practice – the Puritan rise to power, for instance – would be highly problematic, in part because not all the tract writers considered here were even Puritans. As Ringler demonstrates, Gosson was rabidly anti-Puritan and there were a number of Anglican divines who were as disturbed by theatre as Puritan tract writers were. "Regiocentric" attempts to correlate the increase in anxiety about effeminization with the change from Elizabeth to James would pose similar difficulties. It would be necessary to posit an anxiety about effeminization (of the sort Louis Montrose has brilliantly documented) under Elizabeth, a woman sovereign, which should have been but was not ameliorated by the return of a male monarch in James. This hypothesis would imply an increasing anxiety about James' own indeterminacy based on his homosexual proclivities. But, in fact, two kinds of evidence suggest that just the opposite perception of James may have been operative during the period. Jonathan Goldberg has persuasively shown the extent to which James was received and perceived as the father (as his own rhetoric in treatises like *The Trew Law of Free Monarchies* intended) (see *James I and the Politics of Literature* [Baltimore: The Johns Hopkins University Press, 1983], pp. 85–112, especially "Fatherly Authority: Politics of the Family"). And Alan Bray, in demonstrating the difficulty juries and even homosexuals themselves had in recognizing the most flagrant homosexual behavior *as* homosexuality, has suggested the improbability of even ordinary practicing homosexuals' being recognized as such, let alone kings (see Alan Bray, *Homosexuality in Renaissance England* [London: Gay Men's Press, 1982], esp. pp. 48, 67–70). In fact, slander about James and Buckingham more often involved charges about the enormous amount of money spent than it did sexual innuendo. It is precisely the absence of exact cultural homogeneity from tract to tract, the resistance these texts offer to broad categorization along political lines, which forces the reader to approach the issue of effeminization from the standpoint of internal evidence. (Even the internal evidence resists clear categorization along political lines. It is difficult to generalize for instance about the attitude toward magistrates within anti-theatrical tracts. Gosson's *School of Abuse* idealizes Elizabeth as a queen bent on preserving the valour of her men. Prynne's *Histrio-mastix*, on the other hand, was at least taken as a slur on a later queen's prerogatives. *Mirrour of Monsters*, a tract preoccupied with the problem of how to criticize the queen's licensed players without criticizing the queen, lies somewhere between the two.) For a further discussion of why the "Puritan" argument offers an inadequate explanation of anti-theatricality, see William Ringler's "The First Phase of the

Elizabethan Attack on the Stage, 1558–1579," *The Huntington Library Quarterly*, 5 (1942), 391–418.

Since 1986, critical attention has tended to focus not on explaining anti-theatricality, but on answering questions raised by its presence in England. For an analysis of why the English maintained a transvestite stage, given the anxieties anti-theatricalists articulated, for instance, see Stephen Orgel, "Nobody's Perfect: or, Why did the English Stage Take Boys for Women?" *South Atlantic Quarterly*, 88:1 (1989), 7–30. For an analysis of the opportunities for resistance offered by crossdressing, see Jean Howard, "Crossdressing, the Theatre, and Gender Struggle in Early Modern England," *Shakespeare Quarterly*, 29 (1988), 418–40. Because the subject of crossdressing has become the focal point for many different kinds of discussion, only some of which are relevant to anti-theatricality, I confine myself here to differentiating myself from those critics whose explanations of anti-theatricality spring from radically different conceptions of the self than the one I describe, and (in the notes to the introduction) to differentiating myself from those readings of crossdressing which uncover radically different attitudes toward gender than those I identify in attacks against the stage.

5 Jonas Barish, *The Anti-theatrical Prejudice* (Berkeley: University of California Press, 1981), p. 94. Barish also says, "Players are evil because they try to substitute a self of their own contriving for the one given them by God" (p. 93).

6 I include in the first camp Katherine Eisaman Maus as well as Barish. She says, "It must be clear by now that the same assumptions about the structure of personality underlie all these claims. The anti-theatricalists and antifeminists conceive of an inner, 'real,' self, which is too often profoundly private, and an outer self which, though it should express the reality within, too often conceals or distorts it. The histrionic personality of the actor or the seductress is threatening because it alienates appearances from a real state of affairs." See "Playhouse Flesh and Blood: Sexual Ideology and the Restoration Actress," *English Literary History*, 46 (1979), 595–617 for a brilliant discussion. Where Maus sees a parallelism between the structure of truth and the structure of personality ("Both the theatrical writers and the antifeminists assume that their satiric enterprise uncovers the truth by laying bare, by stripping away, until the splendid and multifarious layers of deception have been forced aside" [p. 605]), I see an antithesis between the two, and argue that essentialism is used as a defense against the fear that there is no such thing as a fixed self. Thomas Greene also argues that Jonson's suspicion of theatricality stems from his belief in the "centripetal" or "centered" self. See his influential "Ben Jonson and the Centered Self," *Studies in English Literature*, 10 (1970), 325–48 for this predecessor of the "absolute" self. To it Greene contrasts the "centrifugal" self which seeks constant change. In fact, Greene's categories of "centripetal" and "centrifugal" are replicated in Barish's "fixed selves" and "proteans." Barish accepts the polarity but reverses the values: protean selves become emblems of Neoplatonism and eventually the Hamlets, Edgars and Cleopatras of Renaissance drama. It is not that Barish proposes the "absolute self" as the operative model of the self in the Renaissance – he does not – but that he poses it as the operative problem behind anti-theatricality that is crucial to my discussion. In fact the same polarities govern Greene's, Barish's

and Greenblatt's work, though they lead them to very different conclusions. Greenblatt's discussion of improvisation fastens on the protean side of the polarity.

7 Stephen Greenblatt's *Renaissance Self-Fashioning* (University of Chicago Press, 1980), p. 2.

8 Greenblatt, *Renaissance Self-Fashioning*, pp. 244–5. See Greenblatt's lengthy comment on the analogy between the Lacanian patient in psychoanalysis, the conditions of theatrical identity, and the intensification of "these governing circumstances" of theatrical identity in "the hero's situation" (p. 245). Greenblatt says: "The resemblance is grounded in the dependence of even the innermost self upon a language that is always necessarily given from without and upon representation before an audience" (p. 245).

9 I have singled out Greenblatt as the most interesting challenge to the notion of a fixed self which inadvertently replicates the notion it calls into question, but the tendency to predicate the notion of a self while trying to posit alternatives is common to less radical treatments as well. Greene's claim about Volpone ("Volpone is Protean man, man without core and ... substance") looks as if it should suggest a character without a self, a core, yet embedded in Greene's very notion of a centrifugal self is a "self" as a structure. See also Anne Ferry's *The Inward Language: The Sonnets of Wyatt, Sidney, Shakespeare and Donne* (University of Chicago Press, 1983) where attempts to prove the word "self" was not used in the early Renaissance are nevertheless belied by assumptions about "interiority."

10 Barish states: "One corollary of the concept of an absolute identity was the belief in an absolute sincerity. If it was possible truly to know the 'uniform, distinct and proper being' one had received from God, then it was possible either to affirm that being in all one's acts – to be 'such in truth' as one was 'in show' – or to deny it by disguise or pretense" (p. 94). The use of the words "affirm" and "deny" clearly presupposes a choice and a faculty, an informed will to exercise that choice. In a very different way, Greenblatt's notion of improvisation is also largely a matter of will, "the opportunistic grasp of that which seems fixed and established ... the ability ... to transform given materials into one's own scenario" (p. 227). Though Barish's description of absolute identity presupposes a restraining will and Greenblatt's description of improvisation presupposes a colonizing will, for both critics, embedded in the notion of the self is an informed will. Both think of this faculty as an instrument to power, though the first critic thinks of power as the capacity to stay the same, to "rule" the self, and the second thinks of power as the capacity to change, to assume temporary shapes in order to rule another. In contrast, in the tracts by anti-theatricalists considered here, the will appears to have been rendered inoperative. This is a world in which each action automatically triggers the next without will or volition: "From pyping to playing, from sleepe to sinne, from sinne to death, from death to the Divel," says Gosson.

11 Gosson, *School of Abuse*, p. 10. The suggestion is underlined by the "Dedication to the Gentlewomen," which makes men in the audience into "wild coultes."

12 Anglo-phile Eutheo (Anthony Munday), *A Second and Third Blast of Retrait from Plaies and Theatres* (London, 1580), pp. 100–1. Munday has a great deal

more to say about theatre as enchantment, including the claim that plays are "snares ... such force have their inchantements of pleasure to drawe the affections of the mind" (p. 97).

13 Munday, *A Second and Third Blast*, p. 101.

14 William Rankins, *A Mirrour of Monsters* (London, 1587) and Phillip Stubbes, *Anatomie of Abuses*. For a discussion of possible affinities between theatrical performances and magical rites (with more positive associations) in the mind of the Elizabethan playgoer, see Montrose, "The Purpose of Playing: Reflections on a Shakespearean Anthropology," *Helios*, n.s. 7 (1980), 51–74, especially pp. 61–2. For a brilliant analysis of the way the association between theatre and pestilence (in London's "moral imagination") came to replace the idea of leprosy, see Steven Mullaney, *The Place of the Stage: License, Play, and Power in Renaissance England* (University of Chicago Press, 1988), pp. 27–59, especially p. 50.

15 Stephen Gosson, *Playes Confuted in five Actions*, in Arthur F. Kinney, *Markets of Bawdrie: The Dramatic Criticism of Stephen Gosson*, Salzburg Studies in Literature, No. 4 (Salzburg: Institut für Englische Sprache und Literatur, 1974), pp. 193–4. All subsequent quotations from *Playes Confuted* are taken from this edition.

16 Munday says, "The citie Marsiles, as Valerian writeth, kept so great gravitie, that it would receave into it no stage-plaiers; because their arguments, for the most parte, contained the actes and doinges of harlots; to the end that *the custome of beholding such things might not also cause a licence of folowing them*" (*A Second and Third Blast*, p. 122 [italics mine]). Similarly, Munday describes the way that seducers in the audience immediately make use of what they see on stage and so replicate it. They estimate the compassion of women near them by asking these women about their responses to characters on stage ("is it not pittie this passioned lover should be so martyred. And if he finde her inclining to foolish pittie, as commonlie such women are, then he applies the matter to himselfe and saies that he is likewise carried awaie with the liking of her" [pp. 98–9]).

17 Gosson, *Playes Confuted*, pp. 192–3.

18 Prynne, *Histrio-mastix*, p. 180.

19 Gosson, *Playes Confuted*, p. 178.

20 Thomas Heywood, *An Apology for Actors in 3 Books*, from the Edition of 1612 compared with that of W. Cartwright (London: Shakespeare Society, 1841), p. 45.

21 Heywood offers a kind of genealogy of heroes who watch theatre and become heroes through theatre. Each is shaped and modeled after the hero before him, and the line leads back from Alexander to Achilles and Achilles to Theseus and Theseus to Hercules, and from Hercules back to Jupiter. In each case the tutor of the hero causes history (the history of the previous hero) to be staged for his charge as a model for emulation. See Heywood, *Apology*, pp. 19–20.

22 See Barish, *The Anti-theatrical Prejudice*, p. 117 ("The defenders usually share the assumptions of their opponents"). Barish discusses the way the anecdote about Caesar provides "a perfect instance of what the reformers had all along been saying, that the theatre brought out all that was bestial in its practitioners," thus justifying authorities' suppression of theatre if "actors lost

themselves in their parts so completely as to mistake them for reality" (p. 119). See also Maus, "Playhouse Flesh and Blood," p. 608: "The anecdotes from which Heywood argues seem absurd; his defense of theatre is continually hindered by his tacit acceptance of his opponents' assumptions."

23 Gosson, *Playes Confuted*, p. 181.
24 Gosson, *School of Abuse*, p. 14.
25 Munday, *A Second and Third Blast*, pp. 63 and 71.
26 Munday, *A Second and Third Blast*, p. 64.
27 Gosson, *Playes Confuted*, p. 183.
28 Munday, *A Second and Third Blast*, p. 69. For Gosson plays are dangerous precisely because they cater to this insatiability: "the longer we gaze, the more we crave, so forcible [comedies] are [that] afterwards but being thought upon they make us seek for the like another time" (*Playes Confuted*, p. 186).
29 Gosson, *Playes Confuted*, p. 186.
30 Gosson, *School of Abuse*, p. 34.
31 William Ringler's statement of this is still the clearest. Of the first phase of the anti-theatrical attack, he says "the [anti-theatrical writers] did not at first object to plays and acting in themselves, but only to the abuses for which the theatres were responsible." Of the second phase, he says: "In this phase not only were the abuses of plays and theatres criticized, but acting by its very nature was declared to be sinful and contrary to the laws of God and man" (*Stephen Gosson*, p. 81). Barish follows Ringler, but accounts for the distinction in terms of the institutionalization of theatre: "Discreetly used, these [early anti-theatrical] writers intimate, the stage might serve to educate. It might help form sober citizens and godly parishioners. But with the building of the playhouses toward the end of the century, the creation of a permanent class of professional actors under the aegis of the crown, and the gradual tightening of government control over all theatrical activity – in short, with the theatre more visibly legitimized and institutionalized than at any time since Greek days – the attack moves into high gear" (*The Anti-theatrical Prejudice*, p. 83).
32 Gosson, *Playes Confuted*, see pp. 176–8.
33 My claim here and throughout is not that anti-theatricalists do not make the claims about absolute identity which Barish and others cite, but that these claims are consistently betrayed by anxieties about effeminization, atavism and the constitutive nature of action itself.
34 Prynne, *Histrio-mastix*, pp. 182–3.
35 *Anatomie of Abuses*, sig. F5$^\text{V}$.
36 Gosson, *School of Abuse*, p. 48.
37 Gosson, *School of Abuse*, p. 19.
38 Gosson, *School of Abuse*, p. 22.
39 Gosson, *Playes Confuted*, p. 175.
40 Gosson, *Playes Confuted*, p. 177. For an excellent discussion of this subject, see Maus, "Playhouse Flesh and Blood," p. 604.
41 Gosson, *Playes Confuted*, p. 175.
42 Gosson, *Playes Confuted*, p. 178.
43 Stubbes, sig. F5$^\text{V}$.
44 Stubbes, sig. F5$^\text{V}$.
45 Stubbes, sig. L8$^\text{V}$.

46 Jonathan Goldberg argues that the passage "need not" refer to male/male sex
(though the thrust of his argument is that anyone who says it can refer to
male/male sex is guilty of a "presumptively heterosexual" misreading). The
evidence he brings to bear from within Stubbes' own text is 1) that the other
time Stubbes refers to "playing the sodomite" he is describing an (adulterous)
man and a woman and 2) that "So little can Stubbes imagine the possibility of
members of the same sex having sex together, that he proposes, as a solution to
the incitement to lust that dancing is said to offer, that men should dance with
men, women with women" (*Sodometries* [Stanford University Press, 1992],
pp. 120–1).

The fact that Stubbes describes a man and woman "playing the vile Sodomites together" does, as Goldberg suggests, indicate sodomy "need not" always
describe male/male sex. But the passages about dancing are much more
problematic than Goldberg presents them as being, for many of them seem to
advocate not same-sex dancing, so much as dancing alone. Thus, in Stubbes'
discussion of Jeptha's daughter ("women are to daunce by themselves [if they
wil needs daunce] and men by themselves" [N5^R]), the sense is as much "dance
alone" as it is "dance in the company of others of their sex." This becomes
clearer in the passage about David (cited as an example of "safe" dancing)
"David danced him selfe alone" (N4^V). There is evidence that what bothers
Stubbes about dancing in the first place is the public nature of it, the fact that,
as with plays, people convene in assemblies to do it. ("All lewde, wanton and
lascivious dauncing in publique assemblies and conventicles, without respect
either of sex, kind, time, place, person, or any thing els," Stubbes complains
[N8^R].) The dancing that Stubbes comes closest to endorsing seems to have to
do with dance as an expression of the internal and private mind. Comparing
the Israelites' dancing and the dancing of the present day, he says the Israelites
danced to show their inward joy of mind for the blessings of God (N3^R). He
even cites the story of a possible origin of dancing among the Sicilian people,
when their tyrant forbade them speech and they learned to dance as a means of
constructing a language "to expresse the inward meaning and intentions of the
minde by ... exterior gestures of the body" [O3^R]. The distinction here has to
do with the function of dancing (private/public; as language/as aphrodisiac)
more than it does the gender of the partner. That Stubbes can not "imagine the
possibility of members of the same sex having sex together" is a long way from
"A 'sodomite' need not be a man who sleeps with other men" and does not
seem so clear to me, not only because of the use of the word "Cynoedus"
(Stubbes compares those of all sexes who are accomplished in dancing to
"Cynoedus the prostitute ribauld") but because the claim that after plays they
"play the sodomite or worse" implies such a strong imitative relation between
what goes on onstage and what goes on afterwards.

Because Goldberg seems at times to misunderstand and at times to misre-
present my argument, I deal with his accusation that I make effeminization
constitutive of homosexuality below.

47 Prynne, *Histrio-mastix*, p. 209.
48 Prynne, *Histrio-mastix*, p. 200.
49 Prynne, *Histrio-mastix*, pp. 209–10.
50 As noted above, Bray brilliantly demonstrates the disparity between the

mythology of sodomy, with its associations of sorcery, world anarchy and demonology, and the encountered experiences of sexual – including homosexual – life. See particularly Bray's account of the trial of Meredith Davy, which suggests that for Davy the disparity was so great that he failed to recognize even his own actions as homosexual, so removed were they from the supernatural tradition to which sodomy belonged (Bray, *Homosexuality in Renaissance England*, pp. 48, 67–70).

51 Prynne, *Histrio-mastix*, p. 185.
52 Prynne, *Histrio-mastix*, p. 197.
53 See note 4 above on the difficulties at stake in various "external" explanations of the increasing anxiety about effeminization from tract to tract.
54 This is the passage Goldberg both misunderstands and misrepresents. What I am saying burgeons into a "personal symptomatology" is not homosexuality ("What Prynne's disease is Levine does not exactly say, but the drift seems clear enough: a man so threatened must be what he is describing" [*Sodometries*, p. 110]), but the method of managing contradictory notions of the self by projecting them outward onto others, the method my argument has been charting all along. Goldberg misquotes the relevant passage the claim is built on, which twice says that what burgeons into personal symptomatology is a "cultural prejudice," not a "cultural discourse," that is, the whole constellation of anxieties within anti-theatrical tracts that are themselves homophobic and misogynist.

In my depiction of sodomy as providing a scapegoat or rationale for these tract writers, my argument is practically analogous to Bray's claim that sodomy functions to explain misfortune in the mythology of the period.
55 *School of Abuse*, p. 24.
56 Even when Gosson does imagine a scene in which effeminate clothing is related to the humiliation and effeminization of men, the personal details about effeminization are somehow subordinate to national concerns. When Gosson imagines, for instance, a woman telling men that they are "unworthy of the name of men" – an idea that would strike panic into Stubbes or Prynne – the woman is a Briton and the men are Romans: "Bunduica, a notable woman and a Queene of Englande that time that Nero was Emperor of Rome, having some of the Romans in a garrison heere against her, in an oration which she made to her subjects, seemed uterly to contemn ... them unworthy of the name of men, or title of souldiers, because they were smoothely appareled, soft lodged, daintely ... strewed with poulders, wine swillers, singers, dauncers and players" (*School of Abuse*, p. 28). Not only are the men Romans, but Romans under a play-loving emperor. In contrast, Gosson is quick to point out, England is blessed with Elizabeth, a queen bent on preserving the valor of her men by turning them into soldiers. Neither "Rome nor France, nor tyrant nor Turke dare for their lives to enter the list" (p. 29) with England. Though individual elements of the passage evoke the fears of effeminization that we see in later tracts, they are here contained by the idea of military valor. In fact, Gosson uses them actually to build a case for the bravery of the English military.
57 Gosson, *Playes Confuted*, Dedication to Walsingham.

2 *TROILUS AND CRESSIDA* AND THE POLITICS OF RAGE

1 For a lucid summary of the history of skepticism during the Renaissance and, in particular, the way Reformation and Counter-Reformation debates utilized the arguments of classical skepticism, see Richard Popkin's *The History of Skepticism From Erasmus to Spinoza* (Berkeley: University of California Press, 1979). What the scene on the walls brings about in Troilus is the loss of a criterion, and in this sense he could be said to experience not only the crisis of skepticism but the history of the Renaissance itself, since Reformation and Counter-Reformation history could be characterized as the search to restore that criterion that became dislodged once Luther attacked the Pope as fallible.

   All quotations from *Troilus and Cressida* are taken from *The Riverside Shakespeare*, textual ed. G. Blakemore Evans (Boston: Houghton Mifflin Co., 1974).
2 Stephen Gosson, *The School of Abuse*, p. 19.
3 For the question of "what sexual jealousy has to do with drama," see Katherine Eisaman Maus, "Horns of Dilemma: Jealousy, Gender and Spectatorship in English Renaissance Drama," *English Literary History*, 54 (1987), 561–83. Where Maus focuses on an actual analogy between cuckold and spectator, my interest is on the *function* a theatre which produces rage in its spectator is imagined to have, i.e. a recuperative function. For Stanley Cavell's classic reading of skepticism itself as a "cover story...the attempt to convert the human condition, the condition of humanity into an intellectual difficulty, a riddle" and for the working out of this "cover" in *Othello*, see *The Claim of Reason: Wittgenstein, Skepticism, Morality, and Tragedy* (Oxford University Press, 1982), pp. 483–96, especially p. 493.
4 For the distinction between Academic and Pyrrhonic skepticism, see Popkin, pp. xiii–xv.
5 For classical advocates of Pyrrhonism treating it as a purge, see Popkin, p. xv ("Skepticism was a cure for the disease called Dogmatism or rashness. But, unlike Academic skepticism, which came to a negative dogmatic conclusion from its doubts, Pyrrhonian skepticism made no such assertion, merely saying that skepticism is a purge that eliminates everything including itself"). For Montaigne's allusion to the Pyrrhonist's notion of purge and his repetition of the rhubarb metaphor, see his *Apology for Raymond Sebond* in *The Complete Essays of Montaigne*, trans. Donald M. Frame (Stanford University Press, 1958), pp. 392–3. Montaigne says: "They [the Pyrrhonians] have been constrained to take refuge in their comparison from medicine, without which their attitude would be inexplicable: when they declare 'I do not know' or 'I doubt' they say that this proposition carries itself away with the rest, no more nor less than rhubarb, which expels evil humors and carries itself off with them" (p. 393). All subsequent Montaigne quotations are from this edition and translation. For Montaigne's "skeptical practice of writing," and an account of the assumptions built into the logic of language itself necessitating such a practice, see Victoria Kahn's brilliant discussion of Montaigne in *Rhetoric, Prudence, and Skepticism in the Renaissance* (Ithaca: Cornell University Press, 1985), pp. 115–51. For her discussion of the rhubarb as neither literal nor figurative, see pp. 117–18. For the argument that Tudor plays in general can be thought of as

questions and for the origins of this tradition in the "mental cultivation of ambivalence," see Joel B. Altman, *The Tudor Play of Mind* (Berkeley: University of California Press, 1979), pp. 31–63, especially p. 32 and p. 43.

6 Popkin, p. xv: "Skepticism for them [the Pyrrhonians] was an ability or mental attitude for opposing evidence both pro and con on any question about what was non-evident, so that one would suspend judgment on the question. This state of mind then led to a state of *ataraxia*, quietude, or unperturbedness, in which the skeptic was no longer concerned or worried about matters beyond appearances." For Montaigne on the goal of ataraxy, see p. 372 of *Raymond Sebond*: "Now this attitude of their [the Pyrrhonians'] judgment, straight and inflexible, taking in all things without adherence or consent, leads them to their ataraxy, which is a peaceful and a sedate condition of life, exempt from the agitations we receive through the impression of the opinions and knowledge we think we have of things, whence are born fear, avarice, envy, immodest desires, ambition, pride, superstition, love of novelty, rebellion, disobedience, obstinacy, and most bodily ills."

7 For an analysis of this passage, see J. Hillis Miller, "Ariachne's Broken Woof," *The Georgia Review*, 31:1 (1977), 47–60. For a different sense of the way Cressida (and "woman" in the play) are made to undergo fragmentation, see Carol Cook, "Unbodied Figures of Desire," *Theater Journal*, 38:1 (1986), 34–52, especially p. 36.

8 I call it a play-within-a-play scene in part because the sheer number of asides calls attention to its status *as* performance:

AJAX: A paltry, insolent fellow!
NESTOR: (aside) How he describes himself!
AJAX: Can he not be sociable?
ULYSSES: (aside) The raven chides blackness.
AJAX: I'll let his humors blood.
AGAMEMNON: (aside) He will be the physician that should be the patient.
AJAX: An all men were of my mind –
ULYSSES: (aside) Wit would be out of fashion.   (II.iii.208–16)

While considered as a discrete scene, the moral of II.iii seems to be that things don't exist in themselves, but only in relation to each other – Thersites can't define Agamemnon except in relation to others, Agamemnon tells Patroclus to tell Achilles that virtues don't exist in their own right, but only *in relation* to how they are beheld by the person who possesses them – what the play-within-the-play inside the scene does is teach its unwitting spectator Ajax to forget his "relation," to behold his virtues wrongly.

9 Stephen Gosson, *Playes Confuted in five Actions*, p. 181.

10 Ulysses must know that Troilus loves Cressida. At the end of IV.v, after agreeing to take him to Calchas' tent, he has coyly asked, "Had she no lover there / That wails her absence?" (lines 288–9) and Troilus has virtually admitted that he is that lover:

O, sir, to such as boasting show their scars
A mock is due. Will you walk on, my lord?
She was belov'd, she lov'd: she is, and doth:
But still sweet love is food for fortune's tooth.   (IV.v.290–3)

It is presumably general knowledge in the Grecian camp, since Diomedes has both heard Aeneas say "Troilus had rather Troy were borne to Greece / Then Cressid borne from Troy" (IV.i.47–8) and been told by Troilus "If e'er thou stand at mercy of my sword / Name Cressid, and thy life shall be as safe / As Priam is in Ilion" (IV.iv.114–16). In any case, watching Troilus watch Cressida in V.ii, Ulysses can hardly be in doubt after the first ten lines. Yet some 150 lines later, after watching Troilus rave "Cressid is mine, tied with the bonds of heaven" (line 154) he coyly asks Troilus, "May worthy Troilus be half attached / With that which here his passion doth express?" (V.ii.161–2). The line both establishes his disingenuousness and calls into question his earlier behavior. His injunctions to "contain" have to be seen within a context of actions which manufacture for Troilus feelings increasingly difficult to contain.

11 Gosson, *Playes Confuted*, p. 186.

12 Troilus' use of the word "will" here is, of course, directly antithetical to the sense in which I use it when I claim that Ulysses' model of a self in the degree speech is one with the "will" rendered inoperative. Here, in Troilus' use of the word, the sense is not of a restraining will, a governor of the appetites in the sense in which we use the word, but rather the sense of the appetite itself.

13 For Montaigne, the problem of Pyrrhonism is built into the affirmative nature of language itself. Here is the passage in its entirety:

I can see why the Pyrrhonian philosophers cannot express their general conception in any manner of speaking; for they would need a new language. Ours is wholly formed of affirmative propositions, which to them are utterly repugnant; so that when they say "I doubt," immediately you have them by the throat to make them admit that at least they know and are sure of this fact, that they doubt. Thus they have been constrained to take refuge in this comparison from medicine, without which their attitude would be inexplicable: when they declare "I do not know" or "I doubt" they say that this proposition carries itself away with the rest, no more nor less than rhubarb, which expels evil humors and carries itself off with them. *This idea is more firmly grasped in the form of interrogation: "What do I know" – the words I bear as a motto, inscribed over a pair of scales.* (*Apology*, pp. 392–3, italics mine)

14 On "splitting" as a defense against rage and other destructive impulses during infancy, see Melanie Klein, "The Theory of Anxiety and Guilt," in *Envy and Gratitude & Other Works 1946–1963* (New York: Delta, 1975), p. 34, as well as other essays in this collection.

15 Gosson, *School of Abuse*, p. 14.

16 Thus in every scene he stages, Ulysses offers an assault on the spectator's self and either seeks to or succeeds in enraging his spectator. In his re-enactments of Patroclus' satires, in the conspiracy scene against Ajax, and in the pageant of Greek warriors, that assault is the means of provoking rage. In the scene on the walls, the production of rage is itself the means of destroying the self.

What is interesting about the progression of scenes is that the rage Ulysses produces becomes increasingly less susceptible to being explained as in the service of winning the war. Goading Nestor can be seen as part of a strategy for enlisting Nestor in the lottery plot. Goading Ajax can be seen as stirring up the requisite rage in Ajax to meet Hector's challenge. But even here there is something wrong, for Ajax does not emerge enraged at Hector but enraged at Achilles. The pageant of Greek warriors is clearly in the service of getting Achilles back into the war, but why does Ulysses want Troilus in the war?

17 This is because embedded within the praise, and its implied ideal self, is another vision of an inferior, more degraded self. From the very beginning, this inferior self is dangled before Ajax when Agamemnon acknowledges that Achilles thinks he is better than Ajax. A bit later, Ulysses suggests that for Ajax to "go to" Achilles would be to "stale [his] palm" and "assubjugate his merit." He links, that is, the idea of an inferior Ajax to a line of conciliatory action, by implication makes Ajax's praise and the better self it implies contingent on aggression. By the end of the scene Ajax is ready to kill: "Would he were a Troyan."

18 For Heywood's genealogy of heroes who watch theatre and become heroes through theatre, see Thomas Heywood, *An Apology for Actors in 3 Books*, from the Edition of 1612 compared with that of W. Cartwright (London: Shakespeare Society, 1841), pp. 19–20.

19 In his powerful and influential essay, "The Politics of Desire in *Troilus and Cressida*", Rene Girard argues that Ulysses is "fascinated with the politics of desire" (p. 208). Noting key structural parallels between Ulysses and Cressida in what he refers to respectively as the "political realm" and the "erotic realm," he argues that they adopt identical strategies. What Girard's formulation does not account for is the politics of the rage Ulysses systematically produces, a rage that refuses to compartmentalize the realms of "political" and "erotic," shaping the "political" in its defense against the "erotic." See "The Politics of Desire in *Troilus and Cressida*," in *Shakespeare and the Question of Theory*, ed. Patricia Parker and Geoffery Hartman (New York: Methuen, 1985), pp. 188–209.

20 Eric Mallin reads these lines as primarily built not around an opposition between war and love but an opposition between the sexual objects Achilles can "throw down," Hector or Polyxena. Accordingly, he reads the war as "the use of...woman as pretext and pretense for the enthusiastic display of male desires to and before other men" (p. 162). Where Mallin reads woman (and by extension the war itself) as a pretext for male display, I read the martial "display" as constitutive of masculinity itself. See Eric Mallin, "Emulous Factions and the Collapse of Chivalry: *Troilus and Cressida*," *Representations*, 29 (1990), 145–79.

21 In any case, it is love which is conceived of as effeminizing men, by dragging them away from war. Patroclus says:

> Sweet, rouse yourself, and the weak wanton Cupid
> Shall from your neck unloose his amorous fold,
> And like a dewdrop from the lion's mane,
> Be shook to air.   (III.iii.222–5)

22 For a similar sense of anxieties of effeminization as contagious, see Canidius' claim that "Our leader's led / And we are women's men," in *Antony and Cleopatra* (III.vii.69–70).

23 Operating from very different theoretical premises and in an attempt to solve very different kinds of problems, both Valerie Traub and Linda Charnes have made analogous points. Traub speaks of the military action that "constitutes" the male subject, and Charnes, in the context of a complex argument about

the way Shakespeare solves the representational problems implicit in inheriting his story, says, "Helen and the war she enables provide these male characters with the necessary means for realizing their notorious identities," (p. 437). For Charnes it is Ulysses' "member" that is made "still" in Patroclus' and Achilles' satires (p. 435). For two compelling treatments of the play, see Valerie Traub, "Invading bodies/bawdy exchanges: disease, desire and representation," in her *Desire and Anxiety* (London: Routledge, 1992), pp. 71–87, and Linda Charnes, "'So Unsecret to Ourselves': Notorious Identity and the Material Subject in Shakespeare's *Troilus and Cressida*," *Shakespeare Quarterly*, 40:4 (1989), 413–40.

24 The lack of unanimity within the critical tradition itself suggests the play's refusal to allow us to know what Cressida is. Grant L. Voth and Oliver Evans claim "one judgment [about *Troilus and Cressida*] has remained constant: Cressida is a mere prostitute...Falsehood in Love" and catalogue the string of critics who have seen her this way ("Cressida and the World of the Play," *Shakespeare Studies*, 8 [1975], 231–9). In contrast, Girard makes her the one first betrayed, rather than the betrayer, and takes her speech in I.ii not only as "true" in the sense of offering an index to her own behavior, but as a universal truth about male desire. A third tradition makes her identity either an index to or dependent on the society that defines it. See Gayle Greene, "Shakespeare's Cressida: 'A Kind of Self,'" in *The Woman's Part: Feminist Criticism of Shakespeare*, ed. Carolyn Ruth Swift Lenz, Gayle Greene, and Carol Thomas Neely (Urbana: University of Illinois Press, 1980), pp. 133–49 for a moral version of the claim that "Cressida is the sum total of 'opinions' of men whose opinions are in themselves societally determined" and Jonathan Dollimore, for the claim that "the discontinuity in Cressida's identity stems not from her nature but from her position in the patriarchal order" and that "identity" in general "is a function of position." See *Radical Tragedy: Religion, Ideology and Power in the Drama of Shakespeare and his Contemporaries* (University of Chicago Press, 1984), p. 48. Even within feminist criticism, the splits about how to take crucial moments in Cressida's behavior suggest a basic resistance within the play toward allowing us to know what Cressida is. Greene, for instance, reads the kiss scene as evidence that Cressida has betrayed Troilus, while Charnes reads it as a virtual gang rape. As I do, Janet Adelman argues for a basic inconsistency in the play's characterization of Cressida, which forces us to undergo the same experience as Troilus in V.ii, but for her, the content of that "experience" is "the act of splitting that is essential to the preservation of his union with an idealized maternal figure," (p. 137) rather than the radical doubt that (I argue) the play depicts as the experience of all spectators – all spectators at the hands of Ulysses. For Adelman the inconsistency in Cressida doesn't begin until IV.v, just before it begins for Troilus himself. I would argue that it is there from practically the beginning of the play. See "'This Is and Is Not Cressid': The Characterization of Cressida," in *The (M)other Tongue*, ed. Shirley Nelson Garner, Claire Kehane, and Madelon Sprengnether (Ithaca: Cornell University Press, 1985), pp. 119–41.

25 At the same time, by offering an incoherent Cressida, it prevents a dangerous identification on the part of female spectators in the audience.

26 Gosson, *School of Abuse*, p. 39.

3 "STRANGE FLESH": *ANTONY AND CLEOPATRA* AND THE STORY OF THE
DISSOLVING WARRIOR

1 William Prynne, *Histrio-mastix* (New York: Garland Publishing, 1974), p.
   197.
2 All quotations from *Antony and Cleopatra* are taken from *The Riverside
   Shakespeare*, textual ed. G. Blakemore Evans (Boston: Houghton Mifflin Co.,
   1974).
3 For my discussion of Orgel, Greenblatt, Goldberg and Foucault and others,
   see my introduction.
4 For a brilliant account of the performative notion of gender from a different
   perspective, see Judith Butler's *Gender Trouble: Feminism and the Subversion of
   Identity* (New York: Routledge, 1990), particularly "Subversive Bodily Acts,"
   pp. 139–42. My analysis differs from Butler's in that where she is interested in
   the liberating possibilities implicit in regarding gender as an "act" ("The
   possibilities of gender transformation are to be found precisely in the arbitrary
   relation between such acts, in the possibility of a failure to repeat" [p. 141]), I
   focus on the implicit powerlessness of living in a world in which gender is a
   highly codified, culturally prescribed performance, which by definition simply
   cannot be enacted.
5 In the past decade or so of *Antony and Cleopatra* criticism, two kinds of
   criticism have flourished which are relevant to the argument I pose below. On
   the one hand, a number of critics writing from within feminist and psychoanalytic perspectives have focused on the issue of gender construction in the play.
   On the other, as Renaissance criticism has, in general, grown more preoccupied
   with the issue of theatricality, *Antony and Cleopatra* critics have grown increasingly attentive to issues of theatricality (particularly Cleopatra's) within the
   play. What has not been sufficiently explored (and what lies at the intersection
   of the two approaches) is the way that masculinity itself is presented as a
   theatrical construction in *Antony and Cleopatra*, a role that must be performed
   in order to exist. My argument differs from previous treatments of gender in
   the play, then, first in its focus on masculinity as a performance and the crisis
   generated when this "performance" breaks down. Second, it seeks to ground
   this conception of masculinity as a performance in a culturally specific debate
   during the period, a debate invoked by the play at many points, but not the
   least in the figure of Caesar who parrots the rhetoric of anti-theatrical tracts.
   Unlike those gender critics who approach the problem of effeminization
   within the play by turning to psychoanalytic concepts like regression, fear of
   the mother, the need to differentiate oneself from the mother, I turn to the
   logic provided by attacks against the stage during the period in the narrative of
   the dissolving warrior, a logic in which "doing" leads to "being."
   For important treatments of gender in the play, see Madelon Gohlke's "'I
   wooed thee with my sword': Shakespeare's Tragic Paradigms," in *The
   Woman's Part: Feminist Criticism of Shakespeare*, ed. Carolyn Ruth Swift
   Lenz, Gayle Greene and Carol Thomas Neely (Urbana: University of Illinois
   Press, 1980), pp. 150–70, which argues that although "throughout Shakespeare's tragedies the imagery of heterosexual union involves the threat of
   mutual or self-inflicted violence," Cleopatra is nevertheless Antony's "point of

orientation, his source of signification" (pp. 160–1) and her later "The Boy Actor and Femininity in *Antony and Cleopatra*" in *Shakespeare's Personality*, ed. Norman N. Holland, Sidney Homan, and Bernard J. Paris (Berkeley: University of California Press, 1989), pp. 191–205, which argues that in making Cleopatra allude to her underlying masculinity, Shakespeare is able to equivocate "on the question of gender," to portray woman as "other" and "not other" (192), Carol Neely's "Gender and Genre in *Antony and Cleopatra*" in *Broken Nuptials in Shakespeare's Plays* (New Haven: Yale University Press, 1985), which argues that "in *Antony and Cleopatra* genre boundaries are not dissolved but enlarged ... gender distinctions, too, are not dissolved but are explored, magnified" (p. 165), Constance Brown Kuriyama's "The Mother of the World: a Psychoanalytic Interpretation of Shakespeare's *Antony and Cleopatra*," *English Literary Renaissance*, 7 (1977), 321–51, which sees Antony's dissolution as a regressive aspect of an incestuous fantasy, and Janet Adelman's "Making Defect Perfection," in *Suffocating Mothers: Fantasies of Maternal Origin in Shakespeare's Plays* (New York: Routledge, 1992), pp. 174–92, which argues that "in [Shakespeare's] recovery of Antony through Cleopatra's dream of bounty, Shakespeare brings [Antony's] masculinity back to life" (p. 177). Because this fascinating essay only became available after my own book was done and as it covers some of the same moments (though from a radically different perspective coming to radically different conclusions) I have tried to indicate below some points of difference. For Adelman's earlier treatment of Antony's effeminization in a mythological context, and her discussion of the way that loss of identity for Antony constitutes a kind of identity, see her exhaustive study, *The Common Liar* (New Haven: Yale University Press, 1973), especially pp. 90–92 and 125–50. For a psychoanalytic treatment of the difficulty of establishing masculinity (in other Shakespeare texts) see Coppélia Kahn, *Man's Estate: Masculine Identity in Shakespeare* (Berkeley: University of California Press, 1981).

For crucial treatments of Cleopatra's theatricality, see in particular Ruth Nevo's "The Masque of Greatness," *Shakespeare Studies*, 3 (1968), 111–28, and Phyllis Rackin's "Shakespeare's Boy Cleopatra, the Decorum of Nature and the Golden World of Poetry," *PMLA*, 87 (1972), 201–12, both discussed below. For a crucial reading of Cleopatra as theatricalizing the world for Antony and the proposition that this offers one version of the "overcoming of skepticism" see Stanley Cavell's *Disowning Knowledge in Six Plays by Shakespeare* (Cambridge University Press, 1987), especially pp. 36–7.

6 In a similar way, Gosson displaces all that is effeminizing and dangerous onto Rome. See *School of Abuse*, pp. 24–8, for comparisons between the manliness of old England and the effeminacy of ancient Rome. Shakespeare's cognizance of this, his putting in the mouth of Rome exactly what was said about Rome in anti-theatrical tracts, is one of his ways of ironizing Rome, and hence anti-theatricality itself.

7 Munday, *A Second and Third Blast*, p. 69.

8 Gosson, *Playes Confuted*, p. 186.

9 For the most complete treatment of *Antony and Cleopatra* in relation to its various mythological traditions, see Adelman, *The Common Liar* as cited above. Adelman cites many of the same passages on Antony's effeminization

and loss of identity that I do, but where she argues ultimately that Antony's loss of a self involves a reconstitution of self ("As Antony loses his soldiership, his authority, and even his visible shape, he is nonetheless Antony" [p. 145]), I argue that in the world of this play the masculine "self" is imagined to exist in the first place only through the performance of itself. In contrast to both arguments, Madelon Sprengnether suggests implicitly that it is masculinity that is the underlying reality –"Shakespeare's carefully staged reminders that his women are really men"– and that by alluding to this Shakespeare diminishes the threat of Cleopatra's emasculating powers. See "The Boy Actor and Femininity in *Antony and Cleopatra*" as cited above, especially pp. 202–3.

There are two traditions of the Hercules and Omphale story on which this incident is modeled and these two traditions generate two antithetical interpretations. One originates in the *Heroides*, and the other in the *Fasti*. Deianira's version of Hercules and Omphale switching clothing in the *Heroides* is essentially a story of effeminization, where Hercules' effeminate deeds rob him of utterance itself: "These deeds can you recount, gaily arrayed in a Sidonian gown? Does not your dress rob from your tongue all utterance?" See Ovid, *Heroides and Armores*, trans. Grant Showerman (Cambridge, MA: Harvard University Press, 1977), p. 115. The Fasti version of the story, on the other hand, emphasizes not effeminization, but both the playful quality of the transvestitism and the way it actually constitutes a disguise, a protection, even as it brings about a near encounter with homosexuality. Omphale is protected from the intruder Faunus, as, deceived by the woman's clothing, he gropes Hercules in the darkness:

Next he touched the soft drapery of the neighboring couch, and its deceptive touch beguiled him. He mounted and laid down on the nearer side...There he encountered legs that bristled with thick rough hair. When he would have proceeded further, the Tirynthian hero thrust him away of a sudden, and down he fell from the top of the bed. There was a crash.

See *Ovid's Fasti*, trans. Sir James George Frazer (Cambridge, MA: Harvard University Press, 1951), p. 83.

Sidney's *Arcadia* reinterprets the two traditions of the story when Pyrocles, in love, disguises himself as Zelmane the Amazon. Musidorus takes the position taken by Deianira when he argues that Pyrocles' love has not only "subvert[ed] the course of nature, making reason give place to sense," but that love is essentially contagious, "that it doth transform the very essence of the lover into the thing loved" (i.e. a woman). Pyrocles himself takes a position more like that of the *Fasti*. For although Pyrocles' song confesses him "transform'd" and weakened: ("Transform'd in show, but more transform'd in mind"), and the jewel he wears depicts Hercules "with a distaff in his hand, as he once was by Omphale's commandment," the motto on the jewel is "never more valiant," suggesting that Hercules (and by extension Pyrocles) has never been more valiant than when transformed by love. See Sir Philip Sidney, *The Countess of Pembroke's Arcadia* (Harmondsworth: Penguin, 1977), pp. 131–4.

The Roman point of view about Antony is the logical extension of the views advanced by Deianira and Musidorus (respectively) that shame follows effeminization, and that loving a woman makes you into a woman. Cleopatra's point of view (that Antony is greatest in his love) follows from the motto on

Pyrocles' brooch, and (less obviously) those elements of the *Fasti* story which emphasize sexual play, and religious purification, love being something that Cleopatra presents *as* religion.

10 Jonathan Dollimore calls Antony's obsession with private sword-show with Caesar an "attempt to dissociate Caesar's power from his individual virtue." Describing Enobarbus' amazement at Antony's stupidity, Dollimore says, "in Enobarbus' eyes, Antony's attempt to affirm a self-sufficient identity confirms *exactly the opposite*" (p. 210). At times, Dollimore seems to see Antony's preoccupation with virility as a response to the loss of "real power": "As effective power slips from Antony he becomes obsessed with reasserting his sense of himself as (in his dying words) 'the greater prince o'the world'" (p. 210). At times, as I do, he sees the preoccupation with politics as a response to or defense against anxieties about gender, as when he says, "Correspondingly, [Antony's] willingness to risk everything by fighting on Caesar's terms ... has much more to do with reckless overcompensation for his own experienced powerlessness, his fear of impotence, than the largesse of a noble soul" (*Radical Tragedy*, p. 210).

11 In *Totem and Taboo*, Freud says, "The higher motives for cannibalism among primitive races have a similar origin. By incorporating parts of a person's body through the act of eating, one at the same time acquires the qualities possessed by him" (see *Totem and Taboo*, trans. James Strachey [New York: W.W. Norton, 1950], p. 82). In a similar way, Antony seeks to "incorporate" the sword and the masculinity it signifies back into his own body.

12 Stubbes, sig. F5^V.

13 Gosson, *School of Abuse*, p. 37.

14 Gosson, *School of Abuse*, p. 24.

15 Gosson, *School of Abuse*, p. 24.

16 Where Adelman calls Caesar the "spokesman for the realm of scarcity" and reads the Antony at Modena speech as the locus for his repudiation of appetite, I read that speech as containing within it contradictions which betray Caesar's tacit glorification of the very appetites he would repudiate. Where Adelman reads Caesar's relation to Antony primarily as oedipal (even the encomium which expresses his "longing" serves the function of "recuperating the damaged image of paternal masculinity, in effect re-inventing the father-figure Caesar needs as the basis for his own stringent masculinity," p. 180), I read Caesar's relation to Antony as primarily homoerotic. For me, the crucial rewriting of Plutarch in the Antony at Modena passage lies in the fact that in Plutarch, Antony and Caesar fought on opposite sides. For Caesar to long for the Antony who "ate strange flesh" (when in fact he fought against this Antony) is to long to share these appetites with Antony. Adelman gestures toward this reading in a footnote, but for her the primary relation Caesar bears to Antony is an oedipal one. See Adelman, "Making Defect Perfection."

17 In his second contribution to the theory of sex, Freud says of pregenital organization, "One of the first such pregenital organizations is the oral, or if one will, the cannibalistic. Here the sexual activity is not separated from the taking of nourishment and the contrasts within it are not yet differentiated. The object of one activity is also that of the other: the sexual aim then consists

in the incorporation of the object into one's own body, the prototype of identification" (see *Three Contributions to the Theory of Sex* in *Basic Writings of Sigmund Freud*, ed. and trans. A. A. Brill [New York: Modern Library, 1968], p. 597). In "Instincts and their Vicissitudes," Freud talks about early love in this way: "first devouring, a kind of love which is compatible with abolition of any separate existence on the part of the object and which may therefore be designated as ambivalent" (see *General Psychological Theory*, ed. Philip Rieff [New York: Collier Books, 1963], p. 102).

18 See Appendix V., p. 243 in the Arden *Antony and Cleopatra*, ed. M.R. Ridley (London: Methuen, 1982).

19 See Eve Kosofsky Sedgwick's *Between Men: English Literature and Male Homosocial Desire* (New York: Columbia University Press, 1985).

20 I do not mean to suggest here that there is only one sexual modality per gender or that gender dictates sexuality, but that the operative fantasy is that in "doing" what a woman "does" when she even responds to a man, one becomes like a woman. I hasten to add that this is not my fantasy, but the fantasy of the anti-theatrical tracts Caesar replicates.

21 If Caesar seems to emerge as the villain here, the cause of misogyny I describe, it is not his homoeroticism, but the disallowing of it and of all eroticism which, the play suggests, creates and supports that misogyny.

22 Both Rackin and Nevo make similar points. Rackin's argument differs from mine in that the antithesis she imagines to Cleopatra's show (embodied in the Roman distrust of illusion and show) is neoclassicism, rather than the anti-theatricality of the attacks. Nevo offers quite a detailed argument about the prevalence of Cleopatra's imagery in masques and triumphs of the time and a reading of the anti-masque/masque structure of Caesar's fantasy of triumph and Cleopatra's final scene. My reading differs from hers in the degree to which I see theatre itself as constitutive throughout the play. Thus Cleopatra's presentation of herself as Isis, Venus, mother, wife, constitutes her "self."

23 The first claim comes, of course, from Greenblatt's *Renaissance Self-Fashioning*, p. 1, the second from Goldberg's *James I and the Politics of Literature*, p. 151.

24 For readings which identify Cleopatra with Elizabeth, see Helen Morris, "Queen Elizabeth I 'Shadowed' in Cleopatra," *Huntington Library Quarterly*, 32 (1969), 271–8, and Keith Rinehart's "Shakespeare's Cleopatra and England's Elizabeth," *Shakespeare Quarterly*, 23 (1972), 81–6, both of which draw their arguments from the parallel between Elizabeth's interrogation of Mary's ambassador in 1564 and Cleopatra's scene with the messenger in II.v. My own interest in the parallel has more to do with the attitude toward theatricality both sovereigns exhibit, a topic I pursue in the manuscript essay, "Imagining a Self: Elizabethan Nostalgia and Jacobean Anti-theatricality in *Antony and Cleopatra*." Although Leonard Tennenhouse reads the suicide in just the opposite way, with Shakespeare denying Cleopatra "the privilege of committing suicide in the Roman manner," he too sees the play as an elegy "for the signs and symbols which legitimized Elizabethan power," the single most important of which was "the desiring and desired woman." See Tennenhouse, *Power on Display*, p. 146.

4   THEATRE AS OTHER: JONSON'S *EPICOENE*

1 See Jonas Barish, "Jonson and the Loathed Stage," *The Anti-theatrical Prejudice* (Berkeley: University of California Press, 1981) pp. 153–4. Greene similarly characterizes Jonson as ambivalent, as "taken by [his disguisers'] arts in spite of himself" (*Every Man in His Humor*) and betraying a "half-repressed envy for the homeless and centrifugal spirit" (*Volpone*). See "Ben Jonson and the Centered Self," *Studies in English Literature 1500–1900*, 10 (1970), 336–7.

2 For Thomas Greene, the poems are the defining moments because they provide the greatest intuitions "of the gathered self." For Barish, the tributes to Pembroke, Lady Katherine Aubigny, Penshurst, embody the "real" and the plays are defined in relation to them. ("When we turn to the plays we find that in them Jonson does not shed his anti-theatrical bias: Rather he builds it in; he makes the plays critiques of the instability they incarnate.") See Greene, "Ben Jonson and the Centered Self," p. 331 and Barish, *The Anti-theatrical Prejudice*, p. 145. Stanley Fish's revisionary work on Jonson's poems is both indebted to this tradition and a re-interpretation of it. Fish's argument attributes implicitly anti-theatrical values to Jonson in its claim that Jonson's poems are "anti-representational" ("Representation is the line of work that Jonson's poems are almost never in, except when their intention is to discredit; and indeed, it is a discreditable fact about any object that it is available for representation" [p. 34]). But so powerful is the aura of theatricality that surrounds Jonson's work that Fish's argument is ultimately made in performative terms: Jonson's poems "act out" their anti-representational epistemology (p. 33). See Stanley Fish, "Authors-Readers, Jonson's Community of the Same," *Representations*, 7 (1984), 26–58.

3 See Greene and Barish for readings of Jonson's anti-theatricality springing from moral/philosophical positions. Greene, who set the defining terms for discussion, associates characters who are *not* theatrical with the concept of an "inner moral equilibrium" (p. 329) and talks about the "sinful thirst for perpetual metamorphosis" (p. 339): "*Volpone* asks us to consider the infinite, exhilarating and vicious freedom to alter the self at will once the ideal of moral constancy has been abandoned" (p. 337). Barish, elaborating (and alluding directly to Greene), details Jonson's "puritanical uneasiness about pleasure itself" (p. 135) and argues that Jonson "belongs" in a Christian-Platonic-Stoic tradition. "His nondramatic poems recur repeatedly to the ideal of the unmoved personality, the soul that can sustain itself in virtue when all is flux around it" (p. 143).

The primary difference between Greene and Barish is that for Greene, the concept of anti-theatricality as an objection to the *institution* of theatre remains entirely implicit. Jonson's attitude is "essentially" anti-theatrical, since Greene's concern with theatricality as a mode of existence refuses to make distinctions between theatre as an institution and "theatre" as a characteristic way of addressing the world. In contrast, Barish argues that the institution of theatre (and particularly the audience) was in large part what Jonson hated.

4 One notable exception to this is Phyllis Rackin's "Androgyny, Mimesis, and the Marriage of the Boy Heroine on the English Renaissance Stage," *PMLA*,

102 (1987), 29–41, though Rackin is not really concerned with hostility *to* the stage so much as she is with hostility toward androgyny *on* the stage. See especially p. 30.

5 For the opposing point of view on the status of the masque in the context of Jonson's anti-theatricality, see Barish, *The Anti-Theatrical Prejudice*, p. 152: "The masque proves vulnerable on two related counts – showiness and ephemerality – and the two imply each other. That which is designed for outward show must needs be ephemeral; that which has no solidity to recommend it must perforce resort to display." For Greene, on the other hand, the masques are "the great storehouse of Jonson's centripetal images" (p. 326). For the most complete discussion of the ways in which Jonson's masques incorporated the directives of anti-theatricality, see Stephen Orgel's *The Illusion of Power: Political Theatre in the English Renaissance* (Berkeley: University of California Press, 1975), p. 39.

6 See Edward B. Partridge, *"Epicoene"* in his *The Broken Compass: A Study of the Major Comedies of Ben Jonson* (New York: Columbia University Press, 1958), p. 162. This perceptive essay is one of the first to comment at all on the "epicene" nature of *Epicoene*. It fails, however, 1) to situate the anxiety about androgyny in relation to Renaissance anti-theatricality, 2) to take stock of what happens dramatically to the epicene over the course of time in the play, 3) to notice the dialectic the play presents on the nature of the epicene, a dialectic over whether the epicene is something externally imposed which can therefore be taken away (the anti-theatrical position) or whether it is something inevitable, the result of living in a world of time. Effectively this leads to a failure to discriminate between effeminization and androgyny.

7 These two accounts have been replicated in the play's critical history, with critics tending to ratify one account or the other. Thus for Barbara C. Millard, the unmasking of Epicoene "is the discovery of the androgynous aspects of human nature." In contrast, for Katherine Eisaman Maus, although Jonson raises questions about whether gender is constructed, in *Epicoene* he ultimately cannot relinquish the notion that there is "something 'real' underneath." See Millard, "An Acceptable Violence: Sexual Contest in Jonson's *Epicene*," *Medieval and Renaissance Drama in English*, 1 (1984), p. 143. I thank Katherine Eisaman Maus for sharing her manuscript version, "Prosecution and Sexual Secrecy: Jonson and Shakespeare; Impotence and the Satirist's Vocation." More polemical accounts blame Jonson for not seeing gender as constructed. See, for instance, Karen Newman, "City Talk: Femininity and Commodification in Jonson's *Epicoene*," *Fashioning Femininity and English Renaissance Drama* (University of Chicago Press, 1991), p. 138.

8 All quotations are taken from *The Yale Ben Jonson: Epicoene* (New Haven: Yale University Press, 1971).

9 We tend not to think of the spectator as someone who can be physically damaged by the spectacle in front of him, but increasingly this is the relationship between playwright and spectator which *Epicoene* depicts. Theatre continually bills itself as something which will cure the spectator, only to betray itself as fundamentally an outlet for the playwright's own violence. Thus in IV.ii, Truewit and Clerimont arrange to have acted out before Mrs. Otter a scene of rage which enrages and humilates her. In IV.v Truewit

performs to Daw the theme of Daw's own dismemberment. Truewit recurrently has scenes acted out before him which perform his own aggressive impulses, each masked by the expressed intention of "curing" its spectator (Daw and La Foole of pride, Morose of his aversion to noise, etc.).

10 The sole purpose of the Otters in the play seems to be to confirm this proposition, to argue that men can in fact be effeminized by women, and thus to confirm Morose's worst fears. Thus Otter must refer to his wife as "princess," as she refers to him as her subject: "Is this according to the instrument when I married you? That I would be Princess and reign in mine own house, and you would be my subject and obey me? . . ." (III.i.28–30).

11 Katherine Eisaman Maus has also discussed the analogy between women and theatre which permeates Renaissance culture ("'Playhouse Flesh and Blood': Sexual Ideology and the Restoration Actress," *English Literary History*, 46:4 [1979], 604ff). But for Maus, the analogy rests on the premise that both women and theatre are seen as lies which conceal a "real" core or essence at odds with their seductive appearance. In contrast, *Epicoene* suggests another basis for this association: theatre (in the form of Truewit) continually displaces its own violent tendencies onto women, while maintaining the position that theatre itself is "cure."

12 An analogous instance of theatre billing itself as cure and betraying its own impulse toward violence takes place in the theatrical of the false exorcism that Toby and Maria stage around Malvolio in *Twelfth Night*. See also Massinger's *The Roman Actor* for a theatre whose claims to cure are betrayed as violence.

13 For a compelling analysis of the way impotence trials serve as a model for the satirist's enterprise itself, both in their attempt to ascertain truth through the "bodily fact" and in their ultimate reliance on more dubious commodities like language and reputation, see Maus's "Prosecution and Sexual Secrecy: Jonson and Shakespeare; Impotence and the Satirist's Vocation," forthcoming.

14 For P.K. Ayers, Morose's is a peculiarly urban solipsism: he is "in almost every respect an exemplar of urban schizophrenia." See "Dreams of the City: The Urban and the Urbane in Jonson's *Epicoene*," *Philological Quarterly*, 66 (1987), p. 77. For Anne Barton, Morose's insistence upon preserving a distance between himself and all the rest of the world is "merely a grotesque version of a tendency visible in all the other characters as well." See *Ben Jonson, Dramatist* (Cambridge University Press, 1984), p. 131.

15 And, as I have suggested in my discussions of anti-theatricality, the concept serves a defensive purpose. The relation of the world of self Morose constructs to the self he lacks is roughly the relation of a narcissistic "self" (in the sense of secondary narcissism) to an absent "real" self. See D.W. Winnicott's influential essay, "The True and False Self," in *Maturational Processes and the Facilitating Environment: Studies in the theory of emotional development* (New York: International Universities Press, 1965), also Alice Miller's *The Drama of the Gifted Child* (New York: Basic Books, 1981). Morose's construction of a self through language also lends itself to Lacanian notions of the self, though the "self" Morose constructs through language is less a differentiation from other than it is a denial of other, and the language he constructs this self from less a shared language than a language over which he has sole control.

In Morose's case, what the persistent fantasy of the "other" who can rend or inundate one's boundaries suggests is that these boundaries do not exist in a firm way to begin with, because the self does not exist in a firm way – hence the images of holes and orifices and mouths and penetrable windows. For what self there is is experienced as both violently disruptible from within, and transformable from without. Though Morose claims the inundation comes from outside ("Another flood ... it beats already at my shores"), he himself betrays the fact that the threat comes from inside: "I feel an earthquake in myself for it" (III.vi.4).

The play does contain within it the same recognition of a contradictory version of the self we find at the heart of the anti-theatrical tracts, but it acknowledges the existence of this self only in reference to women. Thus Otter conceives of his wife both as monstrous, "a nasty sluttish animal," "A wife is a scurvy clogdogdo, an unlucky thing, a very foresaid bear-whelp," etc., and as nothing at all, "Wife! Buz! *Titivilitium*! There's no such thing in nature" (IV.ii.49). In an extraordinary passage Otter imagines her taking herself apart every night until there's nothing left (see IV.ii.88–93).

16 Gosson, *Playes Confuted in five Actions*, p. 177 in Arthur F. Kinney's *Markets of Bawdrie: The Dramatic Criticism of Stephen Gosson*, Salzburg Studies in Literature, No. 4 (Salzburg: Institut für Englische Sprache und Literatur, 1974). Prynne also says that God "enjoy[n]es all men at all times, to be such in shew, as they are in truth: to seeme that outwardly which they are inwardly; to act themselves, not others" (p. 159, quoted in Barish as well, p. 92).

17 Anglo-phile Eutheo (Anthony Munday), *A Second and Third Blaste of Retrait from Plaies and Theatres* (London, 1580), p. 115.

18 Munday, *A Second and Third Blast*, p. 115.

19 Barish maintains that the belief in absolute sincerity is the corollary to the anti-theatricalist belief in an absolute identity: "One corollary of the concept of absolute identity was the belief in an absolute sincerity. If it was possible truly to know the 'uniform, distinct and proper being' one had received from God, then it was possible either to affirm that being in all one's acts – to be 'such in truth' as one was 'in show' – or to deny it by disguise or pretense." ("Puritans and Proteans," in *The Anti-Theatrical Prejudice*, p. 94).

20 For Ian Donaldson this constitutes the festive invasion of the public into the private. See "'A Martyr's Resolution': *Epicoene*," in *The World Upside-Down: Comedy from Jonson to Fielding* (London: Oxford University Press, 1970), p. 36.

21 Stephen Orgel, introduction, *Ben Jonson: The Complete Masques* (New Haven: Yale University Press, 1969), p. 13.

22 Stephen Orgel, *The Illusion of Power: Political Theatre in the English Renaissance* (Berkeley: University of California Press, 1975), p. 55. (The Bacon quote is from *The Great Instauration*.)

23 Stephen Orgel, *The Jonsonian Masque* (Cambridge, MA: Harvard University Press, 1965), pp. 14 and 15.

24 *The Masque of Queens*, in *Ben Jonson: The Complete Masques*, lines 158–63 and 166–9.

25 Introduction, p. 5, to *Ben Jonson: The Complete Masques*.

26 *The Jonsonian Masque*, p. 130.

27 *The Illusion of Power*, p. 39.

28 *The Jonsonian Masque*, p. 84.
29 *The Jonsonian Masque*, p. 138. Orgel adds, "though they have become dramatis personae, Good and Evil cannot confront each other, conflict, interact, because their nature forbids it. No drama, then, is possible..." (p. 139).
30 Edward Partridge says,

> Epicoene was first acted by the Children of Her Majesty's Revels at Whitefriars, either in 1609 (as the title page in the Folio of 1616 says) or early in 1610, as E.K. Chambers speculates. Since this company of boy actors, formerly the Children of the Chapel, was not entitled to call itself the Children of the Queen's Revels before its patent of January 4, 1610, early in 1610 may be the better date.

Appendix to *The Yale Ben Jonson: Epicoene* (New Haven: Yale University Press, 1971), pp. 199–200.
31 E.K. Chambers quotes a letter from William Hunnis (appointed Master of the Children on April 22, 1567) in 1583 asking for an allowance – a kind of social security – for children whose voices have changed. *The Elizabethan Stage* (Oxford: Clarendon Press, 1965), Vol. 2, p. 37. It is not clear, however, to what degree the age requirements with their musical basis were still relevant in 1609/1610. The 1616 folio lists Nat. Field (clearly not a child anymore) at the head of the actor list for *Epicoene*, though there are also problems with this folio page, for it ascribes the production to "1609" and to the "Children of the Revels," though the Children were not entitled to call themselves "of the Revels" during 1609. (See Chambers, p. 59.) See Chambers pp. 23–61 for a history of the company. See Charles William Wallace, "The Children of the Chapel at Blackfriars, 1597–1603," *Nebraska University Studies*, 8:2 (1908), 103–321 for a lengthy discussion of the part played by the Children's Companies in the war between London magistrates and the Queen. According to Wallace's calculations, Field would have been thirteen in 1600 (and therefore twenty-two in 1609). See p. 191, note.
32 Herford Percy and Simpson say,

> Killigrew's company moved to Drury Lane in April 1663, and Downes gives the cast for a performance of *Epicoene* on 7 May. Cartwright was Morose; Mohun, Truewit; Burt, Cleremont; Kynaston, Dauphine; Wintershall, La Foole; Shatterel, Daw; Lacy, Otter; Mrs. Knepp, Epicene; Mrs. Rutter, Lady Haughty; Mrs. Corey, Mistress Otter. Mrs. Knepp was the first of a number of actresses who made the part of Epicoene ridiculous by posing as a woman in disguise. Pepys, however, admired her...

Ben Jonson, ed. by C. H. Herford Percy and Evelyn Simpson, Vol. IX, p. 211 (Oxford: Clarendon Press, 1950). In 1664, the King's Company played *Epicoene* at the Inner Temple, and in 1673 went to Oxford. Dryden contributed a prologue and epilogue. It is probable that the productions Dryden saw cast women as Epicoene and certain that they cast women as women.
33 For Dryden, the play itself is associated with the theme of restoration, and particularly with the restoration of a monarch. He calls Jonson "monarchic": "He invades authors like a monarch and what would be theft in other poets is only victory in him" (pp. 111–12). Dryden finds in *Epicoene* an emblem for the return of the muses who have been buried during the civil war, and whose return is the product of the restoration itself. See "Essay of Dramatic Poesy" in *John Dryden*, ed. Keith Walker (Oxford University Press, 1987).

5 THE "NOTHING" UNDER THE PUPPET'S COSTUME: JONSON'S
SUPPRESSION OF MARLOWE IN *BARTHOLOMEW FAIR*

1 All quotations are taken from *The Yale Ben Jonson: Bartholomew Fair* (New Haven: Yale University Press, 1963).

2 Francis Meres' treatise, *"Poetrie"* XXIV, 21–5, rpt. in Don Cameron Allen's *Francis Meres' Treatise "Poetrie," A Critical Edition*, rpt. University of Illinois Studies in Language and Literature, 16:3–4 (1933), p. 84.

3 See Stephen Greenblatt, *Renaissance Self-Fashioning*, p. 220.

4 Ben Jonson's *Timber or Discoveries Made Upon Men and Matter*, ed. Felix E. Schelling (Boston: Ginn & Co., 1892), p. 27.

5 On "aliens" and "strangers" as those whose identity is constituted "at those moments in which order – political, theological, sexual – is violated," see Greenblatt, *Renaissance Self-Fashioning*, p. 222.

6 For an excellent essay on the motives for seeing *Hero and Leander* as an unfinished "fragment," see Marion Campbell's "'Desunt Nonnula': The Construction of Marlowe's *Hero and Leander* as an Unfinished Poem," *English Literary History*, 51 (1984), 241–67.

7 Richard Carew's *The Excellency of the English Tongue 1595–6*, quoted in Don Cameron Allen's *Francis Meres' Treatise, "Poetrie"*, p. 29.

8 Meres, XXIV.i.29–30 and XXV.i.1–2, in Don Cameron Allen, p. 84. The double sense of the word "rival" (competitor, but also friend as in "the rivals of our watch" or lover) suggests the way the two myths keep doubling back on each other, the shepherd turning into the homosexual, the poet into the object of erotic (and therefore "lewde") fascination.

9 See Don Cameron Allen, p. 37.

10 Jonson, *Discoveries*, pp. 21–2.

11 See for instance Barish's *The Anti-Theatrical Prejudice*, pp. 132–54. For readings of the play's use of *Hero and Leander* as an emblem of an ideal that either the stage or the world of the fair debases, see especially Barish, *"Bartholomew Fair* and its Puppets," *Modern Language Quarterly*, 20 (1959), 13–14, which argues that the puppets present the debasement of the great themes of Renaissance literature, love and friendship, and Anne Barton, *Ben Jonson, Dramatist*, p. 218, which argues that Marlowe's poem (among others) points up the deficiencies of those who attend the fair.

12 Broadly speaking my argument differs from two kinds of claims that have been made about Jonson's attitudes toward theatricality in *Bartholomew Fair*. The first kind uses the puppet show as a barometer to Jonson's attitude toward theatre, but generally fails to attend to the specifically sexual material Littlewit excises from Marlowe's poem (and thus fails to notice the concessions the puppet show makes to anti-theatricality). The second reads Jonson's attitude toward theatricality primarily for what it reveals about his attitude toward the crown. I differ from this second approach in understanding anti-theatricality itself (both in pamphlet attacks and in Jonson) not merely as a set of attitudes toward institutions (the crown, licensing, the stage) but as an identifiable set of anxieties about gender and desire. I differ from the first approach in arguing that to locate these anxieties in *Bartholomew Fair* we need to attend to what has been cut from Marlowe's poem.

For readings of the puppet show as a barometer of Jonson's attitude toward theatre, see especially Barish's "*Bartholomew Fair* and its Puppets," and Clifford Davidson's "Judgment, Iconoclasm and Anti-theatricalism in Jonson's *Bartholomew Fair*," *Papers on Language & Literature*, 25:4 (1989), 349–63. For important, powerful readings of the play's attitude toward theatricality and all that it implies about Jonson's attitude toward the crown, see Leah S. Marcus, "Pastimes and the Purging of Theater," in *The Politics of Mirth: Jonson, Herrick, Milton, Marvell and the Defense of Old Holiday Pastimes* (University of Chicago Press, 1986), pp. 28–63, in which the "fairing" offered King James is the "true delight" of seeing his cherished beliefs about the potential function of plays and pastimes reflected in the uncommon looking glass of a play about plays and pastimes. See also Richard Burt, "'Licensed by Authority': Ben Jonson and the Politics of Early Stuart Theater," *English Literary History*, 54:3 (1987), 529–60, on the ways that Jonson registered ambivalence about cultural contradictions in licensing. For an earlier version of the endorsement-of-James argument, see Ian Donaldson on the play as a comedy about extremism or "overdoing," in *The World Upside Down: Comedy from Jonson to Fielding* (London: Oxford University Press, 1970), pp. 47–77, especially p. 73. For a third tradition which locates the play in relation to notions of festival and carnival, see Jonathan Haynes, "Festivity and the dramatic economy of Jonson's *Bartholomew Fair*," *English Literary History*, 51:4 (1984), 645–68, and (for the fullest, most complex reading of the way that Jonson sought to constitute his identity in opposition to the theatre and the fair) "The Fair, the Pig, Authorship," by Peter Stallybrass and Allon White in their *The Politics and Poetics of Transgression* (Ithaca: Cornell University Press, 1986), pp. 27–79.

13 Stephen Gosson, *The School of Abuse*, p. 14.
14 All quotations are taken from *Christopher Marlowe: The Complete Poems and Translations*, ed. Stephen Orgel (New York: Penguin, 1979).
15 Bruce Smith reads the relation between the Neptune episode and Hero and Leander's desire as primarily one of contrast. For Smith "the real subject of desire in these fictions" (epyllia) is the reader. See *Homosexual Desire in Shakespeare's England* (University of Chicago Press, 1991), p. 132.
16 For Gregory W. Bredbeck, the fact that Leander is, in this passage, "*taught* all that elders know" (italics mine) is part of the poem's depiction of desire as social discourse, and thus part of its demonstration of the "relativity of heteroeroticism." (See *Sodomy and Interpretation: Marlowe to Milton* [Ithaca: Cornell University Press, 1991], pp. 131–4.)
17 But there is something contradictory about the notion of authority itself in the poem, for Neptune, the agent of retaliation, is as implicated in the "crime" as Leander – portrayed as both comic and erotically exciting. I am grateful to Stephen Orgel for pointing this out.
18 John Rainolds, *Th' Overthrow of Stage Plaies*, 1599 (rpt. New York: Garland Publishing, 1974), p. 18 D[1].
19 Rainolds, p. 11 C[2]. For Rainolds, like other anti-theatricalists, the fear is that "action" becomes constitutive. He says of the boy actor in women's clothing:

For, the care of making a shew to doe such feates, and to doe them as lively as the beasts themselves in whom the vices raigne, worketh in the actors a marvellous impression of being like the persons whose qualities they expresse and imitate: chiefly when earnest and much meditation of sundry dayes and weekes, by often repetition and represen- tation of the partes, shall as it were engrave the things in their minde with a penne of iron, or with the point of a diamond. (19 [D^2])

The representation of the thing the actor acts is engraved in his mind until he believes he is the representation, behaves like that representation and becomes it. Similarly, Gosson argues that the "impressions" in the actor's mind can be transferred to the gaze of the spectator, *Playes Confuted*, pp. 192–3.

20 William Prynne, *Histrio-mastix: The Player's Scourge or Actor's Tragedy* (New York: Garland Publishing, 1974), p. 209.

21 Prynne, *Histrio-mastix*, p. 197.

22 Prynne, *Histrio-mastix*, p. 209.

23 Leander's golden tresses that were never shorn suggest a childlike as well as a feminine appearance.

24 For a brilliant discussion on the "liminal moment" see Victor Turner's *The Forest of Symbols: Aspects of Ndembu Ritual* (Ithaca: Cornell University Press, 1967), pp. 93–111.

25 Unlike those critics who base the claim that *Bartholomew Fair* constitutes Jonson's grudging acceptance of theatre on Busy's "conversion," I argue that this is a hollow conversion, since the text has already been "converted" to accommodate anti-theatricalism itself. My emphasis lies less on any positive endorsement of theatre than on Jonson's "anti-anti-theatricality." *Bartholo- mew Fair* is less involved in a celebration of theatre than in an acknowledge- ment of its inevitability: except for Trouble-All the play is incapable of imagining anyone not involved in some kind of theatre. For "grudging accept- ance of theatre" positions, see Barish's *The Anti-Theatrical Prejudice*, pp. 134 and 153, and Thomas Greene's "Ben Jonson and the Centered Self."

26 In this sense Ursula is both Ate or Discord, as critics like Cope have argued, and Eve, as critics like Thayer have argued, for from one point of view the two are synonymous. For the claim that Ursula constitutes the "representational archetype" for woman (i.e. as "leakers") see Gail Kern Paster's brilliant essay, "Leaky Vessels: The Incontinent Women of City Comedy," in *Renaissance Drama*, New Series XVIII, Essays on Sexuality, Influence, and Performance, ed. Mary Beth Rose (1987), pp. 43–65. For a brilliant analysis of Ursula as the "celebrant of the open orifice," see Stallybrass and White, "The Fair, the Pig, Authorship," pp. 64–5. For Jackson I. Cope's insistence on Ursula as Ate, see "*Bartholomew Fair* as Blasphemy," *Renaissance Drama*, 8 (1965), 127–52. For Thayer's reading (which Cope rejects) see G.C. Thayer, *Ben Jonson: Studies in the Plays* (Norman: University of Oklahoma Press, 1963), especially pp. 132–6.

27 Wasp is not the only one in the play to display a homosexual fascination – Overdo himself refers to Edgeworth as the "young man I have followed so long in love from the brink of his bane to the centre of safety" (V.ii.120–1). What seems even more important is the simple persistence with which images of dismemberment, dissolution and castration arise. Wasp says that if he lets Cokes alone in the fair he will be lucky to bring him back with one testicle: "If a leg or an arm on him did not grow on, he would lose it i' the press. Pray heaven I bring him off with one stone!" (I.v.107–9) and Edgeworth echoes

later, "Purse? A man might cut out his kidneys, I think, and he never feel 'em" (IV.ii.39–40).

28 See George Speaight's *History of the English Puppet Theatre* (London: G.G. Harrap, 1955), p. 65, for the glove-puppet claim. See Michael Jamieson's note 74, p. 488, *Ben Jonson: Three Comedies* (New York: Penguin, 1966) for the marionette objection (based not on thematic grounds but on practical ones).

29 Stephen Gosson, *Playes Confuted in five Actions*, p. 175.

30 In this analogy, Jonson literalizes and reinterprets one of the tropes of anti-theatrical tracts. *School of Abuse*, for instance, simply assumes that women in the audience will be (or turn into) prostitutes. See Gosson's "Dedication to the Gentlewomen" which accompanies this pamphlet.

31 The most spectacular instance of theatre as a rip-off, of course, is the performance of the ballad "A Caveat to Cutpurses," which effects the theft of Cokes' purse through a performance of a song about the danger of cutting purses.

32 For an instance of the obsession with theatre as an "enormity," see William Rankins' *A Mirrour of Monsters* (London, 1587). Jonson's allusion to this tract establishes a double analogy between Overdo and the anti-theatricalist, since the pamphlet invokes and parodies the title of the work which Overdo too invokes, *Mirror of Magistrates*.

33 Grace Wellborn seems, temporarily, to provide such an alternative to theatre. ("She seems to be discreet, and as sober as she is handsome," says Quarlous [I.v.51–2].) Grace seems at first to constitute a kind of analogue to *Volpone*'s Celia, to offer an instance of the morally "real." But her aversion to going to the fair is based less on any moral fixity, any moral referent outside of the fair, than it is on her recognition that the aristocracy will avoid the place: "Truly, I have no such fancy to the Fair, nor ambition to see it; there's none goes thither of any quality or fashion" (I.v.121–2). And she is specifically identified with the puppet theatre through the word she uses to describe her scheme to distinguish between husbands ("Will you consent to a *motion* of mine, gentlemen?" [IV.iii.38, italics mine]). The word is the one used to describe the puppets.

34 Gosson, *Playes Confuted*, pp. 193–4.

35 Anglo-Phile Eutheo (Anthony Munday), *A Second and Third Blast of Retrait from Plaies and Theatres*, pp. 98–9. Munday describes the way seducers in the audience immediately make use of what they see on stage and replicate it. They estimate the compassion of women near them by asking these women about their responses to stage characters: "is it not pittie this passioned lover should be so martyred. And if he finde her inclining to foolish pittie, as commonlie such women are, then he applies the matter to himselfe and saies that he is likewise carried awaie with the liking of her."

36 Despite *Hero and Leander*'s tribute to the power of rhetoric, it problematizes this very issue by pointing to the failure of rhetoric to achieve its goal. All three seduction stories in the poem characterize the seducer as rhetorician, but in all three rhetoric alone either fails or was unnecessary to begin with: Mercury must give the shepherdess the gift of immortality in addition to his "speeches full of pleasure and delight." Neptune goes off in search of gifts when "deep persuading oratory fails." And Hero is "won" before Leander even begins his speech. More telling is the persona's suggestion that the nature of erotic

experience itself is quintessentially private, cannot be framed in words which have the capacity to transfer the content of the experience from one person to the other: Leander "Entered the orchard of th' Hesperides, / Whose fruit none rightly can describe but he / That pulls or shakes it from the golden tree" (II.298–300).

37 Despite the Induction's relentless tendency to insult its actual spectators, the method of the play itself is to try to bring into existence the spectator able to judge without another man's warrant, by presenting precisely what the puppets have stripped from Marlowe's *Hero and Leander*: ambiguity itself. *Bartholomew Fair* does this by refusing to provide a character who is both virtuous and knowledgeable, a single point of view whose "warrant" the spectator might safely substitute for his own. What it presents instead is a series of relative positions embodied by characters who are all partially flawed, between whom it forces us to choose, then rank. In a literal way, the Induction does this, replacing the stage-keeper with the book-holder, the book-holder with the scrivener and Jonson's "articles" with the play itself. But in a more problematic way, the play itself eliminates successive points of view, refuses to provide a character whose judgments it sanctions. Overdo, the appointed "judge," is wrong in all his judgments, from his assessment of that "proper young man," the cutpurse, to his knowledge of his wife's whereabouts. Grace Wellborn seems to provide a locus for the kind of judgment that Overdo lacks, but relinquishes her most important opportunity to exercise judgment by turning her choice of suitors over to fate, to the "warrant" of a madman. Quarlous himself might be a locus for judgment since, unlike Overdo, he at least has the basis for making a knowledge claim – he knows more than anyone else in the play, knows of the real and false Trouble-All, knows who cut the purse in III.v – but Quarlous is as unscrupulous as he is "quarlous." In him the play splits judgment itself, giving him a claim to knowledge but none to morality.

6 MAGIC AS THEATRE, THEATRE AS MAGIC: *DAEMONOLOGIE* AND THE PROBLEM OF "ENTRESSE"

1 King James the First, *Daemonologie in Forme of a Dialogue* (1597), The Bodley Head Quartos, ed. G.B. Harrison (New York: E.P. Dutton, 1924). All subsequent quotations from *Daemonologie* are taken from this edition.

2 At the beginning of *Ecstasies: Deciphering the Witches' Sabbath*, Carlo Ginzburg cites R. Kieckhefer's distinction of the degree of "scholarly pollution" that characterizes a given text about witchcraft (demonological treatises being the most "polluted" by scholarly ideas and depositions of accusers being the least so). Ginzburg complains, in effect, that most historians of witchcraft deal only with this layer of "pollution" and thus with the "attitudes and behavior" of the persecutors, rather than those of the persecuted. In contrast, in an equally influential essay, "Inversion, Misrule and the Meaning of Witchcraft," Stuart Clark takes as a given that we will find no "empirical verification" for the "actual activities of real agents," i.e. witches, and argues instead that we should approach demonological treatises precisely through what Ginzburg might call their "pollution," their demonstrated similarities to other texts

in the same "language game," texts that share the same conventions for persuasion.

Although my strategy is closer to Clark's (since the "magical thinking" that characterizes witch treatises and attacks against the stage puts them in the same "language game"), my argument in this chapter and the one that follows will differ from both approaches. I differ from Ginzburg (as do most readers of Renaissance witch treatises) in confining myself to an attempt to reconstruct the logic of the examiners, rather than that of the examined. But I differ from Clark in my examination of the way the *narratives* of witch treatises – the stories they tell – actually undermine their more conventional material.

The readings I offer in the chapters which follow differ from broader explanations of witch persecution as a large-scale phenomenon in their attention to the contradictions and tensions of individual texts, but are not incompatible with these. For important versions of broad explanations, see H.R. Trevor Roper's title essay in *The European Witch-Craze of the Sixteenth and Seventeenth Centuries and Other Essays* (New York: Harper and Row, 1967), especially pp. 126–7, for the most famous version of the scapegoat-on-the-basis-of-nonconformity theory of European witch persecution. For examples of "functionalist" approaches to both witchcraft and witchcraft accusations, see Keith Thomas, *Religion and the Decline of Magic* (New York: Penguin, 1971), especially p. 594, for a description of the way religious changes in the mid-sixteenth century that eliminated "ecclesiastical magic" played a role in the "unprecedented volume of witch-trials and executions," and p. 650 for the claim that "the great appeal of witch-beliefs, as against other types of explanation for misfortune, was...that they provided the victim with a definite means of redress," as well as Alan MacFarlane's statistical work in *Witchcraft in Tudor and Stuart England* (London: Routledge & Kegan Paul, 1970). For a crucial critique of Thomas' "functionalist" approach, see Hildred Geertz' "An Anthropology of Religion and Magic, I" in *Journal of Interdisciplinary History*, 6:1 (1975), 71–89 and Thomas' response, "An Anthropology of Religion and Magic, II" in *Journal of Interdisciplinary History*, 6:1 (1975), 91–109. For an evaluation of the degree to which witchcraft was a women's crime, see Christina Larner's "Who Were the Witches?" in her *Enemies of God* (Baltimore: The Johns Hopkins University Press, 1981), especially pp. 100–2. For Ginzburg's claim, see *Ecstasies: Deciphering the Witches' Sabbath*, trans. Raymond Rosenthal (New York: Penguin, 1992), p. 2. For Clark, see "Inversion, Misrule and the Meaning of Witchcraft," in *Past and Present*, 87 (1980), 98–127.

3 See Thomas Laqueur's reconstruction of Paré, Montaigne and Caspar Bauhin on the transformation of the shepherd(ess) Marie into the shepherd Germain-Marie ("Orgasm, Generation, and the Politics of Reproductive Biology," *Representations*, 14 [1986], p. 13). See Ian Maclean, "Medicine, Anatomy, Physiology" in *The Renaissance Notion of Woman* (Cambridge University Press, 1980), p. 39, for the claim that "The few clinical cases attested in the Renaissance are all of women changing into men: this is what would have been expected, as what is perfect is unlikely to change into that which is less so (even though Ambroise Paré talks of women 'degenerating into men')." See Stephen Greenblatt's "Fiction and Friction" in *Reconstructing Individualism* (Stanford

University Press, 1986), for the story of Marie/Marin le Marcis, as well as for the story of Germain-Marie and the claim that the possibility of sex change was "almost always from female to male, that is, from defective to perfect" (p. 40).

Daemonologie calls into question both the claim that such transformations work only up the great chain of being and the claim that a transvestite theatre provides an apt trope for Renaissance anatomy itself ("beneath the imaginary women's bodies, there are other bodies, the bodies of the actors," Greenblatt [p. 52]) since rather than finding in "the woman's secret fold of flesh…a swelling penis" (p. 37) *Daemonologie* seems to imagine the body per se as a collection of orifices and holes.

For important critiques of Greenblatt, see Stephen Orgel, "Nobody's Perfect," p. 18, for a discussion of the fit between French and continental medical materials and the English stage, and Pat Parker's incisive "Gender Ideology, Gender Change: The Case of Marie Germain" in *Critical Inquiry*, 19 (1993), 337–64. For a crucial critique of Laqueur, see Katherine Park and Robert A. Nye, "Destiny Is Anatomy," review of Laqueur's *Making Sex*, *The New Republic*, 18 (February 1991), 53–7. See also the important study by Katherine Park and Lorraine J. Daston, "Unnatural Conceptions: The Study of Monsters in Sixteenth- and Seventeenth-Century France and England," *Past and Present*, 92 (1981), 20–54.

4 In large part through *Renaissance Self-Fashioning*, we have come to understand the connection between theatricality and the capacity to improvise, shape the self and mold reality to one's own scenarios. Additionally, because of continued attention to the way in which James in particular employed masque and Star Chamber interrogations as a staging of royal power, the commonplace that in the Renaissance power expresses itself in theatrical ways has come to be associated with the corollary that theatre is an expression of power, an enabling force which permits a kind of royal self-fashioning.

In this chapter, I identify James' conception of an antithetical kind of theatre which has the capacity to unshape and unfashion the self. In the next, I argue that James' staging of royal power through his spectacular examination of witches was compensatory, responsive to his sense of witchcraft as a kind of theatre with the power to unfashion and unman.

5 In an astute essay about the changes in James' attitude toward witchcraft after 1603, Stuart Clark says that "there is…little that is original in *Daemonologie*," that "it is neither original nor profound," its arguments being the "stock-in-trade of orthodox European demonology." While it is true that *Daemonologie* reiterates many of the stock tropes of European demonology, this begs the question of how to determine what is original in a witch tract, the genre being one that (by definition) repeats conventional material. In this essay my criterion is sequence or chronology. That is, it is true that *Daemonologie* repeats the tropes of earlier demonological treatises (the anal kiss, the incubus) but it does not present these events in the same order as other treatises: not every treatise moves from a vision of foreplay to a vision of penetration, to a vision of the theft of the man's nature. Not every demonological treatise tells the same story. In "Inversion, Misrule and the Meaning of Witchcraft," Clark makes a convincing argument for looking at demonological treatises in terms of the

conventional material they share with other texts in the same "language game," or "total speech situation," but the question this begs is how to differentiate one treatise from another. To determine what is "original" or idiosyncratic to *Daemonologie*, then, we need to examine the way the story it tells undermines the conventional material it shares with other treatises about witchcraft.

Clark's claim denies to the text an unconscious, and Clark's own practice is actually occasionally at odds with this position. For instance, he is unable to regard such "conventional" material as the devil's mark as purely conventional, for he says, "One wonders to what extent [James'] fascination with the details of the North Berwick conventions and with the devil's 'mark' in particular was transmuted into the prurient interest he later showed in the sexual habits of his relations and courtiers" (p. 165). Clark does not treat this piece of witch lore as "conventional" but as idiosyncratic to its author. See "King James' *Daemonologie*: Witchcraft and Kingship," in Sidney Anglo's *The Damned Art* (London: Routledge, 1977), especially pp. 156, 165, 168, 173, as well as "Inversion, Misrule and the Meaning of Witchcraft," cited above in footnote 2.

6 Contemporary accounts of witch hunts during the period suggest that the place could as easily be some part of the body difficult to see, but it was often a genital as the phrase, "secret place," which is virtually synonymous with "private" or "privities," seems to suggest. In *Newes from Scotland*, James finds a devil's mark on one Geillis Duncane, on her throat. But the mark he finds on Agnis Sampson (also called Agnis Tompson) is on her genitals. She has to be shaved before he can find it.

7 This seems key in light of the claim made by Alan Bray that there is no sign in English witch tracts of any homosexual material. After acknowledging that "sexual fantasies do appear in English witch lore, and there is evidence of the belief that the witch had sexual relations with the Devil or a 'familiar' demon," he says, "But this was not homosexuality: if the witch was female the Devil appeared as a man, an incubus, and if the witch was male he appeared as a female, a succubus" (*Homosexuality in Renaissance England* [London: Gay Men's Press, 1982] p. 21). The very claim that "if the witch was ... male" the devil "appeared as a female" belies the claim made a few pages later that "homosexuality had no place in the Kingdom of Hell," for in either case it is a he, the Devil, doing the appearing. In an age in which the representations of men and women on stage always suggested at least the possibility of boys and men in embrace, *this* transvestitism – a transvestitism of bodies, the devil in women's bodies, as he converses with men – seems less unambiguous and unproblematic than Bray makes it. What is interesting about *Daemonologie* though is the way this is figured as a rape, the invasion of and theft from the body of a vital essence.

8 For a discussion of the Renaissance association of women with their orifices and with the orifices of houses, and a critique of the way Bakhtin and Elias fail to take into account the gendered body in their discussion of the grotesque body in terms of orifices and holes, see Peter Stallybrass' brilliant "Patriarchal Territories: The Body Enclosed," in *Rewriting the Renaissance*, pp. 123–42.

9 In fact, the text's attempts to provide a coherent system of knowledge strain

most at the moments of greatest sexual stress. Epistemon has established that the way to tell a real witch from a fake one (a melancholic) is that the confession must be extorted under torture not voluntarily given. But it is exactly at the moment when Epistemon is forced to consider whether the kissing of Satan's "hinder partes" really goes on or not that he raises the possibility that there may be confessions that are neither true or lies, but based on delusion, based on the witch *thinking* she has done the things she confessed to when she has not. This possibility reaches its most elaborate and unwieldy form at the moment Epistemon and Philomathes try to consider the possibility of witches penetrating solid walls. For here they are forced to account for such phenomena by positing a kind of collective delusion, a whole audience of witnesses for out-of-the-body travel who have been deluded into thinking they have seen what they have not because Satan has "ravished" their wits. As the attempts to account for contradictions (that arise at moments of sexual anxiety) become more and more unwieldy they make it harder to identify a systematic epistemology.

7 MAGIC AS THEATRE, THEATRE AS MAGIC: THE CASE OF *NEWES FROM SCOTLAND*

1 *Newes from Scotland declaring the Damnable Life and death of Doctor Fian, a notable Sorcerer who was burned at Edenbrough in Ianuary last* (1591), the Bodley Head Quartos, ed. G.B. Harrison (New York: E.P. Dutton, 1924), pp. 12–13. All subsequent quotations are incorporated into the body of the text.

2 Gosson, *Playes Confuted*, p. 175.

3 In *Discipline and Punish*, Foucault suggests that torture produces knowledge. In *The Body in Pain*, Elaine Scarry says that it pretends to do so. In *Newes from Scotland*, torture produces the sensation of knowledge, of certainty (not in the way that Scarry suggests when she says that torture borrows the certainty of physical pain but in the examiners' insistence on creating a one-to-one correspondence between the "sign" on the body and the "thing": witch). For Foucault on the way torture produces knowledge, see "The Spectacle of the Scaffold," especially pp. 35–42 in *Discipline and Punish* (New York: Vintage, 1978). For Scarry's claim that "although the information sought in an interrogation is almost never credited with being a *just* motive for torture, it is repeatedly credited with being the motive for torture. But for every instance in which someone with critical information is interrogated, there are hundreds interrogated who could know nothing of remote importance to the stability or self-image of the regime..." See *The Body in Pain* (New York: Oxford University Press, 1985), p. 28. For a third position in which the witch's mark represents a "liminal area where inwardness and outwardness met," see Katherine Eisaman Maus, "Proof and Consequences," *Representations*, 34 (1991), 29–52, especially p. 38.

4 In "Who were the Witches?" Christina Larner considers the evidence for "the witch-hunt [as] an attack by the emergent male medical profession on the female healer" and while granting that "there is a certain amount of evidence for this" concludes that "the connection, however, is not direct enough..."

while witchcraft prosecutions may sometimes have married conveniently with the suppression of female healing, male professionalization of healing really cannot account for the mass of prosecutions" (Larner, *Enemies of God* [Baltimore: The Johns Hopkins University Press, 1981], p. 101). In *Newes from Scotland*, the attack on Duncane (which does not come from "an emergent medical profession[al]") seems primarily to revolve around the inexplicability of Duncane's powers.

5 It is difficult to determine what is typesetting and what is history, but this ambiguity has been replicated in the critical history of the text. James Craigie, who edited James' *Minor Prose Works*, treats Agnis Sampson and Agnis Tompson as two separate witches, but then attributes to Sampson actions which the pamphlet attributes to Tompson. Robert Pitcairn, who is one of Craigie's primary sources, and who reproduces the pamphlet along with the trial records of Sampson, Fian and others, treats Sampson and Tompson as the same witch, rationalizing inconsistencies in the pamphlet by putting in parentheses the word "Sampson" each time Tompson is mentioned. Pitcairn's trial records themselves mention no Agnis Tompson among the numerous women tried and convicted for witchcraft and attribute to Sampson many of the actions ascribed to Tompson by the pamphlet (the attaching of human joints to a dead cat in order to raise storms to thwart the king, the association with John Kers, the sailing to North Berwick to meet with the devil).

  For my purposes, however, what is crucial is the pamphlet's own attitude, the fact that it begins by treating the two as separate witches ("*Agnis Sampson* the eldest Witch of them al, dwelling in Haddington, *Agnes Tompson* of Edenbrough" [p. 10]) and ends by conflating them into one person. Thus the pamphleteer will say, "Item, the saide *Agnis Tompson* was after brought againe before the Kings Maiestie" when the only Agnis who has yet been before the king's majesty is Agnis Sampson (p. 13). Or the pamphleteer will say "touching this *Agnis Tompson*" in the middle of recounting what Agnis Sampson said to the king. Similarly, in the middle of a confession by a person called Agnes Tompson, the pamphleteer says, "Item, the saide *Agnis Sampson* confessed before the kings Maiestie sundrye thinges," etc. (p. 15).

  For Craigie's characterization of the two as separate witches, and his attribution to Sampson of the attempt to get the king's linen (which the pamphlet attributes to Tompson) see *Minor Prose Works of King James VI and I* (Edinburgh: Scottish Text Society, 1982), p. 150. For Pitcairn's record of Sampson's trial, see *Ancient Criminal Trials in Scotland* (Edinburgh: Maitland Club, 1833), Vol. 1, Part 2, pp. 230–41, especially pp. 232 and 235–7. For his reproduction of the pamphlet and its rationalization of Tompson *as* Sampson, see particularly pp. 217–18.

6 Allhollon is apparently All Saints Day, November first. Riddles are sieves – wire or mesh strainers, and sieves are witches' sailboats. I have been unable to determine why it is that witches go to sea in strainers, i.e. whether it has to do with the witch's presumed ability to float.

7 Orgel cites Bacon: "it is the glory of God to conceal a thing, but it is the glory of the King to find a thing out" (*The Illusion of Power*, p. 55).

8 For a discussion of sympathetic and contagious magic, see Sir James George Frazier, *The Golden Bough* (New York: Macmillan, 1960), pp. 12–52.

9 One fascinating kind of confirmation for the way "witches" ultimately produced the narratives their inquisitors expected them to lies in Carlo Ginzburg's
   compelling description of the way the Benendanti's very conception of themselves changed through the process of interrogation; before the years of
   interrogation they thought of themselves as going out at night to *fight* witches,
   by the end of the interrogations *as* witches. See *The Night Battles* (Baltimore:
   The Johns Hopkins University Press, 1983).
10 In trial records, Fian is charged with the same kind of conspiracy that Sampson
   is, but the pamphlet suppresses this almost entirely in order to tell the story of
   the three public hairs. See Pitcairn, particularly pp. 211–13.

   In "Discovering Witches," Karen Newman claims that witches threatened
   "hegemonic patriarchal structures" as "cultural producers, as spectacle, as
   representatives – like Margaret, the 'libber' of Fife – of an oppositional
   'femininity'." One limitation to this approach is that it fails to make sense of
   those anomalous instances of men like Fian who elicit *more* torture than female
   witches. For this reason it seems to me necessary to identify the specific ontological system threatened in a given text rather than to generalize. See *Fashioning Femininity* (University of Chicago Press, 1991) pp. 69–70.
11 In *Daemonologie* Epistemon says that necromancers and magicians aren't
   marked the same way witches are, but Fian is not a necromancer or magician:

   "One word onlie I omitted; concerning the forme of making of this contract, which is
   either written with the *Magicians* owne bloud: or else being agreed upon (in termes his
   schole-master) touches him in some parte, though peradventure no marke remaine: as it
   doth with all Witches." (p. 23)

Works cited

Adelman, Janet. *The Common Liar*. New Haven: Yale University Press, 1973
   "Making Defect Perfection," *Suffocating Mothers: Fantasies of Maternal Origin in Shakespeare's Plays*. New York: Routledge, 1992, pp. 174–92
   "'This Is and Is Not Cressid': The Characterization of Cressida," *The (M)other Tongue*, ed. Shirley Nelson Garner, Claire Kehane, and Madelon Sprengnether. Ithaca: Cornell University Press, 1985, 119–41
Altman, Joel B. *The Tudor Play of Mind*. Berkeley: University of California Press, 1979
Ayers, P.K. "Dreams of the City: The Urban and the Urbane in Jonson's *Epicoene*." *Philological Quarterly*, 66 (1987), 73–86
Barish, Jonas. *The Anti-theatrical Prejudice*. Berkeley: University of California Press, 1981
   "*Bartholomew Fair* and its Puppets," *Modern Language Quarterly*, 20 (1959), 3–17
Barton, Ann. *Ben Jonson, Dramatist*. Cambridge University Press, 1984
Boose, Lynda. "The Family in Shakespeare Studies; or – Studies in the Family of Shakespeareans; or – the Politics of Politics," *Renaissance Quarterly*, 40 (1987), 707–42
Bray, Alan. *Homosexuality in Renaissance England*. London: Gay Men's Press, 1982
Bredbeck, Gregory W. *Sodomy and Interpretation: Marlowe to Milton*. Ithaca: Cornell University Press, 1991
Burt, Richard. "'Licensed by Authority': Ben Jonson and the Politics of Early Stuart Theater," *English Literary History*, 54:3 (1987), 529–60
Butler, Judith. *Gender Trouble: Feminism and the Subversion of Identity*. New York: Routledge, 1990
Campbell, Marion. "'*Desunt Nonnula*': The Construction of Marlowe's *Hero and Leander* as an Unfinished Poem," *English Literary History*, 51 (1984), 241–67
Cavell, Stanley. *The Claim of Reason*. Oxford University Press, 1982
   Disowning Knowledge in Six Plays of Shakespeare. Cambridge University Press, 1987
Chambers, E.K. *The Elizabethan Stage*. Oxford: Clarendon Press, 1965
Charnes, Linda. "'So Unsecret to Ourselves': Notorious Identity and the Material Subject in Shakespeare's *Troilus and Cressida*," *Shakespeare Quarterly*, 40:4 (1989), 413–40
Clark, Stuart. "Inversion, Misrule and the Meaning of Witchcraft," *Past and Present*, 87 (1980), 98–127

"King James' *Daemonologie*: Witchcraft and Kingship," *The Damned Art*, ed. Sydney Anglo. London: Routledge, 1977

Cohen, Walter. "Political Criticism of Shakespeare," *Shakespeare Reproduced: The Text in History and Ideology*, ed. Jean Howard and Marion O'Connor. New York: Methuen, 1987, pp.18–46

Cook, Carol. "Unbodied Figures of Desire," *Theater Journal*, 38:1 (1986), 34–52

Cope, Jackson I. "*Bartholomew Fair* as Blasphemy," *Renaissance Drama* 8 (1965), 127–52

Craigie, James. *Minor Prose Works of King James VI and I*. Edinburgh: Scottish Text Society, 1982

Davidson, Clifford. "Judgment, Iconoclasm and Anti-theatricalism in Jonson's *Bartholomew Fair*," *Papers on Language & Literature*, 25:4 (1989), 349–63

Dollimore, Jonathan. *Radical Tragedy: Religion, Ideology and Power in the Drama of Shakespeare and his Contemporaries*. University of Chicago Press, 1984

"Shakespeare, Cultural Materialism, Feminism and Marxist Humanism," *New Literary History*, 21 (1990), 471–93

Donaldson, Ian. *The World Upside-Down: Comedy from Jonson to Fielding*. London: Oxford University Press, 1970

Dryden, John. *John Dryden*, ed. Keith Walker. Oxford University Press, 1987

Erickson, Peter. "Rewriting the Renaisssance, Rewriting Ourselves," *Shakespeare Quarterly*, 38 (1987), 327–37

Ferry, Anne. *The Inward Language: The Sonnets of Wyatt, Sidney, Shakespeare and Donne*. University of Chicago Press, 1983

Fish, Stanley. "Authors-Readers, Jonson's Community of the Same," *Representations*, 7 (1984), 26–58

Foucault, Michel. *Discipline and Punish*, trans. Alan Sheridan. New York: Vintage Books, 1979

Freud, Sigmund. "Instincts and Their Vicissitudes," in *General Psychological Theory*, ed. Philip Rieff. New York: Collier Books, 1963

Three Contributions to the Theory of Sex, in *The Basic Writings of Sigmund Freud*. trans. Dr. A.A. Brill. New York: Modern Library, 1968

Totem and Taboo, trans. James Strachey. New York: W.W. Norton, 1950

Fried, Michael. *Absorption and Theatricality*. Berkeley: University of California Press, 1980

Garber, Marjorie. *Vested Interests*. New York: Harper, 1992

Geertz, Hildred. "An Anthropology of Religion and Magic, 1," *Journal of Interdisciplinary History*, 6:1 (1975), 71–89

Ginzburg, Carlo. *Ecstasies: Deciphering the Witches' Sabbath*, trans. Raymond Rosenthal. New York: Penguin, 1992

The Night Battles, trans. John and Anne Tedeschi. Baltimore: The Johns Hopkins University Press, 1983

Girard, Rene. "The Politics of Desire in *Troilus and Cressida*," *Shakespeare and the Question of Theory*, ed. Patricia Parker and Geoffrey Hartman. New York: Methuen, 1985, pp. 188–209

Gohlke, Madelon. "'I wooed thee with my sword': Shakespeare's Tragic Paradigms," *The Woman's Part: Feminist Criticism of Shakespeare*, ed. Carolyn

Ruth Swift Lenz, Gayle Greene and Carol Thomas Neely. Urbana: University of Illinois Press, 1980, pp. 150–70

Goldberg, Jonathan. *James I and the Politics of Literature: Jonson, Shakespeare, Donne, and their Contemporaries.* Baltimore: The Johns Hopkins University Press, 1983

Sodometries. Stanford University Press, 1992

Gosson, Stephen. *Playes Confuted in five Actions*, in Arthur F. Kinney, *Markets of Bawdrie: The Dramatic Criticism of Stephen Gosson*, Salzburg Studies in Literature, No. 4. Salzburg: Institut für Englische Sprache und Literatur, 1974

The School of Abuse. 1579, London: The Shakespeare Society, 1841

Greenblatt, Stephen. "Fiction and Friction," *Reconstructing Individualism*, ed. Thomas C. Heller, Morton Sosna, David E. Wellbery. Stanford University Press, 1986, pp. 30–52

"Invisible Bullets; Renaissance Authority and its Subversion," *Glyph 8: The Johns Hopkins Textual Studies.* Baltimore: Johns Hopkins Press, 1981

Renaissance Self-Fashioning. The University of Chicago Press, 1980

Greene, Gayle. "Shakespeare's Cressida: 'A Kind of Self,'" *The Woman's Part: Feminist Criticism of Shakespeare*, ed. Carolyn Ruth Swift Lenz, Gayle Greene, and Carol Thomas Neely. Urbana: University of Illinois Press, 1980, pp. 133–49

Greene, Thomas. "Ben Jonson and the Centered Self," *Studies in English Literature*, 10 (1970), 325–48

Haynes, Jonathan. "Festivity and the dramatic economy of Jonson's *Bartholomew Fair*," *English Literary History*, 51:4 (1984), 645–68

Heywood, Thomas. *An Apology for Actors in 3 Books.* From the Edition of 1612 compared with that of W. Cartwright. London: Shakespeare Society, 1841

Howard, Jean E. "Crossdressing, The Theatre, and Gender Struggle in Early Modern England," *Shakespeare Quarterly*, 39 (1988), 418–40

"The New Historicism in Renaissance Studies," *English Literary Renaissance*, 16 (1986), 13–43

James I. *Daemonologie in Forme of a Dialogue* (1597), The Bodley Head Quartos, ed. G.B. Harrison. London: John Lane; New York: E.P. Dutton, 1924

Jonson, Ben. *Ben Jonson*, ed. C. H. Herford Percy and Evelyn Simpson, Vol. IX. Oxford: Clarendon Press, 1950

Ben Jonson: The Complete Masques, ed. Stephen Orgel. New Haven: Yale University Press, 1969

Timber or Discoveries Made Upon Men and Matter, ed. Felix E. Schelling. Boston: Ginn & Co., 1892

The Yale Ben Jonson: Epicoene. New Haven: Yale University Press, 1971

Kahn, Coppélia. *Man's Estate: Masculine Identity in Shakespeare.* Berkeley: University of California Press, 1981

Kahn, Victoria. *Rhetoric, Prudence, and Skepticism in the Renaissance.* Ithaca: Cornell University Press, 1985

Klein, Melanie. "The Theory of Anxiety and Guilt," *Envy and Gratitude & Other Works 1946–1963.* New York: Delta, 1975

Kuriyama, Constance Brown. "The Mother of the World: a Psychoanalytic Interpretation of Shakespeare's *Antony and Cleopatra*," *English Literary Renaissance*, 7 (1977), 321–51

Laqueur, Thomas. "Orgasm, Generation, and the Politics of Reproductive Biology," *Representations*, 14 (1986), 1–41

Larner, Christina. *Enemies of God*. Baltimore: The Johns Hopkins University Press, 1981

Levine, Laura. "Imagining a Self: Elizabethan Nostalgia and Jacobean Anti-theatricality in *Antony and Cleopatra*," unpublished essay.

   "Men in Women's Clothing: Anti-theatricality and Effeminization from 1579 to 1642," *Criticism*, 28:2 (1986), 121–43

MacFarlane, Alan. *Witchcraft in Tudor and Stuart England*. London: Routledge & Kegan Paul, 1970

Maclean, Ian. "Medicine, Anatomy, Physiology," *The Renaissance Notion of Woman*. Cambridge University Press, 1980

Mallin, Eric. "Emulous Factions and the Collapse of Chivalry: Troilus and Cressida," *Representations*, 29 (1990), 145–79

Marcus, Leah S. *The Politics of Mirth: Jonson, Herrick, Milton, Marvell and the Defense of Old Holiday Pastimes*. University of Chicago Press, 1986

Maus, Katherine Eisaman. "Horns of Dilemma: Jealousy, Gender and Spectatorship in English Renaissance Drama," *English Literary History*, 54 (1987), 561–83

   "Playhouse Flesh and Blood: Sexual Ideology and the Restoration Actress," *English Literary History*, 46 (1979), 595–617

   "Proof and Consequences: Inwardness and Its Exposure in the English Renaissance," *Representations*, 34 (1991), 29–52

   "Prosecution and Sexual Secrecy: Jonson and Shakespeare; Impotence and the Satirist's Vocation," forthcoming

McLuskie, Kathleen. "The Act, the Role, and the Actor: Boy Actresses on the Elizabethan Stage," *New Theatre Quarterly*, 3 (1987), 120–30

Meres, Francis. *Francis Meres' Treatise "Poetrie," A Critical Edition*, ed. Don Cameron Allen, rpt. University of Illinois Studies in Language and Literature XVI, no. 3–4 (1933)

Millard, Barbara C. "An Acceptable Violence: Sexual Contest in Jonson's *Epicene*." *Medieval and Renaissance Drama in English*, 1 (1984), 143–58

Miller, Alice. *The Drama of the Gifted Child*, New York: Basic Books Inc., 1981

Miller, J. Hillis. "Ariachne's Broken Woof," *The Georgia Review*, 31:1 (1977), 47–60

de Montaigne, Michel. *The Complete Essays of Montaigne*, trans. Donald M. Frame. Stanford University Press, 1958

Montrose, Louis. "'Eliza, Queene of Shepeardes,' and the Pastoral of Power," *English Literary Renaissance*, 10 (1980), 153–82

   "*A Midsummer Night's Dream* and the Shaping Fantasies of Elizabethan Culture: Gender and Power and Form," in *Rewriting the Renaissance*, ed. Margaret W. Ferguson, Maureen Quilligan, Nancy J. Vickers. University of Chicago Press, 1986, pp. 65–87

   "The Purpose of Playing: Reflections on a Shakespearean Anthropology," *Helios*, n.s. 7 (1980), 51–74

   "The Work of Gender in the Discourse of Discovery," *Representations*, 33 (1991), 1–41

Morris, Helen. "Queen Elizabeth I 'Shadowed' in Cleopatra," *Huntington Library Quarterly*, 32 (1969), 271–8

Mullaney, Steven. *The Place of the Stage: License, Play, and Power in Renaissance England.* University of Chicago Press, 1988

Munday, Anthony. *A Second and Third Blast of Retrait from Plaies and Theaters.* London, 1580

Neely, Carol Thomas. "Constructing the Subject: Feminist Practice and the New Renaissance Discourses," *English Literary Renaissance*, 18 (1988) 5–18

"Gender and Genre in *Antony and Cleopatra*," *Broken Nuptials in Shake-speare's Plays.* New Haven: Yale University Press, 1985

Nevo, Ruth. "The Masque of Greatness," *Shakespeare Studies*, 3 (1968), 111–28

Newes from Scotland declaring the Damnable Life and death of Doctor Fian, a notable Sorcerer who was burned at Edenbrough in Ianuary last (1591), the Bodley Head Quartos, ed. G.B. Harrison. New York: E.P. Dutton, 1924

Newman, Karen. *Fashioning Femininity.* University of Chicago Press, 1991

Orgel, Stephen. *The Illusion of Power: Political Theater in the English Renaissance.* Berkeley: University of California Press, 1975

The Jonsonian Masque. Cambridge, MA: Harvard University Press, 1965

"Nobody's Perfect: or, Why Did the English Stage Take Boys for Women?" *South Atlantic Quarterly*, 88:1 (1989), 7–30

Ovid, Naso. *Fasti*, trans. Sir James George Frazer. Cambridge, MA: Harvard University Press, 1951

Heroides and Amores, trans. Grant Showerman. Cambridge, MA: Harvard University Press, 1977

Park, Katherine, and Daston, Lorraine J. "Unnatural Conceptions: The Study of Monsters in Sixteenth- and Seventeenth-Century France and England," *Past and Present*, 92 (1981), 20–54

Park, Katherine, and Nye, Robert A. "Destiny Is Anatomy," *The New Republic*, 18 (February 1991), 53–7

Parker, Pat. "Gender Ideology, Gender Change: The Case of Marie Germain," *Critical Inquiry*, 19 (Winter 1993), 337–64

Partridge, Edward B. "*Epicoene*," in *The Broken Compass: A study of the Major Comedies of Ben Jonson.* New York: Columbia University Press, 1958

Paster, Gail Kern. "Leaky Vessels: The Incontinent Women of City Comedy," *Renaissance Drama*, New Series XVIII, Essays on Sexuality, Influence, and Performance, ed. Mary Beth Rose (1987), pp. 43–65

Pechter, Edward. "New Historicism and its Discontents: Politicizing Renaissance Drama," *PMLA*, 102 (1987), 292–302

Pitcairn, Robert. *Ancient Criminal Trials in Scotland.* Edinburgh: Maitland Club, 1833

Popkin, Richard. *The History of Skepticism From Erasmus to Spinoza.* Berkeley: University of California Press, 1979

Prynne, William. *Histrio-Mastix: The Player's Scourge or Actor's Tragedy.* New York: Garland Publishing, 1974

Rackin, Phyllis. "Androgyny, Mimesis, and the Marriage of the Boy Heroine on the English Renaissance Stage," *PMLA*, 102 (1987), 29–41

"Shakespeare's Boy Cleopatra, the Decorum of Nature and the Golden World of Poetry," *PMLA*, 87 (1972), 201–12

Rainolds, John. *Th' Overthrow of Stage Plaies.* 1599; rpt. New York: Garland Publishing, 1974

Rankins, William. *A Mirrour of Monsters*. London, 1587

Rinehart, Keith. "Shakespeare's Cleopatra and England's Elizabeth," *Shakespeare Quarterly*, 23 (1972), 81–6

Ringler, William. *Stephen Gosson, a Biographical and Critical Study*. Princeton: Princeton University Press, 1942

"The First Phase of the Elizabethan Attack on the Stage, 1558–1579," *The Huntington Library Quarterly* (1942), 391–418

Scarry, Elaine. *The Body in Pain*. New York: Oxford University Press, 1985

Sedgwick, Eve Kosofsky. *Between Men: English Literature and Male Homosocial Desire*. New York: Columbia University Press, 1985

Shakespeare, William. *Arden Antony and Cleopatra*, ed. M.R. Ridley. London: Methuen, 1982

The Riverside Shakespeare, textual ed. G. Blakemore Evans. Boston: Houghton Mifflin Co., 1974

Sidney, Sir Philip. *The Countess of Pembroke's Arcadia*. Harmondsworth: Penguin, 1977

Smith, Bruce. *Homosexual Desire in Shakespeare's England*. University of Chicago Press, 1991

Speaight, George. *History of the English Puppet Theater*. London: G.G. Harrap, 1955

Sprengnether, Madelon. "The Boy Actor and Femininity in *Antony and Cleopatra*," in *Shakespeare's Personality*, ed. Norman N. Holland, Sidney Homan and Bernard J. Paris. Berkeley: University of California Press, 1989

Stallybrass, Peter. "Patriarchal Territories: The Body Enclosed," in *Rewriting the Renaissance*, ed. Margaret W. Ferguson, Maureen Quilligan, Nancy J. Vickers. University of Chicago, 1986, pp. 123–42

Stallybrass, Peter, and Allon White. *The Politics and Poetics of Transgression*. Ithaca: Cornell University Press, 1986

Stubbes, Phillip. *The Anatomie of Abuses*. 1583, rpt. Netherlands: Da Capo Press, 1972

Tennenhouse, Leonard. *Power on Display*. New York: Methuen, 1986

Thayer, G. C. *Ben Jonson: Studies in the Plays*. Norman: University of Oklahoma Press, 1963

Thomas, Keith. "An Anthropology of Religion and Magic, II." *Journal of Interdisciplinary History*, 6:1 (1975), 91–109

Religion and the Decline of Magic. New York: Penguin, 1971

Traub, Valerie. *Desire and Anxiety*. London: Routledge, 1992

Trevor-Roper, H.R. "The European Witch-Craze," *The European Witch-Craze of the Sixteenth and Seventeenth Centuries and Other Essays*. New York: Harper and Row, 1967

Turner, Victor. *The Forest of Symbols: Aspects of Ndembu Ritual*. Ithaca and London: Cornell University Press, 1967

Voth, Grant L., and Evans, Oliver. "Cressida and the World of the Play," *Shakespeare Studies*, 8 (1975), 231–39

Wallace, Charles William. "The Children of the Chapel at Blackfriars, 1597–1603," *Nebraska University Studies VIII*, No. 2 (1908)

Waller, Marguerite. "Academic Tootsie: The Denial of Difference and the Difference it Makes," *Diacritics*, 17 (1987), 2–20

180   Works cited

Winnicott, D.W. "The True and False Self," *Maturational Processes and the Facilitating Environment: Studies in the theory of emotional development.* New York: International Universities Press, 1965
Woodbridge, Linda. *Women and the English Renaissance.* Chicago: University of Illinois Press, 1984

Index